Dedication

We dedicate the second edition of this guide to all those whose foresight and generosity have made these Peninsula trails possible;

the many citizens who worked for the creation of parks, open space preserves and trails;

the public officials whose decisions supported park and trail programs;

the growing number of volunteers who helped build and maintain trails;

and the individuals and organizations whose gifts have added to our increasing store of public recreation land.

1990 UPDATE for this edition follows page 273.

Peninsula Trails

Outdoor adventures
on the San Francisco Peninsula

Jean Rusmore and Frances Spangle

WILDERNESS PRESS · BERKELEY

PHOTO CREDITS

Carolyn Caddes 12, 162, 172, 209
Courtesy of Garrod Family 222
Crocker Land Co. 32
Alice Cummings—MROSD 145
Ann Duwe 18
Kenneth Gardiner 238, 246, 251
Mary Gundert—MROSD 99
Ellie Huggins 141
Charlotte MacDonald—MROSD 175, 202, 216
Midpeninsula Open Space District 103, 129
Karl H. Riek 35
Jean Rusmore 6, 7 (U.L., L.R.), 25, 58, 61, 65, 72, 77, 85, 91, 107, 111, 115, 123, 139, 181, 199, 225, 227, 231
San Mateo County 55
Frances Spangle 23, 42, 47, 68, 70, 79, 87, 90, 121, 124, 126, 134, 192, 198, 206, 214, 234
State Division of Recreation and Parks 93, 96
Woodside Heritage and Joe Hallet 109
Sheldon Woodward 5, 7, (U.R., L.L.), 51, 165, 183, 187, 188

FIRST EDITION January 1982
Second printing March 1982
Third printing December 1983
SECOND EDITION January 1989
Second printing May 1989
Third printing April 1990

Design by Thomas Winnett
Maps by John Stockwell and Larry Van Dyke
Cover Photo by Diana Venegas-Powers

Library of Congress Card Catalog Number 88-40010

International Standard Book Number 0-89997-097-4

Manufactured in the United States

Published by Wilderness Press
              2440 Bancroft Way
              Berkeley, CA 94704
              (415) 843-8080

              Write for free catalog

Library of Congress Cataloging-in-Publication Data

Rusmore, Jean.
    Peninsula trails.

    Bibliography: p.
    Includes index.
    1. Outdoor recreation--California--San Francisco
Peninsula--Guide-books. 2. Hiking--California--
San Francisco Peninsula--Guide-books. 3. Trails--
California--San Francisco Peninsula--Guide-books.
4. San Francisco Peninsula (Calif.)--Description and
travel--Guide-books. I. Spangle, Frances. II. Title.
GV191.42.C2R87 1988   917.94'6   88-40010
ISBN 0-89997-097-4

Foreword

For many years I worked as a whitewater rafting guide in the Sierra Nevada, and used to regularly pass an old dirt trail that local legend had it could take you all the way to Canada. Whether true or not, every time I went by that place, my imagination would reach out and take me on a momentary journey across thousands of miles. Such is the magic of possibility.

In the Bay Area, there is now the possibility of a Ridge Trail, a five-hundred-mile passage looping around the Greenbelt of open space that frames our metropolis of almost six million people. It will be planned over the next five years, and will take many more to complete. But when it is done, anyone with two good feet, strong legs and a dream will be able to circumnavigate the nine counties that touch San Francisco Bay. A parallel effort is also being undertaken to create a continuous trail around the bay itself.

The trails described by Jean Rusmore and Fran Spangle in this excellent guidebook are integral to this overall regional system of trails. Some of them will actually be Peninsula components of the Ridge Trail itself; others will be branches from the main spine. All are vital public treasures that everyone who lives here can take advantage of, because of the guidebook.

Look into the future: you are hiking in Rancho San Antonio Park, or Windy Hill, or McNee Ranch. You come across a side trail with a sign that says "To the Ridge Trail." Maybe you're there with a full pack, ready to begin a journey of many days. Or maybe you pause just to look up the side trail. For a moment you feel flowing through your imagination the richness that lies out there, and then with a knowing smile, you walk past that portal and continue on your way.

—Larry Orman
Executive Director
Greenbelt Alliance

Acknowledgements

We enjoyed the company of our families and the many friends who joined us in exploring these trails. To them and to all those who helped and encouraged us during the preparation of this second edition of *Peninsula Trails,* we extend our gratitude.

We are grateful to the directors and staffs of the public agencies who manage our parks and preserves: Golden Gate National Recreation Area— Brian O'Neil, Superintendent; State Department of Parks and Recreation— Carol Nelson, Superintendent, San Mateo Coast District; San Mateo County Parks and Recreation Department—David Christy, Director, and Harry Dean; Santa Clara County Park Department—Douglas J. Gaynor, Director, and Felice Errico; Midpeninsula Regional Open Space District—Herbert Grench, General Manager, and David Hansen, Del Woods, Mary Gundert, Alice Cummings and Mary Hale. Their lively interest encouraged us, and their generous contributions of up-to-date information, photographs, maps and trail data were indispensable.

We appreciate the cooperation of the Bayside cities who furnished valuable information on the trail system now taking shape along San Mateo County's Bay shoreline.

To the many park and preserve rangers we offer special thanks for the wealth of detailed information on the trails in their care. We share their enthusiasm for the lands under their jurisdiction.

Our thanks to photographers Carolyn Caddes, Kenneth Gardiner, Charlotte MacDonald and Sheldon Woodward, whose works grace these pages. We acknowledge the assistance of the agencies and organizations who made available to us their photographs: the Midpeninsula Regional Open Space District, Peninsula Open Space Trust, the San Francisco Water Department, the County of San Mateo and the Woodside Historical Society.

To the San Mateo County Historical Society for help on local research, many thanks.

We extend our appreciation to Thomas Winnett, Editor and Publisher, and his staff at Wilderness Press for their help throughout the production of this guidebook.

Jean Rusmore   Portola Valley, California
Frances Spangle   November 1988

Preface

In the years since 1982, when the first edition of this guide was published, many thousands of acres of parks, open-space preserves and Baylands have been added to the Peninsula's enviable store of public recreation lands. Now an expanded greenbelt in the mountains and foothills spills over on both sides of the Skyline ridge, and a fringe of marshes, wildlife refuges, parks and trails provides newfound public access on the shores of San Francisco Bay.

Today in these 33,000 acres of parks, Bayfront lands, watersheds and open-space preserves more than 300 miles of trails provide superb opportunities to hike, ride and run through evergreen forests, beside crystal-clear lakes, over foothill meadows and ridgetop grasslands and along the Bay's edge. On new trails beside San Francisco Bay walkers, runners and bicyclists can see shorebirds in marshlands, watch windsurfers skim the water, and savor views of distant mountains encircling the Bay.

We have hiked all the trails described in this guide, and we marvel anew at the treasury of public land so close to Peninsula homes. We hope to kindle the reader's interest in exploring these public places, where a wealth of beauty, wildness, serenity and charm awaits. We think that those who come to know these mountains, meadows, streamsides and Baylands will cherish them with a heightened sense of stewardship.

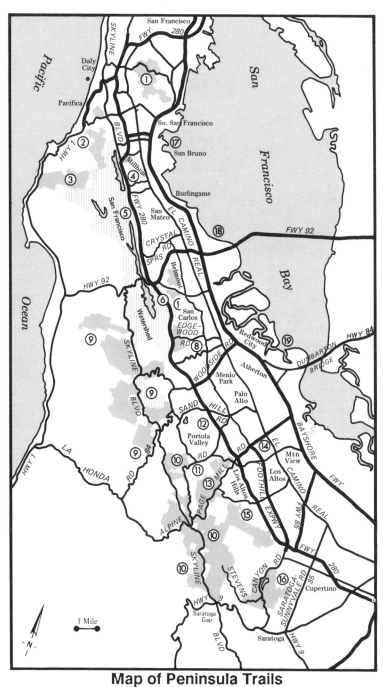

Map of Peninsula Trails

Numbers in circles refer to Part II of Contents.
Shaded areas are parks and preserves.

Contents

Introduction

This second edition will guide trail users over 33,000 acres of parks and preserves in the forests, foothills and ranchlands east and west of the crest of the Santa Cruz Mountains and on new paths beside the Bay. Fresh views of the San Mateo County coast reward those who climb the ridges high on the western slopes of the mountains. For the energetic there are day-long excursions into deep canyons where tiger lilies bloom by year-round creeks.

This guide describes the public trails of the San Francisco Peninsula on the slopes of the Santa Cruz Mountains from San Bruno Mountain in northern San Mateo County to Saratoga Gap in Santa Clara County, and from the Bay west over the Skyline ridge through the parks and preserves touching the Skyline. Some trails are in redwood forests, once logged over and now grown to tall trees again. Some are on ranches where barns and fences remind us of early days. Others are on untouched hillsides where little has changed over the centuries. Some are on the Bay's edge, newly accessible to the public.

Old ranch and logging roads, bayside levees and newly constructed trails make easy routes for us to walk, ride and run—under old oaks, through pungent chaparral and beside blue Bay waters—to enjoy our heritage of forests, meadows and Baylands.

The Peninsula is blessed with a remarkable diversity of landforms, plant life and microclimates. The hiker can choose steep mountains, level creeksides, deep forests or open meadows to suit his mood. The gentle Mediterranean climate, with dry summers and mild winters, makes our trails inviting the year around. They appeal to hikers during our temperate winters, our flowery springs, our summer days whether hot or foggy, and our bright, crisp days of autumn.

The main part of this guide is a trail-by-trail account of trips through our parks and open-space preserves. The description of each trip gives the length and grade of the trail and an estimate of time required to make the trip. Also mentioned are special features of each trail, such as a bit of historical or geological information, and plant and animal life seen along the way. The accompanying maps show the location of trailheads and parking areas and, of course, the trail routes.

Part 1: Background

The Peninsula Setting

Geography

The Santa Cruz Mountains are part of the Coast Ranges of California. They run northwest to southeast, extending from Montara Mountain near San Francisco to Mt. Madonna near Watsonville. At the Highway 17 pass to Santa Cruz, a natural divide splits the range into two parts. The Spaniards called the southern section the Sierra Azul (blue mountains) and the northern part, the Sierra Morena (brown or dark mountains). The area covered by this guide is in the Sierra Morena. The highest mountain in the Sierra Morena is appropriately called Black Mountain.

The east side of the Santa Cruz Mountains, steeper than the west, is cut into deep canyons by streams running generally at right angles to the main axis. San Mateo, Belmont, Redwood and Cordilleras creeks are the main streams flowing east in central San Mateo County. The San Francisco Watershed drains into the Crystal Springs reservoirs and San Mateo Creek. The large drainage basin of San Francisquito Creek and its tributaries is fed by streams from Woodside and Portola Valley. Along with Los Trancos Creek, it forms a natural boundary between San Mateo and Santa Clara counties.

In Santa Clara County are Matadero, Adobe and Permanente creeks. At the south end of the area covered by this guide is Stevens Creek, which rises near the Skyline ridge, flows south between Monte Bello Ridge and the Skyline ridge, then bends around the southeast end of Monte Bello Ridge and turns due north on its way to the Bay.

The upper reaches of these creeks, which still flow more or less untrammeled down through the mountains and the foothills, are some of the main delights of our mountainside parks. Where these creeks meandered across the Bay plain, they were once the dominant features of the landscape, being bordered by huge oaks, bays, alders and sycamores. Now they have all but disappeared from sight in the flatlands, often being confined to concrete ditches and culverts and bordered by chain-link fences. Two happy exceptions are the lower reaches of Los Trancos and San Francisquito creeks, which still retain their parklike tree borders as they wind through Portola Valley and the undeveloped lands of Stanford University. They are the sites of popular creekside trails.

The principal streams on the western slopes of the Santa Cruz Mountains are San Pedro, Purisima, El Corte de Madera, La Honda, San Gregorio, Mindego and Pescadero creeks. These creeks or their tributaries, many of them perennial, flow through state and county parks and open-space preserves. Still coursing relatively uninterrupted through forests and grasslands and across coastal terraces, they empty into the Pacific Ocean. Present-day trails follow the routes of early roads beside these creeks.

Geology

The Santa Cruz Mountains were formed over the millenia by the uplifting, folding and faulting of rocks. Frequent earthquakes in the area tell us that forces deep within the earth continue to shape and reshape the land.

The San Andreas Fault, which extends the length of California, is the most conspicuous feature of the Peninsula landscape. It runs in a northwest-southeast direction roughly parallel to the main ridge of the Santa Cruz Mountains. Linear valleys lie along the fault, and the main ridge of the mountains stands to the west of it. Monte Bello Ridge and the lower hills stand to the east.

A dramatic vantage point from which to view this fault is the top of Los Trancos Open Space Preserve on a fault saddle between the Skyline ridge and the Monte Bello Ridge. You can see the rift valley running south toward Mt. Umunhum and north up the Crystal Springs Valley as far as San Andreas Lake, about 25 miles in each direction.

In the 1890s Andrew Lawson, a noted geologist visiting California, saw these straight valleys and recognized them as typical of a rift zone. He named the fault for the northernmost of the rift-valley lakes. The great earthquake of 1906, centered about 25 miles north

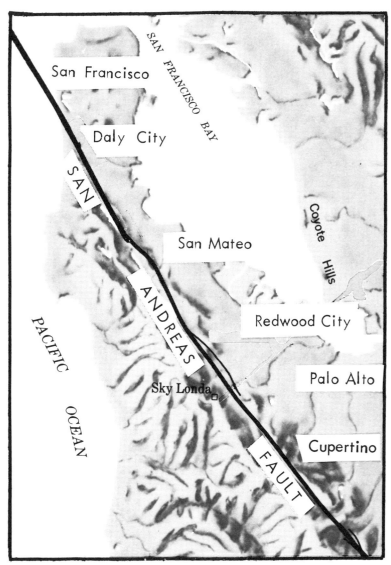

The San Andreas Fault

of San Francisco, made the San Andreas Fault famous around the world.

The Santa Cruz Mountains are very young geologically. The oldest exposed rocks on the Peninsula were formed only 100 million years ago, whereas the oldest known rocks on earth are four billion years old. In spite of its youth, Peninsula geology is extremely com-

plex because the area lies at the boundary between the Pacific and
the North American plates. These plates have been and are still
moving very slowly past each other. The movements of these large
blocks of the earth's crust are explained by the modern concept of
plate tectonics.

From the concept of plate tectonics, and the kind of bedrock
formation found in the Santa Cruz Mountains, the following geologic
history can be inferred. Between 100 and 65 million years ago, massive quantities of lava flows, red ooze, sand and mud accumulated in
complex layers on the Pacific Plate in a location west of what is now
the California coast. These deposits on the ocean floor were
hardened to rock, partly crushed and thoroughly mixed as the
Pacific Plate was pushed under the North American continent, thus
moving what is called the *Franciscan Formation* to its present location on the east side of the Purissima and San Andreas faults. This
formation is composed of shale, siltstone, limestone, sandstone,
chert and greenstone, occurring sometimes as a melange and sometimes as discrete beds. Outcrops of these rocks occur on Sweeney
and Sawyer ridges, San Bruno Mountain, Belmont Hill and Monte
Bello Ridge. For the past several million years the San Andreas
Fault has formed a boundary between the Pacific and the North
American plates, the land west of the fault, the Pacific Plate, moving
northwest in relation to the North American Plate, at an average
speed of 1 to 2 inches per year. As a result of movements along the
fault, granitic rocks originally formed about 90 million years ago in
the area now occupied by *Southern California* now underlie all the
land west of the San Andreas fault at depth, and are exposed on
Montara Mountain.

Serpentine, the California state rock, occurs in outcrops along
Sawyer Camp Trail, in road cuts along Freeway 280 from Woodside
north, in Edgewood Park and in scattered locations on Monte Bello
Ridge.

The linear fault valleys of the Peninsula exist because rock
broken by fault movements erodes more rapidly than rock farther
from the fault. However, you can see other and more recent signs of
faulting in the Peninsula. Where the fault crosses the ridge at the top
of Los Trancos Open Space Preserve, the crushed rock has eroded to
form a fault saddle. Sag ponds at the preserve result from earth
movements that allowed parts of a hillside to sink. Earthquake
movements have changed stream-courses along upper Stevens Creek
Canyon. Landslides occur frequently in the steep Santa Cruz Mountains; many were triggered by the 1906 quake and earlier ones.

The San Andreas Fault Trail in Los Trancos Open Space Preserve is a good place to learn about the effects of fault movement. As a joint project of the Midpeninsula Regional Open Space District and Foothill College, geologists interpret for you evidence of earthquake activity along a self-guided trail through an area changed by the 1906 earthquake and earlier ones. After you have completed the trail and look straight down the rift valleys, you will sense the awesome force of the constant movement of the segments of the earth's skin as they float on top of the deeper mantle of semimolten rock beneath.

Plant And Animal Life

Looking up at the Peninsula hills from several vantage points along Freeway 280, it is possible to identify four of our main plant communities. (A plant community is a group of plants with similar tolerances and similar adaptations to environmental conditions.) First, you see the rounded forms of the oaks, madrones, bays and buckeyes of the mixed woodlands, which cover much of our hillsides. A noticeably different community is the open, rolling grasslands of mountainside meadows and foothill pasturelands, mostly imported annual grasses. Green in winter, dry and golden in summer, they are characteristic of California and other areas of Mediterranean climate, distinguished by winter rains and summer drought.

On the Skyline ridge you see the jagged silhouettes of firs and redwoods in the conifer forest. Although the redwoods were cut over

L. to R. blue oak, coastal live oak, black oak, valley oak

in the 19th century, extensive stands have grown again. This third plant community covers thousands of acres in the Skyline ridge watersheds, parks and sheltered canyons. A fourth plant community, chaparral, thrives on hot, dry slopes. This dense growth of shrubs and trees is specially adapted to our winter rains and long, dry summers. Their leathery or waxy evergreen leaves, sometimes curled inward, conserve moisture, and their long taproots reach water deep below the surface. These plants form a scratchy thicket, unfriendly to the hiker but home to many species of wildlife. The Spaniards are said to have named the vegetation "chaparral" after a Spanish evergreen oak, the chaparro.

After you note the general appearance of Peninsula plant groupings from a distance, you will be surrounded by a great variety of trees, shrubs and flowers on the trail. More than 1700 species grow in the Santa Cruz Mountains.

You will also see and hear unnumbered birds, and if you look closely you will notice lizards, salamanders and the myriad spiders and insects of the earth. Larger animals, once so plentiful, are now rarely seen, though you may have the pleasure of catching sight of a deer in the woods, squirrels in the trees or an occasional rabbit in the brush. But footprints in the wet earth by a stream or in the dust on a sunny trail will tell you there is still animal life nearby. Small holes in the ground and tunnels underfoot are probably all you will see of the many burrowers, such as badgers, voles, field mice and gophers. In thick woodlands you may find the three-foot-high piles of sticks that are the homes of woodrats.

In this guide we mention some of the trees, flowers and creatures you may encounter, but we can touch only briefly on a few of the thousands of species. Fortunately for those whose curiosity is aroused, there are many excellent publications that focus on the plants and wildlife of the Bay Area and California. See Appendix II.

California buckeye has spikelike blossoms.

Sticky monkey flower

Hound's tongue

Sun cups

Clematis

The Peninsula's Past

Although man has lived on the Peninsula for 3000 years (some think for much longer), it is only in the past 200 years that he has significantly changed the natural landscape. Spanish newcomers in the 18th century hunted game with their guns, brought herds that grazed the hills, and introduced annual grasses that supplanted the native bunchgrass. By the mid-19th century, Anglos from the East were changing the face of the Peninsula, logging over the forests, and farming the valleys and foothills.

But it was not until the mid-20th century that the settlements that were scattered down the length of the Peninsula suddenly spread over the valley, reshaped the hills and replaced woodlands and orchards with houses, roads and shopping centers.

However, the Peninsula, which three decades ago was seemingly about to be engulfed in buildings, is now witnessing renewed efforts toward containing its urban spread. Public and private groups are setting aside parks, preserves and trail corridors that complement the increasingly dense settlement patterns of the Bayside. An expanding system of public greenbelts now gives us the opportunity to walk through the lovely foothill landscape, follow a stream, or climb a trail up our steep mountains to thousands of acres of forest on both sides of the Skyline ridge. The recent acquisition of parks and preserves on the west slopes of the Santa Cruz Mountains set aside 10,000 acres of ranchlands and forests for public use.

Earliest Inhabitants

The first people to walk these hills were the Ohlone Indians, a tribe of hunters and gatherers, who lived along the Bay and Pacific shores and in the foothills between San Francisco and Monterey.

When the first European explorers came along the Peninsula, they found their way crisscrossed by trails worn by the bare feet of the Indians as they went to the shores of the Bay and into the hills from their villages. The explorers came across small tribelets of these Indians living in reed huts in villages built beside creeks west of the Bayside marshes and below the first rise of the hills. Our first Peninsula cities were built on many of these same pleasant sites. Before the Spanish era the Peninsula supported one of the densest

Indian populations in the country. Nearly 10,000 Ohlone Indians lived between San Francisco and Monterey.

The Ohlones lived well without cultivating the land. They thrived on the incredible bounty of Peninsula woodlands, streams and shores. Elk, deer, antelope, coyote, fox, bear and mountain lion roamed the hills, along with plentiful small game. Birds, particularly waterfowl, filled the air in sky-darkening numbers. Acorns, the staple of the Indians' diet, were gathered from the thick stands of oak in the hills and on the valley floors. Families returned to ancestral groves year after year to harvest. Welcome seasonal additions to their diet were the plentiful grass and flower seeds, roots, fruits and berries. They also used the bountiful supply of fish and shellfish from the Bay and the creeks. Indeed, when early explorers were offered gifts of food, they commented that Indian fare was palatable, even tasty.

Although the tribelets moved between Bay and foothills most of the year, they did not stray far from the small territories they considered their own. Spring and summer migrations for hunting and gathering were not extensive. A few groups made longer expeditions to trade with other groups for beads, salt, pine nuts, obsidian, abalone shells and wood for bows. Regular trade routes crossed the hills between Bay and ocean.

From the great size of the shell mounds found along the Peninsula it is believed that the Indian population lived here with little change for thousands of years. Theirs was a successful culture that provided well for these people, who lived in relative peace with their neighbors and in harmony with the land.

Save for the periodic burning of the native bunchgrasses in the meadows to keep them open for better hunting and the paths worn deep by centuries of their footprints, the Indians had little impact on the land or the animals around them. Early Europeans reported that the Indians moved among the wildlife and small game without arousing their fears. As Malcolm Margolin states in *The Ohlone Way,* "animals and humans inhabited the very same world, and the distance between them was not very great."

The coming of the European, with his guns, horses and cattle, changed all this. The antelope and elk soon disappeared, and other animals retreated from sight. Changes in the land were profound. Cattle grazing and the inadvertent introduction of European oat grass nearly eliminated the native perennial grasses.

For the Indians, change was swift and complete with the advent of the Spanish missions.

The Spanish-Mexican Period

Two centuries after Europeans first explored the California coast by ship, the overland expedition of Gaspar de Portolá discovered San Francisco Bay in 1769. This event paved the way for permanent Spanish settlement. Mission Dolores and the Presidio of San Francisco, as well as Mission Santa Clara, were founded in 1776. A year later, the Pueblo of Guadalupe in San Jose was built.

After the founding of these missions and their supporting ranches and outposts, the Padres baptized the Indians and drew them into the mission system. By the end of the 18th century, most of the Indians had been moved from their villages to missions and ranches, their families broken up, their old ways lost. The mission founders' dream of small farms run by Christian Indians did not come to pass. In just over half a century the stable Indian culture that had changed little over thousands of years disappeared. In the final tragedy this whole people succumbed by the thousands to imported diseases to which they had little or no resistance.

In the brief period of Mexican rule the missions and their supporting farms were secularized, and the ensuing disruptions of mission life further demoralized the remaining Indians.

Then, with the Gold Rush came land-hungry Easterners, who gained title to the lands occupied by the few remaining Indians, displacing these first Americans who had lived in harmony on the Peninsula for so long. The United States census of 1860 listed only 62 persons as Indians on the Peninsula.

In the early Spanish days the entire Peninsula was divided into a few vast supporting ranches for the missions and the Presidio. Great herds of cattle and sheep grazed over the hills. Grains, vegetables and fruits from the ranches on the Bayside near San Mateo supplied these Spanish outposts.

When Mexico gained independence from Spain in 1821, the government secularized the missions and their ranches. To encourage settlement of the land the Mexican governors of California made grants of land to individuals. They divided the Peninsula into huge ranchos, as large as the 35,000-acre Rancho de las Pulgas. East of the Skyline ridge in the area covered by this guide were the Ranchos Guadalupe, BuriBuri, Feliz, Raimundo de las Pulgas, Martinez, Corte de Madera, Purissima de Concepcion, and the Rancho San Antonio. West were Ranchos San Pedro, Corral de Tierra, Cãnada Verde y Arroyo de la Purisima and San Gregorio.

The brief flowering of these Mexican ranchos ended in 1848 when the American flag was raised over California. The Treaty of

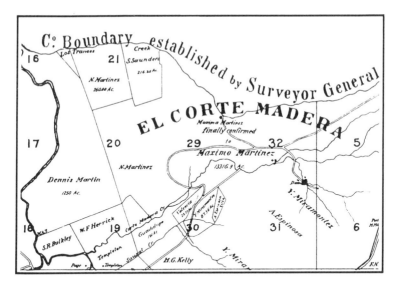

Maximo Martinez, together with Domingo Peralta, was granted the Rancho Corte de Madera, which took its name from the wood cut in the forests of present day Portola Valley. The Martinez home near Alpine Road was torn down in 1940.

Guadalupe, intended to protect the titles of Mexican land grants, failed to do so. Hordes of Americans from the east, eager for land after the discovery of gold, poured into northern California. The great ranchos were soon divided and sold or even usurped by squatters.

Logging

The Spanish had dealt lightly with the forested Peninsula hills. The redwoods cut to build their missions they felled by ax. In fact, they later expressed concern over unrestrained logging by the Anglos.

The greatly increased demand for lumber to build Gold Rush San Francisco brought the first major change to the Sierra Morena, particularly to that part known as the Pulgas Redwoods—the forest above present-day Portola Valley and Woodside. The new owners of these lands logged them heavily with whipsaws. They built sawmills powered first by water, then by steam engines. As many as 50 sawmills operated in these forests, turning out lumber to build San Francisco and then rebuild it after its fires. By 1870 the huge trees, some 10 feet or more in diameter, were gone. Hardly a redwood tree remained standing east of the Skyline, but logging continued in the vast forests on the western slopes.

Farming and Ranching

With the redwoods gone in eastern San Mateo County, some of the lower slopes of the mountains were planted with orchards and vineyards. Dairy farms and large estates covered the foothills. During the late 1800s in northern Santa Clara County, ranchers planted vineyards and orchards of plums, apricots, peaches, pears and cherries on the valley floor and in the lower foothills. This area became one of the most productive fruit-growing areas in the world. The scent of blossoming trees filled the air every spring. Ripening fruits on the trees and trays of apricots, peaches and prunes drying in the fields made summers colorful in the peaceful orchard country. On western slopes open land became livestock and dairy farms.

The Peninsula Bayside Becomes Urban

In eastern San Mateo County a century of settlement saw the gradual break-up of large estates and the burgeoning of towns. By 1863 tracks for the San Francisco and San Jose Railroad had been laid as far as Palo Alto and soon they extended to San Jose. By 1900 a string of suburban towns had grown up along the railroad, which shaped the growth of the Peninsula until the coming of the automobile.

The Santa Clara County orchards survived until the middle years of this century, when people poured into the Peninsula after World War II. Industry expanded in the Santa Clara Valley, and orchard after orchard gave way to housing tracts. Towns grew until their borders touched to form the present unbroken urban band along the Bay.

Cities now cover the Bay plain.

Although houses had been built on the gentler slopes of the eastern foothills, the steeper hillsides, where road building was too difficult, remained wild. By the mid-1950s there were still many undeveloped hillsides, forested slopes and canyons in a relatively natural state. As the concept of public open space evolved, the precipitous canyons and oak-covered hills were seen as welcome breaks between subdivisions. These are the lands that have become parks and open-space preserves where miles of trails beckon hikers today. By the 1980s many forests and ranchlands west of the Skyline were acquired for parks and preserves.

San Francisco Watershed Lands

The vast San Francisco Watershed lands in the heart of San Mateo County have remained wild, their hills spared from development and their reservoirs forming a sparkling chain of lakes. The Watershed deserves special mention because at present San Mateo County's important north-south trail corridor runs the length of these lands, and in the future the thousands of acres east of the lakes are slated for some recreation use, including more trails.

The 23,000-acre Watershed belonging to the City of San Francisco lies between the wooded northern Santa Cruz Mountains and the lower hills to the east. It once drained into upper San Mateo Creek, which was dammed in the late 1800s. The resultant Crystal Springs Lakes and San Andreas Lake to the north are now water-supply reservoirs for San Francisco and much of the Peninsula.

The 15-mile linear valley running through the Watershed was formed over the millenia by movements along the San Andreas Fault as the Pacific Plate slid against the North American Plate. For perhaps thousands of years before the coming of the Spanish this valley was the site of Indian villages. From then until the dams were built, it was a place of small, fertile farms and a few inns. The Crystal Springs Hotel, built in 1855, a popular spa of its day, gave the lakes their name.

When San Francisco needed more water than local wells could supply, the city's Spring Valley Water Company began buying up lands in the Watershed and building reservoirs. In 1862 they dammed Pilarcitos Lake in the northwest part of the Watershed, bringing water by gravity to San Francisco along a 32-mile wooden flume. Next they built the San Andreas Dam and the two Crystal Springs dams. The last of these dams, built across the gorge of San Mateo Creek, was completed in 1896, the engineering feat of its

time. Although it is in the fault zone, it withstood the earthquake of
1906.

When San Francisco's needs were again outpacing its water
supply, the City acquired the private Spring Valley Water Company
and started the ambitious project of bringing water from the Sierra
Nevada. In 1934 O'Shaughnessy Dam at Hetch Hetchy was completed and a pipeline was built across the San Joaquin Valley. Sierra
waters flowed into the Crystal Springs lakes through the Pulgas
Water Temple, built to celebrate this event.

The entire Watershed now belongs to the City of San Francisco.
The location of Freeway 280 through the Watershed south of
Highway 92 required prolonged negotiations that involved the
federal government, the State of California, the City and County of
San Francisco and San Mateo County. An agreement was finally
reached in 1969 to place the freeway farther east of the lakes than
originally proposed. This agreement granted two easements affect-
ing the Watershed lands and guaranteed certain scenic and recreation rights in perpetuity to the people of the United States.

Roughly 19,000 acres on the west side of the lakes are designated as scenic. They must remain undeveloped—preserved for
watershed capacity and scenic quality.

East of the lakes, 4,000 acres of the Watershed will continue to
be set aside for scenic value and watershed purposes, but may also
be used for recreation.

**Before building of the Crystal Springs Dams, San Mateo Creek flowed
through the San Andreas Valley and was joined by Laguna Creek from
the south.**

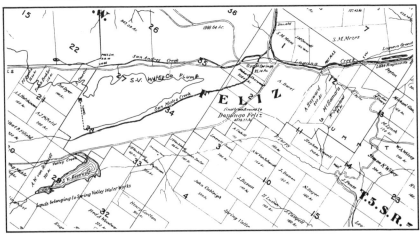

Peninsula Trail Planning

History

As the Peninsula became more urban, opportunities for walking, riding and picnicking diminished. NO TRESPASSING signs and houses appeared where once you could climb a fence to walk or picnic. The counties began to recognize the recreation value of some of the steep canyons, hillsides and once-cut-over lands.

In 1924 Santa Clara County acquired lower Stevens Creek Canyon, its first county park, which has been a favorite place for hiking and riding ever since. Also in 1924 the Spring Valley Water Company laid out 10 miles of equestrian trails near Lake Merced in northern San Mateo County, probably the earliest formal trails built on the Peninsula. According to a bulletin of the Spring Valley Water Company, "These trails were planned to give riders as great a diversity of scenery as possible while at the same time minimizing the danger of trespassing on Lake Merced, the golf courses and vegetable gardens." To this day these concerns remain for trail planners as they seek routes through the countryside that will not conflict with the interests of farmers and property owners.

San Mateo County in the mid-1930s began requiring dedication of riding-trail easements as a part of land subdivisions. In the Woodside and Portola Valley area in particular, this requirement was used to prevent loss of pre-existing trail links when land was subdivided.

The continued interest in trails, particularly for riding, was manifested in the late Forties and early Fifties in a grand plan for a statewide California Riding and Hiking Trail system. In San Mateo County, with the support of horsemen's associations and hikers and with some funding by the state, trails were laid out over easements through private property along the Skyline ridge, through the San Francisco and Bear Gulch watersheds, and along the right-of-way of Skyline Boulevard and Cañada Road. The California Riding and Hiking Trail was marked by posts with gold symbols of horseshoes and hiking boots. Regrettably, in time, a number of easements through private property lapsed and freeway building obliterated parts of the trail near San Andreas Lake and below Crystal Springs Dam. But many miles of the trail survived, and San Mateo County's north-south trail corridor from San Andreas Lake to Wunderlich Park and Skylonda uses much of this same route.

The Forties saw the acquisition of Huddart Park and the development of riding and hiking trails there. San Mateo County, with trail-club cooperation, laid out still more hiking and riding trails on road rights-of-way along Cañada, Whiskey Hill and Portola roads through the present-day towns of Woodside and Portola Valley.

In a burst of trail-planning activity in the Fifties and Sixties, San Mateo County mapped over 400 miles of trails in the City/County Regional Plan for Parks and Open Space, adopted in 1968. Unfortunately, at that time neither the funding nor the support for trails seemed sufficient to bring these trails into being.

However, with funding from a federal pilot project to encourage trails in urban areas, three important trails were built in 1969—the Waterdog Lake and Sheep Camp trails from Belmont to Cañada Road and the Alpine Road Hiking, Riding and Bicycle Trail.

In the Seventies, with renewed appreciation for the remarkable potential for hiking and riding trails in the Peninsula mountains and foothills, conservation, hiking and riding organizations pressed for specific programs and funding for trails.

Voters in San Mateo County adopted a Charter for Parks establishing a special tax for park purposes, and Santa Clara County voters passed a park bond issue. In 1974 a gift of Wunderlich Park's 942 acres of conifer forest and meadows provided hikers with many more miles of trails. The City of Palo Alto bought 1400 acres of hillside woodland, which have become the much prized Foothills Park. Other cities reserved canyons, streamsides and hillsides for public use.

But the citizens of the Peninsula, still concerned with the rapid disappearance of open space and the slow pace of park acquisition, proposed by initiative a Midpeninsula Regional Park District. Northwest Santa Clara County voters formed this district in 1972 and were joined by voters in southern San Mateo County in 1976, after which the name was changed to Midpeninsula Regional Open Space District.

The District's major purpose is to acquire and preserve foothill and Bayland open space outside the urbanized areas of the Peninsula for public use and enjoyment. These lands provide protection for natural vegetation, wildlife and areas of scenic beauty. The District's goal is to help preserve a greenbelt of open space linking District lands with state and county lands. By 1988 the District had acquired 28,000 acres in San Mateo and Santa Clara counties. This greenbelt is creating a system of regional trails with outstanding opportunities for hiking, riding, bicycling and running.

The Peninsula Open Space Trust, a nonprofit land conservancy, takes another approach to open-space acquisition. The Trust is dedicated to private and public preservation of open space in San Mateo and Santa Clara counties. Organized in 1977, the Trust by 1987 had acquired 3 300 acres of open-space lands preserved directly through purchases, gifts or easements and another 14,000 acres preserved indirectly by assistance to other organizations.

During the Seventies trail interest in Santa Clara County focused on the preparation of a Trails and Pathways Master Plan, developed with the participation of representatives of the County Board of Supervisors and each city's planning commission and council. The plan, accepted by the Board of Supervisors in 1978, is based on the concept of trails and trail corridors for bicyclists, hikers and equestrians in a system linking urban areas and parks. In the late 1970s San Mateo County adopted priorities for implementing its trail system.

Pressure for trails sparked state legislation for funding major trails to link state and county parks. Growing interest in regional trails led to bold programs initiated in 1987 for two Bay Area trail systems—the Bay Trail circling San Francisco and San Pablo bays and the Ridge Trail, a 400-mile-long trail along ridgetops ringing the Bay.

Hostels and Overnight Camping

As the Peninsula sections of long-distance trails take shape, more camping and hostel facilities will be needed. In the area covered by this guide, backpack camping by reservation is possible at Huddart Park and at the MROSD camp on Black Mountain in Monte Bello Open Space Preserve. Hidden Villa Hostel in Los Altos Hills, the first and oldest hostel in the West, is the only one in the area of this book. (Hidden Villa Hostel is closed in summer to accommodate a youth camp.) Another hostel is proposed in Palo Alto's Arastradero Preserve.

When the trail network is expanded farther west, hikers will be able to reach camps in some of the coastside parks—Portola State Park, Pescadero and Memorial county parks—or stay in the Sierra Club Hikers' Hut in Sam McDonald County Park, or at the lighthouse hostels at Montara and Pigeon points. Trails now go south from Saratoga Gap to Sanborn Park, where there is a hostel in the historic Welch-hurst home.

**Volunteers from the Trail Center help rangers build the
Redwood Trail in Purisima.**

Trail Building and Maintenance

The success of trail programs depends to a great extent on careful operation and maintenance. The Santa Cruz Mountains Trail Association, horsemen's associations, Scouts, Sierra Club groups and school groups are making valuable contributions in trail building and clean-up projects. They also perform an important role in promoting a sense of stewardship for public land and respect for private property.

The Trail Center, a nonprofit organization established in 1983, recruits, trains and encourages volunteers to help public agencies build and maintain local trails. The Trail Center is located at 4898 El Camino Real, Office 205A, Los Altos, CA 94022. Phone: 415-968-7065.

Trails in The 1990s

As the five-year goal for a San Francisco Bay Area Ridge Trail is reached and the plans for a Bay Trail realized, trail users will have an unparalleled opportunity to explore our region at its highest elevations and at sea level along the Bayfront. Local pathways, like spokes of a wheel, will eventually connect our communities with both these encircling trail systems.

The Ridge Trail is being developed by the Bay Area Ridge Trail Council with the sponsorship of the National Park Service, local park departments, Greenbelt Alliance, regional and open-space districts and water agencies. In the area covered by this guide, it will link Peninsula trails from the Golden Gate National Recreation Area in San Francisco through San Mateo County to the mountainside parks of Santa Clara County.

The Bay Trail planning, headed by the Association of Bay Area Governments staff and assisted by an Advisory Council, will spur the completion of trails and the closing of gaps in the existing trail system along the Peninsula Bayside.

For information on these ongoing projects contact the National Park Service, Interpretation and Visitor Services, Golden Gate National Recreation Area, Fort Mason, Building 201, San Francisco, CA 415-556-3535, the Association of Bay Area Governments, P.O. Box 2050, Oakland CA 415-464-7975 or Greenbelt Alliance, 116 New Montgomery, Suite 640, San Francisco, 415-543-4291.

Using This Guide

The main focus of this guide is to describe trips through our parks and preserves, giving a detailed account of each trail and information on elevation change, terrain, orientation, trip distance and hiking time. The authors have drawn on their own experience of hiking on all the trails in this guide. Their enthusiasms are, of course, subjective, but directions, trail distances and details of natural features are intended to be objective and concise.

Travel times are based on a moderate hiking pace, which averages about two miles an hour, taking into account the difficulty of the terrain and the elevation gain. Trip distances are stated as one-way, loop or round trip. Trip times are those required to complete the trips as described. Of course, time for bicyclists or equestrians will differ from that for hikers.

Figures for elevation change tell the vertical footage gained or lost from the start to the highest or lowest point of the trip. These figures do not include minor elevation changes along the way. When the outward leg of a loop or a round trip is uphill, the elevation change is given as a gain; then, of course, the return leg will be an elevation loss. Conversely, when the outward leg is downhill, the elevation change is given as a loss.

To estimate the time required for a trip where the cumulative gain is more than 1000 feet or where there are steep climbs within a short distance, the authors used an old hiking rule: for every 1000 vertical feet gain, add ½ hour to the time that would be required on level ground.

These trails include not only long hikes in big county parks and major open-space preserves, but also strolls on paths in city parks and by the Bay that offer pleasant, brief respite from the urban scene. The many choices for hikes near home range from steep mountain climbs to gentle paths through the woods to level paths past tidal marshes.

Every effort has been made to make this guide up-to-date, but new parks and preserves opening in the future undoubtedly will provide new trails.

On the *Map of Peninsula Trails* in the beginning of this book the general locations of trails are numbered to correspond with the table of contents. Trails are listed from north to south, and page numbers refer to detailed trail descriptions.

"Trails for Different Seasons and Reasons" in Appendix I groups trails for a variety of purposes and situations. These suggestions may help those unfamiliar with the Peninsula to find a suitable trail or perhaps inspire seasoned hikers to try new trails in our parks and open-space preserves. It is not an exhaustive list. Each hiker can add his favorites.

How To Get There

This guide includes maps and directions to each park and preserve by car. Directions give routes from the nearest freeway or major road, and indicate parking areas and points of access to the trail.

Where bus transportation is close to a trail head and schedules convenient, the bus route number is given. For up-to-date information in San Mateo County, call SamTrans. In Santa Clara County, call County Transit District.

Information and Maps

Maps of all the parks and preserves, specially prepared for this book, show trail routes and entry points, main natural features, elevations, park facilities and parking areas for cars and horse trailers. These maps are a valuable reference for hikers, runners, bicyclists and equestrians, as well as for those who wish to picnic or just relax in public recreation sites on the Peninsula.

Although most major parks and preserves offer maps of their trails, these are not always at hand. To secure more information, leaflets and maps, write, phone or visit:

San Mateo County Parks and Recreation Department
County Government Center
590 Hamilton St.   Phone: 415-363-4020
Redwood City, CA 94063   Reservations: 415-363-4021

Santa Clara County Parks and Recreation Department
298 Garden Hill Drive   Phone: 408-358-3741
Los Gatos, CA 95031   Reservations: 408-358-3751

Midpeninsula Regional Open Space District
Old Mill Office Center, Bldg. C, Suite 135
201 San Antonio Circle
Mountain View, CA 94040   Phone: 415-949-5500

For free docent-led walks and tours in MROSD preserves, call the District Office—415-949-5500.

In addition to these public agencies, the Trail Center, a volunteer organization, serves as a source of information about local trails and trail activities. Among publications available are a four-county parks map; and books on trails, parks, open-space preserves and wildlife refuges in San Francisco, San Mateo, Santa Clara and Santa Cruz counties. A monthly activity schedule lists upcoming hiking, running, equestrian and bicycling events. See page 18 for address and phone.

Excellent topographic maps are available from the United States Geological Survey headquarters and from many sporting-goods stores. The western district headquarters of the USGS is right here on the Peninsula at 345 Middlefield Road, Menlo Park. The map sales and information office, Building 3, a fascinating place worth a trip in itself, is open from 8 A.M. to 4 P.M. Maps come in 15- and 7.5-minute series. The larger scale, on the 7.5-minute series, where one inch represents 2,000 feet, is more useful for hikers. At $2.50 per quadrangle, they are a great buy.

Some local trails are shown on these maps, but it is the topographic information that is of particular interest to the hiker—contours and natural features, such as wooded areas, clearings, creeks, lakes and mountains. Although "topos" are not necessary for hiking on the trails in this guide, they can add to your understanding of the terrain. After you have learned to read the contour lines, you can visualize the shape and elevation of the land they represent. Then you can tell by the spacing of the contour lines whether the grade on the trail will be steep or gentle.

The area of this guide is covered by eight quadrangles of the 7.5-minute series, listed here from north to south: *San Francisco South, Montara Mountain, San Mateo, Woodside, Palo Alto, Mindego Hill, Cupertino and La Honda.*

Rules For The Trail

Park and open-space preserve regulations are few, but they are important. Based on common sense, they are necessary for your own safety and the protection of our parklands. To preserve the beauty of the natural setting, all plants, animals and natural features are protected. Leave them undisturbed for others to enjoy. Don't smoke on the trail, and build no fires except where permitted in established fireplaces. Firearms and bows and arrows are prohibited.

Leave dogs at home. Dogs are prohibited in all San Mateo County parks; in lands of the Midpeninsula Regional Open Space District, except for a few preserves where dogs are allowed on leash in specified areas; and in Santa Clara County parks, except for some parks that permit dogs on a short leash in picnic areas, but never on trails. The presence of a dog, even a well-behaved one on a leash, disturbs wild creatures.

Stay on the trail. Shortcuts across trail switchbacks break the trail and accelerate erosion.

In addition to these regulations, good trail manners assume that you will preserve the quiet of the natural scene. Leave your radio at home so you and others can listen to the songs of the birds and the sounds of the forest.

Parks and preserves generally open at 8 A.M. and close at dusk.

For your own safety, stay on the trail. Cross-country travel through steep, brushy, unfamiliar land can get you into real trouble (and poison oak).

Also, for safety's sake, walk with companions rather than alone. If you need to find someone to go with you, get in touch with one of the many organizations that conduct hikes, such as the Sierra Club, the Committee for Green Foothills, the Audubon Society and city and county parks departments. The Peninsula Conservation Center in Palo Alto (415-494-9301) is an excellent source of contacts for such groups, and itself conducts hikes from time to time.

Some senior centers organize walks and provide transportation to trails. Or you can form your own walking group of friends and neighbors who travel at your pace. You will find trail companions available just for the asking. See Appendix III for organization lists and phone numbers.

Sharing the Trails

Many Peninsula trails are shared by hikers, runners and equestrians. Some trails are shared with bicyclists too. The use of trails by these several users creates the need for the further development of trail etiquette and in some cases trail rules.

Hikers and runners should stand quietly when horses are passing, as sudden movements can startle horses.

Bicyclists have long used paved paths, and some paths have been built principally for their use. When sharing these paths, bicyclists should warn of their approach when overtaking walkers, runners and an occasional equestrian.

The new trail users of the 1980s are the mountain bicyclists, whose new equipment takes them up steep and unpaved trails. It will take time to work out reasonable rules that will be fair to potentially conflicting uses of trails and will protect all trail users. It is generally agreed that bicyclists should yield to horses and hikers.

At this writing, Santa Clara County does not allow mountain bicycles on its trails. A few San Mateo County parks allow mountain bicycles on wide service roads, noted in the text and Appendix I. MROSD, while developing a set of standards and guidelines for trail use, allows bicycles on most of its preserves.

Two Hazards For Hikers

Poison Oak: This plant, *Rhus diversiloba,* is widespread through most of the Peninsula hiking country. It is not necessary to remember its Latin name, but it is essential to learn to recognize this

Poison-oak plant

ubiquitous plant with its three-lobed leaves. It looks different according to the season and the environment where it is growing. In spring its gray branches send out reddish buds, then shiny, young, light-green leaves. In autumn it has rosy red leaves that are brilliant in the woods and along the roadsides.

Watch out for it in its various habits, from stunted bushes on dry slopes, to luxuriant shoulder-high plants, to climbers twining 20 feet or more up a tree. To touch the twigs or leaves is to court the outbreak of an uncomfortable, itchy, blistering, long-lasting rash. **Avoid it!** Wear long sleeves and long pants for protection; bathe with cool water and soap when you get home. If you have unavoidably brushed against some poison oak, wash the area in the nearest stream or even use water from your canteen.

Rattlesnakes: The other, and far less common, hazard is the rattlesnake. It has a triangular-shaped head, diamond markings or dark blotches on its back, and from one to seven rattles (segments) on its tail. It is the only poisonous snake native to our hills; it inhabits many hillside parks, though it is rarely seen. The rattlesnake will avoid you if it possibly can. Just watch where you put your feet and hands, and stay on the trails.

Weather

The vagaries and variety of our local weather require some flexibility in planning hikes. Summer weather can vary from day to day, even from hour to hour where coastal fogs and winds influence the temperature. The Skyline ridge and the northern Peninsula are often windy and dripping with fog in summer while the rest of the Peninsula is mild and sunny. In other seasons the mountains can be drenched in rain when the Bayside cities are merely cloudy.

Summer and fall bring sunny, hot days to the southern Peninsula. Midday hiking is best then in the cool, forested canyons. In any season, south- and west-facing slopes are the warmest. A winter hike on such slopes is delightful on a sunny day.

Although we all welcome the many clear, mild days of our incomparable Peninsula climate, there are hikers who find particular joy in a bracing hike on a cold day. And there is even a unique pleasure in walking through the woods in the gentle rains of early spring when pale green new leaves begin to appear on the trees.

What To Wear

Walking is surely the prime low-cost sport. The rewards are unrelated to the outlay for equipment, since the only essential is comfortable, sturdy footgear. The many available walking and running shoes with good treads are fine for Peninsula trails. Some hikers still prefer boots for the protection they give on rough terrain and on wet trails. Some experienced hikers suggest that you "dress like an onion," so you can peel off layers as needed. A sweater and a windbreaker provide for the extremes of weather and temperature you may encounter during a day. If you are susceptible to poison oak or are not yet familiar with it, a long-sleeved shirt and long pants offer protection to sensitive skin. With a hat for shade in summer and a scarf or warm cap for cold and windy days, you are well-equipped for enjoying the trail.

Put the extra clothing in a light, inexpensive day pack, add a snack or lunch, a canteen of water and perhaps this guidebook. Binoculars for birds, a magnifying glass for flowers, lichen and insects, and a flower or bird guide won't add much weight. An all-purpose bandana and pocket knife come in handy. Most of the latter may be just frills, but the water is a must, since streams are infrequent and their water is unsafe to drink.

Wildland signs stand at entrances to many open-space preserves.

Map Legend

▬▬▬ Freeway	Ⓟ Parking
—— Road	Ⓟ̸ No parking
– – – – Trail	ⓁⓅ Limited parking
•••••••••• Hiking-only trail	ⒺⓅ Equestrian parking
○ ○ ○ ○ ○ ○ ○ Proposed trail	■ Restroom
—•—•— Park boundary	▲ Picnic area
— – — Watershed boundary	▢ Park office or headquarters
—•••— Stream	School
➤ Park entrance	Church
➤ Trail entry point	
⊢—⊣ Gate	

Part 2:
The Peninsula Trails

The Northern Peninsula
From the San Francisco County Line to Highway 92

San Bruno Mountain
State and County Park

San Bruno Mountain rises starkly from the Bay to an elevation of 1314 feet, dominating the northern Peninsula landscape, its bare, steep flanks creased by narrow ravines and a few wooded canyons. The cities of San Francisco, Brisbane, South San Francisco, Colma and Daly City surround the mountain.

From the top of this seemingly barren mountain rising above the cities encircling it, you see the other Bay Area landmark mountains, the Pacific Ocean, the skyscrapers of San Francisco and the ships on its great Bay.

In 1978 the mountain became San Bruno Mountain Park with the purchase by the State of California and San Mateo County of 1500 acres and the gift of 500 acres by the property owner. Later additions brought the park's total to 2266 acres.

Guadalupe Canyon Parkway, running generally east-west across the park, leads to the park entrance. North of the parkway is a relatively level area known as the Saddle, where visitors find beautiful views and attractive picnic areas screened by native oaks and sheltering low walls. A day camp nestles in the center of the Saddle and trails loop around the perimeter.

South of the parkway, trails ascend the mountain's steep sides. A road to the summit leads to trails along its high ridges. Superb views from this mountaintop make it a fine place to take visitors for an orientation to the Bay Area, all laid out before you.

More than 11 miles of trails take the visitor over the mountain's varied terrain on short, easy nature trails accessible for the physically limited, on moderate loop hikes, and on longer trips up the mountain. Although the ridges of the mountain are exposed to the prevailing winds and fog from the ocean, and buffeted by the storms of winter, the ravines in the lee of the main ridgeline are often sunny and relatively warm. After winter rains clear, the superb 360° views are worth a trip to the mountain with windbreaker, binoculars and camera. Even in blustery weather, the hiking is good if you are prepared with proper clothing.

Geography and Geology

Considered an outlier of the Santa Cruz Mountains, San Bruno Mountain is an elevated fault block composed largely of a dark gray rock of the Franciscan Formation with the catchy name of graywacke (three syllables). You can see jumbled outcroppings of this rock above Guadalupe Canyon Parkway as you come up the canyon from the west.

History

Some evidence of Indian habitation has been found in Buckeye Canyon and shell mounds are known along the edge of the Bay below. A few years after the Portolá expedition discovered San Francisco Bay in 1769, Captain Fernando Rivera, the principal officer of Father Francisco Palou's exploring party, climbed the mountain with four of his men to watch the sunrise. Man has since greatly altered the land they saw around them, but the mountain itself remains very little changed. It is believed that the mountain was named for the patron saint of Captain Bruno Heceta, who commanded an inland party mapping the Bay and the surrounding lands.

From Spanish times the mountain was considered good pasture, and from those times until World War II cattle grazed these grassy slopes.

In one of the early grants of the Mexican regime in 1836 Governor Luis Arguello bestowed on Jacob Lesse, a naturalized Mexican citizen, the Rancho Cañada de Guadalupe, Visitacion y Rodeo

Viejo. The Ranch took in the whole mountain, Visitacion Valley and the old rodeo grounds near the Bay. Over the years the ranch changed hands many times as it was traded, sold and divided, until 1872 when the Visitation Land Company secured the largest holding. In 1884 H. W. Crocker acquired the company's 3814 acres. This large holding remained for nearly a century in the Crocker Estate, until the establishment of the park.

The Mountain's Special Flora

The mountain, so dun-colored from a distance after its grasses dry up, is at close view colorful and lively with a great variety of plants, lichen-covered rocks and fern-lined canyons. In spite of over a century of grazing, San Bruno Mountain is a botanical island with vegetation typical of that which once covered the San Francisco hills. A great number of native species of plants grow on the mountain—384 have been counted, including some rare and endangered species and a few unique to this special environment.

Nearly 50 varieties of grasses grow here, half of them native, including many of California's perennial bunchgrasses. In the grasslands from February on, you can see impressive displays of wildflowers—sheets of pearly everlastings, colonies of goldfields, clumps of Johnny jump-ups, slopes covered with Douglas and coast irises, and steep hillsides of brilliant, showy, red California fuchsias. The mountain's most extensive and varied displays of annual flowers are found on some 150 acres on the April Brook slopes known as the Flower Garden.

Four rare butterflies, among them the endangered Mission blue, the San Francisco silverspot and the San Bruno elfin, live and feed on the plants of San Bruno Mountain.

Habitat Conservation Plan

Long years of concern over potential effects of construction on the mountain's flora and its rare and endangered species led to a landmark decision in 1982. Known as the Habitat Conservation Plan, it granted developers a 30-year permit to build on some of the endangered species' habitat in return for their funding programs to enhance the species' chances of survival on the park lands.

This plan sets up an annual fund which will be used to eliminate invasive gorse and eucalyptus and to seed host plants, such as lupine and goldfields, for food and refuge for the endangered species.

Time will tell how well these fragile species can survive in limited space and in close contact with urban development. In the meantime, building moves right up to the boundaries of the park.

Jurisdiction   State of California and San Mateo County.

Facilities   Picnic areas, barbecues, meadow play area, restrooms, day camp.

Park Rules   8 A.M. to sunset. No dogs allowed in the park. Bicycles allowed on Radio Road and the Saddle Loop Trail only.

Maps   San Mateo County *San Bruno Mountain Park* and USGS topo *San Francisco South.*

How To Get There   From Freeway 280: (1) Southbound, take the Eastmoor Avenue exit and turn left on Sullivan Avenue, which parallels the freeway. At the first street on the left turn left onto San Pedro Road, which goes over the freeway. Across Mission Street San Pedro Road becomes East Market Street, which becomes Guadalupe Canyon Parkway. The park entrance is on the north side of the parkway. (2) Northbound, take the Mission Street exit. At the first stop sign, turn left on Junipero Serra Boulevard, then right on San Pedro Road and follow the directions above.

San Bruno Mountain County Park

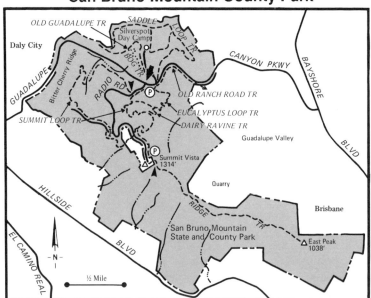

Two Trips on the North Side of the Parkway
Trip 1.   Saddle Loop Trail

Circling the northern Saddle area of the park, this is an invigorating hike when fresh breezes sweep in from the Pacific. Views stretch beyond San Francisco to its dramatic setting of Bay and mountains.
Distance   2.7-mile loop.
Time   1½ hours.
Elevation Gain   150'

TRAIL NOTES

Marked off in ½-mile segments, this loop is a longtime favorite of joggers. Now open to bicyclists too, it is becoming an even more popular trail.

Starting on the Old Guadalupe Trail on the west side of the north parking area, follow this former ranch road lined with eucalyptus and Monterey cypress. It traverses the sides of a ravine, where moisture-loving plants grow by the path. On foggy days the aroma of eucalyptus leaves is intensified when they are crushed underfoot.

In 0.8 mile veer right, past new subdivisions crowding the park boundary, to climb into open grasslands where you have long views out to the Pacific Ocean and Pt. Reyes. If the day is very clear, the Farallon Islands seem closer than their 40-mile distance.

The trail arcs right, staying close to the boundary of the park, with flowers brightening the way at most any season. Particularly brilliant in spring with goldfields, lupines and some rare species, this path even in summer is dotted with magenta farewell-to-spring and white yarrow.

Downtown San Francisco highrises puncture the skyline and the Bay Bridge stretches across to Oakland. As your trail continues to its highest point, the view spreads toward the South Bay shoreline. From about the halfway point of this loop, a service road cuts straight back to the park entrance, passing the pleasant day-camp area enroute.

As you continue around the Saddle Loop, the view changes to take in the full height and breadth of San Bruno Mountain. It beckons the hiker to cross the parkway and climb its trails to even wider views of the entire Bay Area.

Heading back to the parking area, you pass the gorse elimination projects. European gorse has taken over large areas of this saddle, threatening to wipe out the host plants for the rare and endangered butterflies. Because gorse seeds can live for six to eight years, gorse is very difficult to eradicate.

Looking north from San Bruno Mountain's summit

In small ravines coastal scrub harbors many bird species. You may recognize the quail's warning call and see wren-tits and song sparrows flitting from shrub to shrub. These birds and the rare plants and butterflies of the mountain are now protected through the establishment of San Bruno Mountain Park.

Trip 2.   Bog Trail

A short nature trail aligned on a gentle grade and having a stable surface skirts a little swale west of the park entrance. A bridge over an intermittent stream leads from it to the Old Guadalupe Trail.

This 0.4-mile trail, accessible to the physically limited, offers an opportunity for all nature lovers to enjoy the riparian environment. A self-guiding pamphlet explains the plants and animals of this environment.

The Bog Trail, together with a section of the Old Guadalupe Trail (the first leg of the Saddle Loop Trip), makes a loop of less than a mile. Try this before sitting down to lunch at one of the picnic sites just beyond the old cypress trees at the park entrance.

Four Trips on the South Side of the Parkway
Trip 1.   Eucalyptus Loop Trail

A relatively easy trail samples the lower slopes of the mountain with views up to its long ridgetop.

Distance 1-mile loop.
Time ½ hour.
Elevation Gain 170′

TRAIL NOTES

This trip is just right for a brisk walk before lunch. After learning about the natural wonders of the mountain from the exhibits on the display board by the trailhead at the south-side parking area, set off left on this loop trip.

As you come out of the big eucalyptus trees and around a few bends, you see the deeply furrowed sides of the mountain, dark green against the sky. Water rushes down the mountain in winter, carving still deeper furrows in the mountain's side. After a few bends in the trail, your way straightens out above the eucalyptus grove to cross Dairy Ravine. High above, the long spine of the park extends for more than 2 miles southeast. Up close, the mountain has a magnificent profusion of poppies and goldfields glowing golden in spring and early summer.

A last turn right takes you into the trees and thence back to the trailhead. For lunch you can take the footpath through the underpass to the north-side picnic area by the old Monterey cypresses that mark the north entrance to the park.

Trip 2.   Dairy Ravine Loop

Climbing higher on the mountain, this trip zigzags up and down the sides of Dairy Ravine past trailside gardens of remarkable beauty.

Distance 1 ¾-mile loop.
Time 1 hour.
Elevation Gain 325′

TRAIL NOTES

In return for the extra elevation gain and extra mileage, this loop offers the delights of coming upon different rock gardens at every turn. Lichen-covered rocks shelter gray-green sedums, their tall flower stalks bearing coral and yellow blossoms.

Starting from the trailhead on the south side of Guadalupe Canyon Parkway, take the left branch of the Eucalyptus Loop Trail and at the first junction bear left onto the Dairy Ravine Trail. This ½-mile-long trail climbs the east side of Dairy Ravine in wide switchbacks to meet the Summit Loop Trail at the head of Dairy Ravine.

When you meet the Summit Loop Trail, veer right on it, and see the San Francisco skyline looming in the distance. Below are the old cypress trees in Dairy Ravine. The name and these trees are all that remain of the dairy farm that once operated at the foot of the ravine.

The trail crosses over and makes a switchback above the steep east side of Cable Ravine, then descends quickly through waist-high cream bush, coffee berry and snowberry to meet the Eucalyptus Loop Trail. Here you take a left turn to return to the south-side parking area.

Trip 3.   Summit Loop Trail

This mountaintop climb takes you past the Flower Gardens of April Brook Ravine, along the west ridge for its views, and down the steep north face below the summit.

Distance   3.1-mile loop.

Time   2 hours.

Elevation Gain   725'

TRAIL NOTES

Although you can complete this trip in two hours, you may want to linger longer in spring to enjoy the views and the flowers at every step of the way. From the trailhead on the south side of Guadalupe Canyon Parkway, take the path to the right through the eucalyptus grove.

After crossing the road, you soon come out into dense, waist-high growth—tall cows parsnip with its flat clusters of white blossoms, honeysuckle, and California bee plant with its dull red flowers. Along the way you come across the many wet places in the trail where even in summer water is seeping from springs above.

You are soon at the ravine where April Brook flows into willow-bordered Colma Creek. It's a protected little swale that catches the noontime sun. The brook is heavily lined with sword ferns, and big clumps of coastal iris edge the trail. In winter, you can distinguish the coastal iris from the Douglas iris, also found on the mountain, by their straplike leaves that are green on both sides; in contrast, Douglas iris leaves are shiny green on top and dull-grayish green

**Summit of San Bruno Mountain,
from northwest of Guadalupe Parkway**

below. Come back in April and May to see the long-petaled flowers in shades of blue.

But even in winter you can see the promise of spring in the emerging foliage of California poppies, lupines and other annual flowers. Stone outcrops by the trail form rock gardens of such satisfying design as to serve as models for our domestic landscaping efforts. Needlepoint-textured, orange and gray lichen cover the rocks; pink-hued succulents, small polypody ferns and thick-leaved daisies fill the crevices.

The trail crosses April Brook Ravine and ascends via switchbacks to Bitter Cherry Ridge, where the skyscrapers of San Francisco and the blocks of Daly City homes come into view. East of April Brook in the sloping meadow below Radio Road is the Flower Garden, a carpet of color from early March through May.

At the very top of the ridge the trail joins a paved road, where you turn left. Southwest and far below are the cemeteries of Colma, with lawn, lakes and headstones. After a few minutes' walk east on top of this ridge, look for the continuation of the trail on the south side. Keep to the narrow trail going uphill and avoid an old jeep road that contours around to a lower destination.

The first stretch of the trip goes through a brilliant summer garden of knee-high golden yarrow, contrasted with purple pennyroyal, crimson pitcher sage, white yarrow and pink owl's clover. If you look back over this sea of blooms, you will see up the coast all

the way to Pt. Reyes. A few steps farther around the east side of the
hill the stony slopes are encrusted with low, pink-edged succulents
and gray-leaved, lemon-yellow-blossomed Indian paintbrush. Below
the next bend in the trail the saucer of a telephone relay rises like a
giant white bloom from this stony garden.

A switchback in the trail takes you up to Radio Road, where
above you rises a spindly forest of antennas springing from the commercial communications installations in an enclave of private
property. Cross the road and start north down the mountain in wide
switchbacks with ever-changing vistas and a succession of trailside
gardens as varied as the views. Just 400 feet down the Summit Loop
Trail you pass the Ridge Trail going east. You could turn here and
walk out to the East Peak and back, thus extending your trip by 5
miles.

Continuing down the Summit Loop Trail, you pass a rocky
promontory where rare varieties of huckleberry and manzanita form
ground-hugging mats. This species of manzanita, found only on San
Bruno Mountain, is now sold in nurseries as a drought-resistant
ground cover.

From the promontory you can see down the flank of the mountain to the Bay. After a hairpin turn you look east to Blue Blossom
Hill, mantled with deep-blue wild-lilac blossoms in early spring.

At the next trail junction you can choose the east or the west
ridge above Dairy Ravine. Both have fine views and remarkable
flower displays, long after the spectacular spring show. To stay on
the Summit Loop Trail bear left (west). On this long traverse you
pass a series of little gardens in a sheltered spot. Low-growing pink
daisies are blooming along with blue brodiaeas, accented with
crimson sage, and a patch of pennyroyal is splashed with scarlet
paintbrush. Here and there are clumps of iris edged with monkey
flower.

At the next trail junction, veer left and follow the Eucalyptus
Loop Trail around a big bend down into the trees at the parking area.

Trip 4.   Ridge Trail to East Peak Vista

An invigorating hike goes out to East Peak for commanding
views of the Bay Area and far out over the Pacific Ocean.

Distance   4.8 miles round trip from summit; 8 miles round trip
from lower south-side trailhead.

Time   2½ hours from summit; 4½ hours from lower trailhead.

Elevation Loss   310′ from summit; **Gain**   from lower trailhead
725′

TRAIL NOTES

Drive up Radio Road to begin this trip at the east end of the summit parking area. Or, for a more challenging 8-mile hike, start at the lower south-side parking area and take the Summit Loop Trail up to the Ridge Trail, which is on the northeast side of the summit. Then follow the Ridge Trail, contouring east below the mountaintop, to join the trail from the summit parking area to the East Peak. In either case, this trip calls for windbreakers against the usual mountaintop winds and sturdy shoes for the often rocky Ridge Trail.

Only ¼ mile out on the trail you can begin to take in the wonderful panorama. You stand with the San Francisco skyline in view in one direction, the Bay in front of you, and over your shoulder the blue Pacific Ocean. Right at your feet is the mountain, its grassy slopes flowering in early spring. You can see down into the steep ravines, the first to the southwest, Sage Ravine, grayed with artemisia. The northeast slopes tend to be brush-covered or wooded. Past the quarry, rock outcroppings, tall chaparral and trees cover Buckeye Ravine.

On either side hawks ride the updrafts. You may see one make its swift glide for a ground squirrel in the grass below. If it has a wing spread of 4 feet or more and a tail that shows reddish orange against the sky, it is a red-tailed hawk, the most common kind on the mountain.

By late February wildflowers begin to bloom through the grass, earlier here than elsewhere on the Peninsula. Clumps of California poppies and ground-hugging Johnny jump-ups color the ridgetop. Creamy yellow wallflowers blow in the breeze on ten-inch stems, and blossoms of white milkmaids are sprinkled down the shadier northeast slopes.

The East Peak, unmarked except by the transmission towers, is a good place to turn back. The ridge falls off rapidly a little beyond, which makes for a very steep climb back. Returning to the summit, the ocean is before you. On a clear day you can see Pt. Reyes on the northwest horizon.

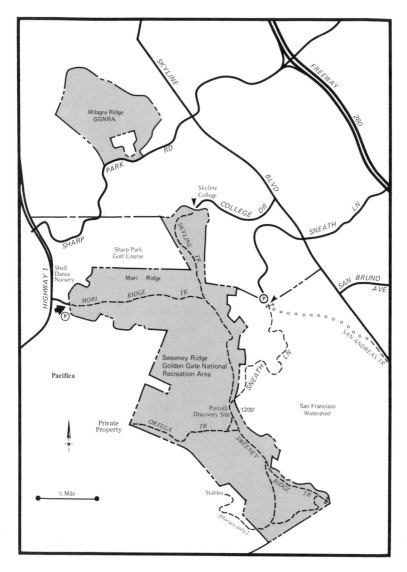

Sweeney Ridge Golden Gate National Recreation Area

The Sweeney Ridge addition to the Golden Gate National Recreation Area takes in the high ridge just north of Montara Mountain. Its grassy hilltop commands sweeping views of ocean and Bay.

From this site Gaspar de Portolá's scouts first saw the expanse of water we know as San Francisco Bay.

In 1980 the Golden Gate National Recreation Area expanded its jurisdiction south from Marin County and San Francisco to include 26,000 acres of land within San Mateo County. Much of this land was already in public ownership, though not some 1,000 acres along Sweeney Ridge. The GGNRA purchased this land in 1982 to "preserve the natural, cultural and recreation values of the ridge." Included in this acquisition was the Portolá Discovery Site, already owned by the City of Pacifica and San Mateo County. In 1987 the GGNRA assumed jurisdiction of San Mateo County's adjacent Sweeney Ridge Skyline Preserve and Milagra Ridge Preserve less than a mile north.

In addition to their place in history as the spot from which Europeans first saw San Francisco, these wind-swept, foggy heights were grazing lands for Spanish ranches. By 1875 these lands, ideal for dairy farming, were acquired by the enterprising Richard Sneath, for whom the lane is named. He operated his dairy here until well into the 1920s. His barns were on Sneath Lane at El Camino Real.

From the rounded ridgetop, steep slopes and narrow, brush-filled canyons descend. At the northwest end of the preserve Mori Ridge reaches beyond Highway 1 to Mori Point.

Sweeney Ridge's hogback is flanked east and south by San Francisco Watershed lands; west is the City of Pacifica. Only a few thousand feet from the southern boundary of the preserve is San Pedro Valley County Park.

Described here are three trips, one from each of the present access routes to the preserve. The quickest and most direct for those living on the Bayside is the approach from Skyline Boulevard on Sneath Lane. From the north there is a direct route from Skyline College to the ridgetop. From Pacifica, a trail up Mori Ridge leaves Highway 1 just north of Vallemar.

Sweeney Ridge is a key segment of the San Francisco Bay Area Ridge Trail. Proposed trails will reach the ridge from the existing San Andreas Trail beside San Andreas Lake to the southeast, and other, as yet undesignated, routes will connect to the ridge from the south. Northwest are several routes from Sweeney Ridge to Mussel Rock through Milagra Ridge and along utility easements and road rights-of-way. From Mussel Rock north to Thornton Beach there is an opportunity for a spectacular trail along the ocean's edge on the route of the Shoreline Railroad and old Highway 1.

Jurisdiction   Golden Gate National Recreation Area.

Facilities   Trails for hikers, equestrians and bicyclists.
Maps   GGNRA *Sweeney Ridge,* USGS topo *Montara Mountain.*
Park Rules   Open from 8 A.M. to dusk; no dogs on trails.
Connecting Trail   Proposed access from San Mateo County's San
Andreas Trail northwest to Sneath Lane.

Trip 1.   From Sneath Lane to the Discovery Site

Up the lane to the Discovery Site and down Sweeney Ridge to its
south end is a bracing hike with superb views.
Distance   1.8 miles one way from end of Sneath Lane to the
Discovery Site; and a 2½-mile loop from the Discovery Site to the
south end of the preserve and back, altogether a 6-mile round trip.
Time   3 hours round trip.
Elevation Gain   700'
Connecting Trail   Proposed extension of San Andreas Trail to
Sneath Lane.
How To Get There   Turn west off Skyline Boulevard on Sneath
Lane. Continue for 2 miles to gated entrance to preserve and park by
roadside. Better parking is planned for this entrance.

TRAIL NOTES

Enter through the stile to the paved service road through the San
Francisco Watershed lands. You descend by a willow-bordered
watercourse that flows into San Andreas Lake. Close by will be the
junction with the proposed extension of the San Andreas Trail. The
road soon starts its rise in and out of ravines that furrow the eastern
slopes. From the outer bends of the road you catch glimpses of San
Andreas Lake below. The grade is easy and the only traffic an occasional official vehicle or a few bicycles.

Partway up you will see a yellow stripe in the center of the pavement, making a "fog line" to guide cars and bicycles when dense fog
blankets the hills. A word of caution about the ridge on foggy days: A
walk in the fog is a bracing experience, but stay on roads or well-
defined trails. When visibility is close to zero, a hiker can become
disoriented and find himself lost on these moors.

Where the service road reaches the ridgetop, you are in the
GGNRA. Turn left for the Discovery Site, which is marked by a dark
granite cylinder. Carved around it are the outlines of the landmarks
in the sweeping views around you, such as Mt. Tamalpais, San Bruno
Mountain, Mt. Diablo and Montara Mountain.

From this point on the ridge Gaspar de Portolá's scouts saw "a
great estuary . . . extending many leagues inland." They were in

search of Monterey Bay, however, and felt misgivings that that bay and the ship they wished to rejoin might lie behind them. It was only several years later, and after subsequent expeditions, that the Spaniards recognized the importance of San Francisco Bay and its magnificent harbor.

From the Discovery Site the Sweeney Ridge Trail heads south toward the boundary of the preserve. For more than a mile you go over grasslands, past rock outcroppings and through patches of coastal scrub. In spring this is a flowery way, with carpets of goldfields, patches of blue lupine and great clumps of blue coastal iris. On fine days you can see forever. The dark outline of Montara Mountain is before you, and on either side the ocean and the Bay. As you go along, listen for the sharp cries of a kestrel, a small hawk with white undersides that searches the meadows for field mice and gophers.

Toward the south end of the preserve are a spring-fed marsh and a small reed-rimmed pond. The trail splits at the marsh. Our route goes left of the marsh and returns on the west side of the low hill beyond. Follow this trail to the southeast corner of the preserve, where a gate for equestrians with permits leads into the San Francisco Watershed.

To continue on the loop, turn right at the gate and skirt the hill. You pass through a thicket of coastal scrub enlivened by apricot-colored monkey flowers, white heads of pearly everlastings and here and there clumps of bright red and yellow Indian paintbrush.

On the west side of the hill an equestrian trail takes off steeply downhill to stables at the end of Linda Mar Valley. Beyond the preserve boundary the trail is for equestrians only. Our route turns north back to the Discovery Site where the Ortega Trail, named for Portolá's scout, turns downhill. This trail goes down a ridge to end a mile below at private property beyond the preserve boundary. Ranger-led walks up into the preserve from Pacifica are available occasionally.

Trip 2.   Up Mori Ridge to the Discovery Site

This trail heads straight up the steep grassy slope of Mori Ridge to superb views of the coast.

Distance   5 miles round trip.

Time   3½ hours.

Elevation Gain   1600′

How To Get There   From Highway 1 going north just beyond Vallemar, turn abruptly right at the Shell Dance Nursery. When

The Mori Ridge Trail is a steep climb for bicyclists.

going south on Highway 1, a left turn is not advisable because of the poor sight distance. Rather, continue to Vallemar, make a U-turn and go back to the Shell Dance Nursery. Drive up through the nursery grounds to a broad parking area where there is a signed entrance to the preserve. An improved entrance to Mori Ridge is planned.

TRAIL NOTES

From the preserve entrance gate a service-road trail begins a steep, steady ascent up a grassy slope. Views open out over the Pacific Ocean and north to the Farallones, Pt. Reyes and Mt. Tamalpais. In the foreground the suburban community of Pacifica contrasts with the austere outlines of Pedro Point.

In spring the grasslands are bright with flowers. You will be glad to stop the stiff climb now and then to look at them more closely. A half-hour's hike brings you to scattered old plantings of Monterey pines. One by the trailside provides a welcome shady stop on a bright day. Often, however, this exposed ridge is swept by winds and fog.

Soon you are on a gentler slope where grasses give way to low bushes. On Sweeney Ridge is found one of the best examples of the lively combination of low shrubs and flowers called coastal scrub. In spring and summer this scrub takes on a brilliance that belies the harsh, negative connotation of its name. It blooms then with white pearly everlastings; patches of blue coast iris; Indian paintbrush in red and yellow; daisies in yellow, lavender and white; yellow yarrow;

coffeeberry; greasewood and blue wild lilac. The ever-present poison oak is red and rose by the end of summer.

After about an hour you reach an intersection with the Skyline Trail from Skyline College. The ridge flattens out as you continue through the waist-high scrub. San Francisco is in view, including the antenna on Sutro Heights and the towers of the Golden Gate Bridge. East is San Bruno Mountain and the East Bay Hills beyond.

From the intersection the trail turns southward along Sweeney Ridge, skirting an old Nike site. These blocky cement buildings and battered fences will be torn down some day. Our trail continues for a mile on a paved, level road that is the upper end of Sneath Lane, leading to the Discovery Site.

Trip 3.   Skyline Trail from Skyline College to the Discovery Site

This route takes you quickly to a ridgetop from which there are wide views. However, after ½ mile you must make a steep descent into and out of a ravine—losing 300 feet in elevation before you make the final gentle climb past the Nike site to the Discovery Site.

Distance   4 miles round trip.

Time   2 hours.

Elevation Gain   500', plus loss and gain of 300' in the ravine.

How To Get There   To reach the trailhead, take College Drive from Skyline Boulevard and go through Skyline College. Park in lot 2 and walk east to a gated service road where a sign marks the entrance.

SamTrans buses reach Skyline College from Pacifica, Daly City BART and Serramonte-Tanforan, some with weekend schedules.

TRAIL NOTES

On a clear day the view is unlimited, all around the compass. However, this bald hilltop can get the full force of the wind from the ocean—be prepared. On the other hand, if the day is clear and warm, take a lunch to this hilltop, where you can look down at the coast from Mussel Rock to San Pedro Point. Pacifica is below you, and the green of Sharp Park Golf Course contrasts with the deep blue of the ocean. White breakers curl into the sandy curves of the beaches.

But if the Discovery Site is your destination, continue on and scramble down into and out of the ravine ahead (a better alignment for a trail route is planned) and take the Sweeney Ridge Trail to the Discovery Site.

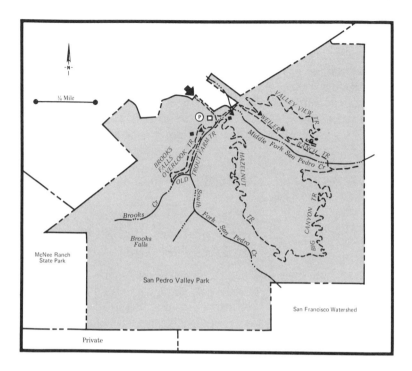

San Pedro Valley Park

The park's 1000 acres include the narrow valley along San Pedro Creek's middle fork and the steep ridges draining the south fork.

San Pedro Valley has a significant place in early Bay Area history as the site of Indian villages and the site of Gaspar de Portolá's camp from which his scouts climbed the ridge to get their first view of San Francisco Bay. An early outpost for Mission Dolores was in this valley, as was the adobe home of Francisco Sanchez, still standing and now a County museum.

Park trails offer a number of easy, level strolls and some vigorous climbs to the ridges above the valley. The creeks run clear, and are still spawning grounds for steelhead trout that migrate upstream to the park each winter. The creeks furnish a substantial part of Pacifica's water supply.

Jurisdiction   San Mateo County.

Facilities   Visitor center, picnic tables and barbecues for families and groups; trails for hikers; self-guiding nature trail, wheelchair accessible.

Park Rules Trails for hikers; bicycles permitted on Weiler Road; no dogs; open 8 A.M. to dusk; fee $2 per car, seniors free week days.
Maps San Mateo County *San Pedro Valley Park;* USGS topo *Montara Mountain.*
How To Get There From Highway 1 in the south end of Pacifica turn east on Linda Mar Boulevard and drive to the park entrance.

Trip 1.   Up the South Fork of San Pedro Creek to the Old Trout Farm

From the picnic grounds a short, pleasant walk up the Old Trout Farm Trail beside the creek is just right to occupy the time before lunch.
Distance 0.8-mile loop.
Time Less than an hour.
Elevation Gain Relatively level.

TRAIL NOTES

Take time to explore the visitor center, which has something for the whole family. Children will enjoy display cases of the park's animals, and botany buffs delight in the well-mounted specimens of a surprising variety of plants. Photographs trace San Pedro Valley's long history.

Near the beginning of the trail look for the tanks that are all that remain of the trout farm washed away in the floods of 1962. Under overhanging trees by the rippling creek, the trail continues for almost a mile. Turn back when you will, or find the Brooks Falls Overlook Trail where stone steps start up the hillside, and follow that trail back to the picnic grounds.

Trip 2.   North Ridge Loop

This trip climbs a west-facing slope on the Valley View Trail and then descends to join Weiler Ranch Road farther up the valley.
Distance 2-mile loop.
Time 1 hour.
Elevation Gain Valley View Trail 600′

Cross the creek on a bridge from the main parking lot to the left of the visitor center. Continue past the group picnic area under walnut trees. Turn right on Weiler Ranch Road, then almost immediately veer left on the Valley View Trail, which takes off uphill.

If you want a short level walk, continue on the road to one of the two picnic tables between the beginning and the end of the Valley

View Trail. But for a brisk walk up the ridge before lunch, you can take the Valley View Trail and be back in less than an hour. In spring the meadow-side tables look out over a field of poppies, lupines, buttercups and wild mustard.

The Valley View Trail climbs a sunny slope, welcome in cool weather, through a eucalyptus grove and then fragrant chaparral. You can look south to the heights of Montara Mountain. In April blue coast iris blooms in clearings. From the ridgetop easy switchbacks bring you down to Weiler Ranch Road. For a longer walk you can follow this easy road to the upper end of the valley, where hills rise steeply to Sweeney Ridge a thousand feet above.

Ocean fogs often roll in to shroud surrounding ridgetops, but San Pedro Mountain tempers winds from the west, sheltering the sunny valley. The same mild climate that led the Ohlone Indians to build their village by the creek makes San Pedro Valley Park a place to return to in all seasons.

Trip 3.   A South Ridge Loop Trip

After a climb up the high ridge on the Big Canyon Trail, you return on the Hazelnut Trail to the visitor center.

Distance   4.3-mile loop.

Time   3 hours.

Elevation Gain   800′

TRAIL NOTES

On the Weiler Ranch Road, walk about a mile up the valley and cross a bridge over the creek. Continue to the head of the valley, where the Big Canyon Trail turns off on your right. It makes a wide swing west, then continues on switchbacks up the canyon wall. After a wide traverse east you zigzag up a ridge, gaining 400 feet in elevation.

At the high point of the trail you come to a gentler grade and meet the Hazelnut Trail in high chaparral of coffeeberry, Montara manzanita, wild lilac and scrub oak. On this trail you are soon down on a high saddle between San Pedro Creek's middle and south forks. A huge eucalyptus grove dominates the northwest end of the flat just before you begin the steep pitch down the Hazelnut Trail.

As the trail turns down in earnest, it doubles back and forth through a thicket of hazelnut, the shrub that gives it its name. You are soon at the foot of the hillside and crossing a sloping, flower-filled little meadow behind the visitor center, the end of the trip.

In the contemporary visitor center are displays
of San Pedro Valley's long history and abundant wildlife.

A trail connection between San Pedro Valley Park and the
adjoining McNee Ranch State Park is in prospect after the 1987 purchase of a strategic parcel of land between the two parks. This trail
would cross the steep southwestern slopes of San Pedro Valley Park
and join McNee Ranch State Park high on the saddle between San
Pedro Mountain and Montara's peaks.

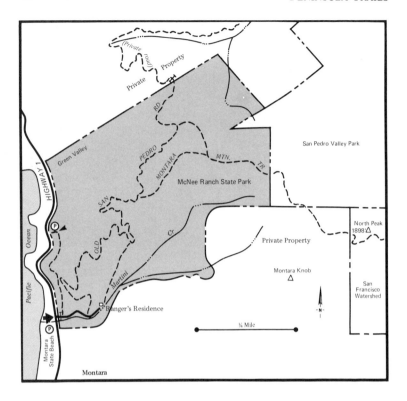

McNee Ranch State Park

Rising steeply from rocky seacliffs, McNee Ranch State Park's rugged slopes reach an elevation of 1500' near Montara Mountain's peaks. The 700-acre park includes the saddle between San Pedro Mountain and Montara Mountain. Over this saddle went the Indian trail followed by Gaspar de Portolá's party in 1769. Later it was the route of early wagon roads between coastal ranches. And in the 20th century the winding old San Pedro Road carried automobiles over the saddle until it was abandoned for the cliff-side Devil's Slide route. Today the old road serves as a trail for hikers.

Plans for McNee Ranch State Park, which is a part of Montara Beach State Park, are in process at this writing. Meanwhile you can explore the park on informal paths along the lower hillsides, and on the trips described here following Old San Pedro Road and a service road up the mountain.

The State of California Division of Parks and Beaches purchased the land for McNee Ranch State Park in two parcels to
accommodate a right-of-way for a possible Highway 1 bypass, and
has the right of refusal in case the right-of-way is not used. A bypass
would require a 250-foot cut in the saddle of San Pedro Mountain
and other massive cuts and fills which would interrupt park trails and
impair scenic values. At this writing a decision on the bypass is still
in the courts.

Jurisdiction   State of California.

Facilities   Trails for hikers, equestrians and bicyclists.

Park Rules   Open from 8 A.M. to dusk.

Map   USGS topo *Montara Mountain.*

How To Get There   An unmarked entrance gate on Highway 1,
just north of Montara State Beach, leads into the park. There is
ample parking at the beach, or use Gray Whale Cove parking area on
east side of Highway 1 and take trail south paralleling highway to
park entrance gate.

The trips described start along the road leading east to the
ranger's residence and then follow a service road up to Old San
Pedro Road. The lower part of this old road is badly gullied and
eroded. However, you can find its start near the ranger's residence.

Trip 1.   Old San Pedro Road North Across the Park

For fine views of the ocean and hills, this route takes you up to
the saddle of San Pedro Mountain.

Distance   5 miles round trip.

Time   3 hours.

Elevation gain   900′

TRAIL NOTES

From the unmarked entrance gate, walk ahead on the short
cypress-lined road to the ranger's residence, then take the service
road straight uphill. In ½ mile you meet Old San Pedro Road and
turn left on it. Because the first section of this old road is badly
gullied, though passable on foot, it is better to reach the old road at
this junction.

From this junction you see below fields planted with rows of
vegetables and flowers on the far side of Martini Creek. Above you
tower Montara's peaks, chaparral-covered and formidable. Broad
Montara State Beach stretches south, and on a rise out of sight is
Montara Lighthouse. Now an American Youth Hostel, it is an
appealing place for an overnight stay while exploring the park.

The old road you take upward was for many years the principal north-south highway along the coast. Its pavement is now worn and eroded, but yellow and blue bush lupine and sagebrush cover its banks. A half mile from the junction, a steep service road turns to the right up the mountain to communications installations on its peaks, the route of our other trip in the park. Keep to the left on Old San Pedro Road. A short section of this road is washed out soon after this junction, but it is possible to scramble down and back up to the old road level. From there the next ½ mile is on an easy grade.

It is worth the climb to reach the high flower garden that this old roadway becomes in late spring and summer. Its banks then bloom in brilliant variety, with red and yellow Indian paintbrush, purple pussy paws, orange wallflowers, blue-eyed grass, buttercups and more. West over the steeply descending hillside is the blue of the Pacific Ocean.

As you continue around the hillside, you come to large outcrops of granite. This light-colored igneous rock is exposed on this mountain and in only a few other places in the Bay Area, such as the Farallon Islands and Inverness Ridge. This is the same kind of rock from which Yosemite Valley was carved, formed beneath the surface many eons ago.

The road continues around the mountain, passing a service road turning right, uphill. Old San Pedro Road, which we have been following, veers left and continues to a gate marking the park's boundary. From the gate Old San Pedro Road goes on over the saddle through private property and down to San Pedro Valley. You can retrace your steps from here.

Trip 2.   A Hike to Montara Mountain's North Peak

A steady, 3-mile climb brings you to rewarding top-of-the-world views.

Distance   6 miles round trip.
Time   4 hours.
Elevation Gain   1898'

TRAIL NOTES

To take the service road up Montara Mountain, again start from the ranger's residence as in Trip 1, then follow Old San Pedro Road to the turnoff (right) up the steep service road. On this road you are soon in tall chaparral of wild lilac, coffeeberry, scrub oak, and here and there a few chinquapins—that sturdy tree with burrs and yellow-backed leaves, occurring on some dry slopes like these.

As you rise along the road and round the mountain, views are to the north and the east. You soon cross a flat where giant outcrops of granite stand like great monuments. From this high plateau you are ½ mile from Montara's peaks. Now continue up the mountain to North Peak.

On a clear day, views from the mountaintop are awesome. Southeast are the green heights of Scarper's Peak and the ridges of the Santa Cruz Mountains. Below lie the coastal terrace of Half Moon Bay and its beaches. West and north you see Mt. Tamalpais, the Bay and the skyscrapers of San Francisco, east the bridges, the East Bay hills and Mt. Diablo.

Below are the slopes of adjoining San Pedro Valley Park. The 1987 purchase of a key parcel of land makes possible a long-planned-for trail connection between these parks.

You can return on the north leg of the service road, which leads steeply down to the right to Old San Pedro Road. Turn left (south) on Old San Pedro Road to traverse the flowery upper section of this road and then return as you came up, on the service road.

Fog rolling eastward over the hills

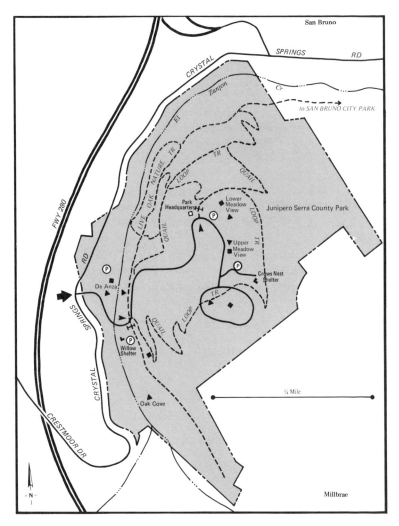

Junipero Serra County Park

This 100-acre wooded park in the curve of Junipero Serra Freeway 280, just minutes from homes in San Bruno, provides a quick retreat from the urban scene into protected meadows and woods. The park, situated on a long ridge that had been quarried for its Franciscan sandstone, offers several miles of trails, attractive picnic sites and a visitor center.

From the park entrance, meadows, picnic grounds and parking areas extend left and right. On weekends these are heavily used by families and groups who gravitate to the sheltered canyon. The entrance road winds uphill past park headquarters, the visitor center and the picnic tables, continuing to the very top, where still more picnic tables are nestled in a eucalyptus grove. This hilltop site offers spectacular views.

From these wide views of mountains and Bay, the eye and the ear are drawn to the San Francisco Airport. Air-age, flight-minded children (and others too) delight in the bird's-eye view of planes taking off and landing.

In the visitor center at park headquarters are native bird and mammal displays and an exhibit of Indian history. A self-guiding nature trail through a wooded glade and a loop trail to the park's summit make good warm-up trips before a picnic spread at one of the many picnic tables in this attractive setting.

Jurisdiction   San Mateo County.

Facilities   Trails for hikers and a nature trail. Picnic areas with barbecues and covered shelters, visitor center at park headquarters, youth-group camp.

Park Rules   Open from 8 A.M. to sunset. Fee: $2 on weekends and holidays.

Maps   San Mateo County *Junipero Serra Park,* USGS topo *Montara Mountain.*

How To Get There   From Freeway 280: Southbound, take the Crystal Springs Road exit and turn right on Crystal Springs Road 0.7 mile to the park entrance on the left. Park at the lower picnic areas or continue to more parking on the hilltop. Northbound, take the San Bruno Avenue exit and turn left on San Bruno Avenue. Go under the freeway and turn left back on 280 south. Immediately exit at Crystal Springs Road and follow directions for southbound above.

Trip 1.   Hike to the Hilltop on the Quail Loop Trail

Gaining altitude quickly on a zigzag climb, this trip leads to flowers in grasslands and woods and to protected slopes on the park's east side.

Distance   1.4-mile loop.
Time   1 hour.
Elevation Gain   300'

TRAIL NOTES

To the right of the park entrance find the signed beginning of the Quail Loop Trail. You start climbing immediately, with oak trees overhead and patches of bright flowers at your feet. Early in spring false Solomon's seal plants droop with clusters of small white flowers, which later form panicles of red-brown berries. Switchbacks take you up the mountain, first out into an open grassy slope where sun-loving orange poppies and yellow mule ears dot the hillside. At the next switchback you are under the cover of oaks and toyons with ferns and snowberry underneath.

Toward the top of the hill you encounter Monterey pines and a large grove of mature eucalyptuses. Here the trail crosses the picnic grounds to reach the wide meadow beyond. On a clear day the brilliant Bay waters are set against the backdrop of East Bay cities and tree-topped hills. After taking in the sweep of Bay from north of San Francisco to its southern shores, continue on the Quail Loop Trail past the Crows Nest picnic shelter and bear left to descend across the meadow.

At the first trail junction you could turn left to reach the visitor center at park headquarters, but instead stay on the Quail Loop Trail, which swings right. From the next trail junction the Quail Loop Trail goes left on a long traverse through oak woodlands back to the picnic areas near the park entrance.

If you would like to extend your trip, pass up the left Quail Loop Trail turnoff and continue on down the hill for about 1000 feet to the next trail junction. Park signs offer the choice of going to San Bruno City Park or back to the park entrance on the Live Oak Nature Trail. If you take the San Bruno option, this trail, following El Zanjon Creek down to the park and back, adds 3 miles to this hike.

If you ignore this side trip to San Bruno City Park, you will take the left turn to descend quickly on the Live Oak Nature Trail. In about 200 yards, take either leg of this trail to return to the meadows below.

Trip 2.   Two Short Walks in the Canyon

The ½-mile Live Oak Nature Trail leaves the lower meadow parking area going left on the hillside just above El Zanjon Creek. The creek probably got its name from a Spanish word meaning "deep ditch" or "slough." Through an oak glade follow the numbered signs keyed to a self-guiding pamphlet explaining the microclimates of this trail. Pamphlets are available from the ranger and at park headquarters.

Now crossing open grasslands, you come to a pipe spyglass pointed at Mt. Diablo, the main reference point for surveying in northern California. The trail circles back on the shady upper hillside, then drops down to return to its starting point.

Another short walk goes by the Willow Shelter to the right of the park entrance on a service road above El Zanjon Creek, past picnic tables in the shade of oak groves. From the end of this road it is just ⅓ mile back to the park entrance.

From the upper meadow you can watch the airport.

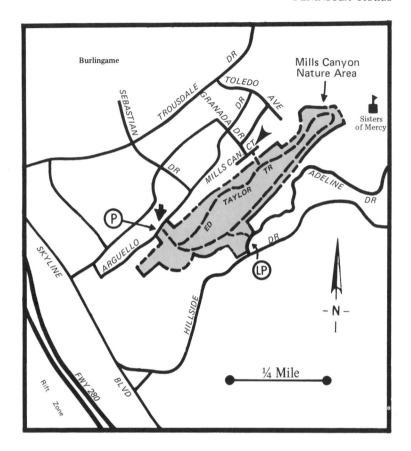

Mills Canyon Nature Area

A loop trail through an unspoiled canyon in suburban Burlingame traverses open northwest slopes, then dips down into deep woods beside Mills Creek.

Distance   2.5-mile loop.

Time   1¼ hours.

Elevation Loss   250′

Jurisdiction   City of Burlingame.

Facilities   Trail for hikers only.

Park Rules   Open 8 A.M. to dusk.

Map   USGS topo *Montara Mountain.*

How To Get There   From Freeway 280 or El Camino Real in Burlingame take Trousdale Drive, then turn south on Sebastian

Drive. In two blocks, turn right on Arguello Drive. The park entrance is on the south side of the 3000 block of Arguello Drive. On-street parking near entrance.

TRAIL NOTES

Under Mexican rule Mills Canyon was part of Rancho Buri Buri, which included most of northeast San Mateo County, extending as far south as what is now the City of San Mateo. In the early 1860s Darius Ogden Mills and his brother-in-law, Ansel Easton, each bought 1500 acres of Rancho Buri Buri. The division between their two holdings ran straight through this canyon. Most of Mills' estate was in present-day Millbrae, but this land, including the upper part of this canyon which takes his name, was eventually annexed to Burlingame. The city acquired the canyon as a park and wildlife area and in 1978 volunteers built a delightful creekside trail and one on the hillside above.

Today this entire trail loop is called the Ed Taylor Trail, in honor of the man who inspired the volunteers and led the first work parties. Dedicated in September 1983, the trail is maintained by local volunteers with the help of the City of Burlingame.

Access to the preserve is possible from Arguello Drive, Adeline Drive and Mills Canyon Court. However, the parking is best on Arguello Drive, where just inside the entrance a handsome wooden sign proclaims the name and the way to the Ed Taylor Trail.

Start your trip by going downhill about 150 yards to a small path cut into the hillside on the left. Follow this path through willows, coyote bushes and toyons for about 20 yards to a trail junction. The Creekside Trail turns off sharply to the right, while the Northwest Trail continues straight ahead on the upper hillside.

For the best views, take the Northwest Trail first, returning on the trail by the creek. On the Northwest Trail you follow a shady path under huge, high-branched live oaks. When this trail emerges onto the open hillside, you see the rooftops and chimneys of the Sisters of Mercy Convent rising from their spacious grounds below. The Bay and a few highrise buildings on the Bayfront are framed by this V-shaped canyon. Beyond, airplanes in the landing pattern descend low over the water. In the distance you see the Bay curving out to wooded Coyote Point.

In about ½ mile you descend along the upper edge of a tributary to Mills Creek. Now madrone trees shade the trail as it drops into the cool canyon. When you reach Mills Creek you start upstream, following its north bank in a dense stand of oaks and bays over-hanging the creek.

Continue along the creek bank, over a few protruding tree roots and in and out of little ravines. You soon come to a tall, picturesque rock outcropping where lichen-covered ledges invite you to stop and enjoy the sounds of the creek. As you stroll along the streamside, you will see remnants of an old fence, perhaps the boundary between the two early estates. In the spring look for small patches of iris, blue-and purple-flowered on long, straight stems.

Shortly you come upon a plank bridge with chain handrails that crosses to the south side of the creek. This bridge leads to a service road from which a trail climbs the steep south side of the canyon to another preserve entrance on Adeline Street.

Continuing on the path upstream past mossy rocks and lacy wood ferns, you come to a succession of miniature cascades and small pools in the shady depths. Before long the path to the main entrance turns uphill, and you leave this little creek, which below the park flows beside homes and schools, under streets and finally into the Bay at Burlingame's Shoreline Bird Sanctuary.

On a summer day this canyon is a cool, sheltered place for a leisurely walk along a little watercourse, relatively unchanged since the early settlers came here. On fair winter days the southern sun shining on the northwest hillside will warm you while you enjoy the views down the canyon.

A trail under the oaks leads to open hillsides

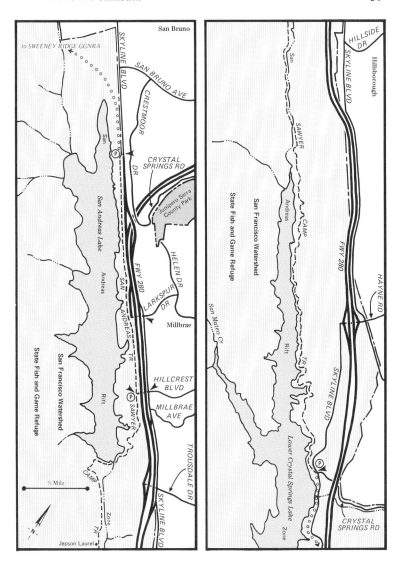

San Andreas Trail

The wide, paved San Andreas Trail follows the eastern boundary of the San Francisco Watershed, giving views of the lakes and the wooded mountains. At Larkspur Drive it becomes a hiking and equestrian path, winding through the trees and underbrush in a fenced right-of-way until it reaches Hillcrest Boulevard.

Distance   2.1 miles one way.
Time   1 hour.
Elevation Change   Relatively level.
Connecting Trails   Proposed trail west to Sweeney Ridge, Sawyer Camp Trail south.
Jurisdiction   State of California Department of Transportation (Caltrans).
Facilities   Trail for hikers, bicyclists, equestrians.
Rules   Open dawn to dusk.
Map   USGS topo *Montara Mountain.*
How To Get There

By Car   From Freeway 280: (1) North entrance: (a) northbound, take Skyline Boulevard to a point ¼ mile south of San Bruno Avenue, where the signed trail entrance is on the west side of the road; (b) southbound, take the Sneath Lane exit and continue south on the frontage road to San Bruno Avenue, where you turn right; at Skyline Boulevard turn left and go ¼ mile to the entrance. (2) South entrance: (a) northbound, take Millbrae Avenue exit, go north on the frontage road to Hillcrest Boulevard, then west (left) under the freeway to parking at the trail entrance on the right; (b) southbound, take the Larkspur Drive exit, go under the freeway and turn south on the frontage road to Hillcrest Boulevard; turn right under the freeway to the trail entrance.

By Bus   One of the few trails with good bus access. The south entrance can be reached by bus 33B on weekdays and Saturdays.

TRAIL NOTES

As you start down the San Andreas Trail from the north entrance, you can see directly in the west the spot on the ridge from which Gaspar de Portolá first saw San Francisco Bay in 1769. An extension of this trail will someday reach this "Discovery Site."

The San Andreas Reservoir now fills the valley, which for centuries before the coming of the Spaniards was the site of Indian villages. As Portolá's party was searching for a site for a mission and presidio in the northern part of the Peninsula, his diarist and historian, Father Francisco Palou, and his scout, Captain Fernando Rivera, went through this valley on November 30, 1774. Palou named it San Andres, honoring that saint's feast day.

Later, the earthquake-fault valley north of the present damsite was included in the Rancho Feliz, where Spaniards grazed cattle and grew wheat. There were no Spanish settlements here, reportedly because of trouble with bears. It is now surmised that the bear

On the San Andreas Trail

population may have exploded when the cattle provided an increased food supply.

With the coming of the Anglos in the 19th century the valley became a place of small farms and a dairy. In the mid-1880s farmers and herdsmen were still hunting down marauding bears and mountain lions that were attacking their cattle.

San Francisco's Spring Valley Water Company bought up the farms in the valley by the 1860s, and the lands have been kept as a watershed from that time. The bears are now gone, but the vast and still-wild watershed (also a State Fish and Game Refuge) harbors a great variety of animals, probably including wildcats and a few eagles.

The first 1½ miles of the San Andreas Trail are paved, from the Skyline Boulevard entrance to Larkspur Drive. From the end of this paved path to the Sawyer Camp Trail entrance at Hillcrest Boulevard, hikers and equestrians take a cleared and maintained 0.6-mile path in a wooded corridor next to the freeway. Runners use the trail frequently, perhaps because the forest floor is springy underfoot and the air fragrant with the scent of pine needles. Bicyclists must travel on Skyline Boulevard to Hillcrest Boulevard, where they turn right to the paved Sawyer Camp Trail.

In spite of the noisy presence of the freeway, you can enjoy the outlook to the west as the path winds through groves of Monterey pines and old plantings of cypresses, with vistas of the lake below and the western hills beyond.

Sawyer Camp Trail
(Map on page 59)

A historic road of singular beauty extends for 6 miles through the San Francisco Watershed lands past the sparkling San Andreas and Crystal Springs lakes. The road is paved, but open to hikers, equestrians and bicyclists only.

Distance   6 miles one way.

Time   3½ hours. A car shuttle is practical here. Shorter round trips on part of the trail from either end make good hikes.

Elevation Loss   400′ from north to south.

Connecting Trails   San Andreas Trail north. Crystal Springs Trail south. Note: The first 1.6 miles of the Crystal Springs Trail south of the Sawyer Camp Trail are not built at this writing, but the trail resumes at the Freeway 92/Skyline Boulevard intersection.

Jurisdiction   San Mateo County.

Facilities   Trail for hikers, bicyclists and equestrians. Picnic tables, restrooms and telephone.

Park Rules   Open dawn to ½ hour after sunset.

Maps   San Mateo County *Jogging, Exercise and Bicycle Trails* and USGS topos *Montara Mountain* and *San Mateo*.

How To Get There

By Car   From Freeway 280: (1) North entrance at Hillcrest Boulevard: (a) southbound, take the Larkspur Drive exit and go south on Skyline Boulevard to Hillcrest Boulevard, then west under the freeway to the trail entrance on the right; (b) northbound, take the Millbrae Avenue exit and go north on Skyline Boulevard, then west on Hillcrest Boulevard to the trail entrance. (2) South entrance at Crystal Springs Road: (a) southbound, take the Hayne Road exit and go south on Skyline Boulevard to parking beside the entrance gate on the west side of the road; (b) northbound, take the Bunker Hill Drive exit, cross over the freeway, then go north on Skyline Boulevard past Crystal Springs Dam to the entrance gate.

By Bicycle   Use the same approaches from Skyline Boulevard as for cars.

By Bus   North entrance: Take SamTrans Bus 33B from Millbrae Train Station on Millbrae Avenue to Hillcrest Boulevard and Skyline Boulevard. Walk under the freeway to the trail entrance.

The Story Of Sawyer Camp Road

The camp that gave the road its name was in a small flat in the San Andreas Valley where in the 1870s Leander Sawyer trained performing horses for circuses. Later he ran an inn here for travellers on their way to Half Moon Bay.

The sunny meadow by the creek where Sawyer had his camp had earlier been home to the Shalshone Indians (a tribelet of the Ohlones), who hospitably offered wild fruits and seed cakes to Gaspar de Portolá's expedition when it passed this way in 1769. During Sawyer's day wagons pulled by teams of eight horses hauled wood over the road on their way to San Francisco, and stage coaches used it as an alternative route to Half Moon Bay.

When San Francisco took over the Watershed lands, narrow, winding Sawyer Camp Road was kept open, and later fenced on either side for protection of the Watershed. In 1978 San Mateo County closed the road to motorized vehicles, and it is now Sawyer Camp Trail.

TRAIL NOTES

Entering the trail at the north end, you descend for the first ¾ mile from Skyline Boulevard to San Andreas Lake and its dam. The woods and lake are a pleasant introduction to the trail. Summer winds often ruffle the lake, and drifts of fog sweep over the hills. On the far side of the dam a commemorative plaque marks the hundredth anniversary of the dam's completion in 1869. The trail heads south along a shady walk between the creek and a hillside of bay trees. Fern-covered banks bloom with purple iris and scarlet columbine. Look here for the very rare shrub leatherwood, with its small yellow blossoms. It is found in only a few places in San Mateo County (one of them is Edgewood Park). The Indians used its tough, flexible branches for lacings.

In a small clearing along the way, about 30 yards west of the trail, is the venerable Jepson Bay Laurel, thought to be one of the oldest and largest in the state. It was named in honor of Willis Jepson in 1923. He was one of California's noted botanists. The flowery little meadow around the tree was popular as a picnic spot in Mexican and early California times. Today the tree is fenced to protect it, and there is a picnic area nearby. Once again picnickers are enjoying this retreat beside the famous bay tree.

Here and there you will come to benches beside the trail for a place to rest, picnic, or enjoy the sound of a stream or a view of the lake. At about its halfway point the trail crosses San Andreas Creek where it enters Lower Crystal Springs Lake. From here on, it borders the east side of the lake, giving a succession of views out over the bright waters to the wooded Watershed hills. The Peninsula's own "Lake District" has a special enchantment whether mists are shrouding the mountains or the lakes are reflecting a blue sky.

A few hawks sail overhead. Grebes, ducks and other waterfowl bob on the water, and the oaks by the trail are alive with countless small birds—countless except to the Audubon Society, which enumerates the species meticulously in its annual Christmas bird count; a recent count totaled 190 species. Bring your binoculars and favorite bird guide.

Along the road cuts you will see the greenish-gray serpentine, a rock that occurs through the foothills in San Mateo County. It is frequently found in major earthquake fault zones, and is associated with some of our finest wildflower displays.

The south end of the trail is on Skyline Boulevard at Crystal Springs Road, close to the Crystal Springs Dam across the gorge of San Mateo Creek. This is a good starting point for a 3-mile walk north by the lake, with vistas of the shimmering waters around each bend. Your return trip brings you new views as you retrace your steps. Walk here in late winter when clouds are moving across the sky and sunshine alternates with light showers. The hills are already green, drifts of magenta Indian warriors bloom under the trees, and the first buds of iris appear. This is one of the Peninsula's best walks for any time of the year.

The Sawyer Camp Trail is good for an early-morning family ride.

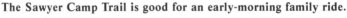

The Central Peninsula
From Highway 92 to Highway 84

Crystal Springs Trail

Bordering Upper Crystal Springs Lake, this trail traverses the linear valley of the San Andreas Rift Zone, known by the Spaniards as Cañada de Raimundo, then continues through a corner of the Watershed and up through Huddart Park to the Skyline. Views of lakes, mountains and hills make this a beautiful trail for short trips along its segments. Connections with trails east and west make it a useful route for longer expeditions. The trail is part of San Mateo County's north-south trail corridor, and it provides access to the regional Bay Area Ridge Trail.

The Crystal Springs Trail follows the easement of the old California Riding and Hiking Trail between the boundary fence of the Watershed and Cañada Road, from Freeway 92 to Huddart Park and up to the Skyline. Although the trail easement extends north to the Sawyer Camp Trail, a 1.6-mile segment from Freeway 92 to Bunker Hill Road is not built.

The nearly 10-mile Crystal Springs Trail is covered in this book in three sections: (1) from Cañada Road at Freeway 92 to Edgewood and Cañada roads, (2) from Edgewood Road to Huddart Park and (3) through the park to the Skyline. This last segment is covered in the section on Huddart Park.

The Pulgas Water Temple grounds are closed to cars and there is no roadside parking within a mile on either side. However, the lovely water temple and its reflecting pool and grounds, open to pedestrians and bicyclists, make a fine destination from either end of the trail.

Jurisdiction   San Mateo County.

Facilities   Trail for hikers and equestrians.

Park Rules   Open from 8 A.M. to ½ hour after sunset. No bicycles.

Maps   USGS topos *San Mateo* and *Woodside*.

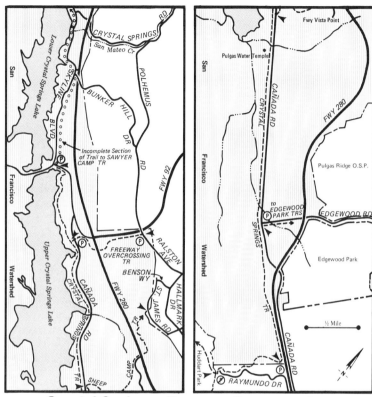

Crystal Springs, Freeway Overcrossing, Sheep Camp Trails

How To Get There   From Freeway 280: (1) North entrance: (a) southbound, take the Half Moon Bay exit to Skyline Boulevard (Highway 35), go south to Freeway 92, and then turn east. Turn south on Cañada Road and go 0.2 mile to the trail entrance on the west side of the road just opposite the Freeway 280 Overcrossing Trail junction; (b) northbound, take the Freeway 92 exit west to Cañada Road. Turn south for 0.2 mile to the trail entrance. (2) South entrance: take the Edgewood Road exit, go west to the Edgewood/ Cañada Road intersection, where there is parking. No parking at the Raymundo Drive cul-de-sac entrance to Huddart Park. Note: Cañada Road is closed to motor-vehicle traffic from the intersection of Freeway 92 to Edgewood Road for "Bicycle Sunday," a popular event held on the first and third Sundays in the months of April through October.

Trip 1. Freeway 92 to Edgewood and Cañada Roads

The first part of the trail to the Water Temple is close to the lake, where you can enjoy the blue waters and the flocks of birds. South from the Water Temple the trail takes you through the broad, parklike Watershed valley past spring wildflowers against a backdrop of the wooded slopes of the Santa Cruz Mountains.

Distance   4 miles one way.
Time   2 hours.
Elevation Gain   Relatively level.

TRAIL NOTES

Start your hike by going down the path from Cañada Road 0.2 mile south of Freeway 92 and just across the road from the western entrance to the Freeway 280 Overcrossing Trail. You can also walk north along this lakeside trail as far as the intersection of Freeway 92 and Skyline Boulevard. This trail at times swings away from the road, coming close to the lake, or leads down below road level through oak groves.

The lake is a resting place for water birds in the Pacific Flyway, so take your binoculars. Even without them you will easily identify the big, brownish Canada geese that winter here. Flocks of them are often gathered along the shores. In the early morning and evening you may see herds of deer grazing in the fields or drinking at the water's edge.

**Through this temple with its classic colonnades
rush Sierra waters before flowing into Crystal Springs Lakes.**

Soon after the trail leaves the lakeside it passes the point where the Sheep Camp Trail joins the east side of Cañada Road. From here to the Pulgas Water Temple the trail is on the bank above the road.

The Water Temple grounds, open to pedestrians and bicyclists from 8:00 to 4:30, include lawns for picnicking and sunning, and the Water Temple itself. At the end of a long reflecting pool is the classic little Pulgas Water Temple, where waters from high in the Sierra thunder into the sluiceway to the Crystal Springs Lakes. Inscribed around the pediment are words from the Book of Isaiah, "I give waters in the wilderness and rivers in the desert to give drink to my people."

Continuing southward, you see on the valley floor to the west open fields and groves of stately oaks, a part of the Filoli estate, which once belonged to W. B. Bourn, president of the Spring Valley Water Company. The name for the estate was coined by Bourn from "Fidelity," "Love" and "Life." Completed in 1916, Filoli was the last of the great mansions built in San Mateo County.

Bought by the Roth family in 1934, the estate was given by Mrs. William Roth to the National Trust for Historic Preservation in 1975. It is now operated by the Filoli Center, a nonprofit organization. The mansion is hardly visible from the trail, but its beautiful formal gardens and the mansion itself, as well as its nature trails, can be visited on tours by arrangement with the Filoli Center. Phone: 415-364-2880.

From the Filoli gates our trail passes more oak-bordered meadows to reach the stone gates at the foot of Edgewood Road, the end of this trip. The Crystal Springs Trail continues on to the Skyline Trail through Huddart Park.

Trip 2.   Edgewood and Cañada Roads to Huddart Park

A short trip over a hill through the watershed and down to West Union Creek in Huddart Park.

Distance   2.4 miles one way.
Time   1¼ hours.
Elevation Gain   200'

TRAIL NOTES

As you pass the stone gates at the foot of Edgewood Road, fields extend on either side of Cañada Road. Come this way in April and May to see some of the Peninsula's most dazzling displays of wildflowers. They thrive on the thin, magnesium-rich soil over serpentine

The Crystal Springs Trail enters a redwood glade near West Union Creek.

rock outcroppings. Swatches of intense blue larkspur bloom against great drifts of cream cups, goldfields, poppies, lupine and owl's clover. Admire these flowers from the roadside paths, photograph or paint them, but do not cross the fence and walk among them. The fields have been set aside as a preserve in the Watershed, and these flowers, if left undisturbed, will continue to bloom year after year to amaze and delight our great-grandchildren.

Where Cañada Road turns east to cross under the freeway, the trail continues south beside it for nearly a mile between wire fences, the freeway on one side and the Watershed lands on the other. It's not so attractive a stretch for walkers, but the cinderpath surface is popular with equestrians and joggers.

The Crystal Springs Trail emerges from the cinderpath at Runnymede Road at the Woodside Town boundary. From here another fenced trail goes across a corner of the Watershed and south on an easement to Raymundo Drive. From this point walk west on Raymundo Drive 0.2 mile to its cul-de-sac.

The trail leaves the south side of the cul-de-sac, descending into oak woods on switchbacks for 0.3 mile to the redwood groves beside West Union Creek. Here a footbridge takes you across to forested Huddart Park. The Crystal Springs Trail continues upstream by the creek, then turns up through the park on the 3½-mile trip to the Skyline described in the section on Huddart Park.

For those with a backpack excursion in mind, there is a trail camp (by reservation) about 1¼ miles up the trail on the park's secluded north side. From there you can explore the miles of trail in the park, or climb up the mountainside to the Skyline Trail and across to Purisima Creek Redwoods Open Space Preserve.

Sheep Camp Trail
(Map on page 67)

This walk from the eastern crest of the Watershed winds downhill above Crystal Springs Lake to cross under Freeway 280. On the far side the trail meanders through sheltered oak groves and small meadows to join the Crystal Springs Trail at Cañada Road.

Distance   1 mile one way.

Time   ½ hour.

Elevation Loss   400'

Connecting Trails   Waterdog Lake Trail east to Belmont; Crystal Springs Trail north to Freeway 92 and south to Water Temple and Huddart Park; Cross Country Running Course and Watershed boundary trails on the east.

Jurisdiction   San Mateo County.

Facilities   Trail for hikers and equestrians.

Rules   Open 8 A.M. to sunset. No dogs or bicycles.

Maps   USGS topos *San Mateo* and *Woodside*.

How To Get There   From Freeway 280 take Freeway 92 east to Ralston Avenue, turn south on Hallmark Drive, west on Benson Way and south on St. James Road. The gate to the Watershed is on the right.

TRAIL NOTES

Enter through the green gates to the Watershed. Walk straight ahead on the gravelled road over the grassy slope to the sign "Sheep Camp Trail. Cañada Road 1.6 km." No sheep are in sight, but around the bend is a view of eight concrete lanes of the Junipero Serra Freeway, which would surprise its namesake, the Franciscan Father who trod a more modest path between his missions.

Keep going downhill on the road and cross under the freeway. As the road starts up the hill to the vista point, go instead through a gate on the right. From here a dirt-and-gravel road takes you away from the freeway roar into quiet oak woods with small meadows. About ½ mile from the gate you reach Cañada Road. On the far side is the Crystal Springs Trail, which goes south to Huddart Park and north to Freeway 92. Just 0.4 mile south is the Pulgas Water Temple, a pleasant picnic destination.

For an interesting 6.2-mile loop trip on the Sheep Camp Trail and other trails in this area, see the description of the Freeway Overcrossing Trail, below. Someday it will be possible to make a 9-mile loop hike using the Sheep Camp, Crystal Springs, Edgewood, Pulgas Ridge and Watershed boundary trails. Only a short connection from Pulgas Ridge Open Space Preserve to the Watershed boundary trail is missing at this writing.

The Sheep Camp Trail passes through oak woods west of the freeway underpass.

Freeway 280 Overcrossing
(Map on page 67)

A wide, mile-long pedestrian, equestrian and bicycle path and freeway overpass crosses high above 10-lane Junipero Serra Freeway 280 at its interchange with Freeway 92. It connects the bike path on Ralston Avenue in Belmont to Cañada Road north of the Sheep Camp Trail junction.

Distance   1 mile one way.
Time   ½ hour.
Elevation Loss   125′
Connecting Trail   Crystal Springs Trail at Cañada Road.
Jurisdiction   San Mateo County.
Facilities   Pedestrian, equestrian and bicycle path.
Rules   Open sunrise to sunset.
Map   USGS topo *San Mateo*.
How To Get There   (1) East entrance: From Freeway 280 take the Freeway 92 exit east, then take the Ralston Avenue exit. At the first traffic signal, ⅛ mile east of the Ralston/Polhemus/Freeway 92 interchange, park on the south side of Ralston Avenue. (2) West entrance: (a) From Freeway 280 northbound take Freeway 92 west to Cañada Road. Go south on it 0.2 mile to the gate on the east side. Parking is on either side of the road. (b) From Freeway 280 southbound take the Half Moon Bay exit to Skyline Boulevard (Highway 35) and continue south to Freeway 92, then turn east to Cañada Road. Go south on it 0.2 mile to the gate on the east side.

TRAIL NOTES

This is no quiet country trail, but a paved, fenced path and concrete structure vaulting over the freeway. It is the only way to cross the freeway on foot or bicycle at this point.

The overcrossing path from Ralston Avenue goes through a gate to the Watershed lands and descends along chaparral-covered slopes. It curves south and then rises steeply to the arched structure over the freeway. A swift drop on the other side and a sharp turn bring you down to Cañada Road. On the west side you can pick up the roadside Crystal Springs Trail.

An interesting 6.2-mile circle hike starting at the Ralston Avenue entrance combines the Overcrossing Trail, part of the Crystal Springs Trail, the Sheep Camp Trail and the upper part of the Waterdog Lake Trail. When the Waterdog Lake Trail reaches Hallmark Drive, walk north on it to Ralston Avenue, then west on the Ralston bike path to where you started. These trails are described more fully in their separate chapters.

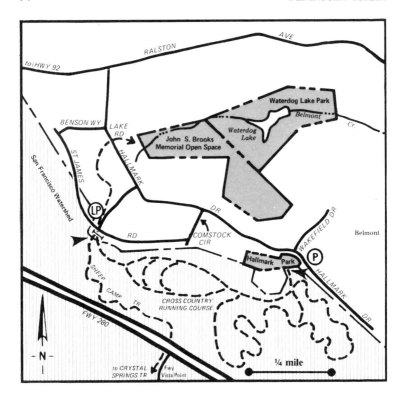

Cross Country Running Course

Considered one of the best running courses in the Bay Area, this course's location on the eastern crest of the Watershed makes it a good walking trail as well. Here is a chance to check your pace on carefully measured and marked loop paths.

Distance   0.5 to 7.5 miles.

Time   15 minutes to 4 hours, or as long as you like.

Elevation Change   Relatively level.

Connecting Trails   Sheep Camp Trail west to Cañada Road, Waterdog Lake Trail east to Belmont and Watershed boundary service roads to the west and southeast.

Jurisdiction   San Francisco Water Department; maintained by College of San Mateo.

Facilities   Trails for runners, joggers and hikers. Drinking fountains.

Rules Open to runners, joggers and hikers except during competition events. No dogs. No bicycles.
Maps City of Belmont *Jogging Trails,* available at the Parks Department, and USGS topo *San Mateo.*
How To Get There From Freeway 280 take Freeway 92 east. Take the Ralston Avenue exit and turn right on Hallmark Drive. Go past Wakefield Drive to Hallmark Park on the right. Park on the street. Enter the course on a path by the tennis courts between Wakefield Drive and Paddington Court.

TRAIL NOTES

This championship course was started some 25 years ago by two College of San Mateo coaches. Although the course had to be rerouted because of the construction of Freeway 280, its popularity has continued to increase. Local, regional and state high-school and community-college competitions are held during the months of September, October and November.

Care of the course is under the direction of the College of San Mateo track and cross country coaches. Volunteers do cleanup, mowing and course conditioning. Walkers, hikers and joggers can use the course, but should respect competitions by staying off the course during races. Dogs are not allowed on Watershed lands and are particularly unwelcome along the running course. No smoking is allowed on Watershed lands.

From the start of the course at Hallmark Park the paths extend in loops west and south. The openness of the rolling hillsides and the views over Crystal Springs Lakes to the Santa Cruz Mountains make this an exhilarating walk at any time of the year. In spring, poppies, lupines, daisies, blue-eyed grass and brodiaea bloom at your feet. In summer, coastal breezes cool what could be a hot, sunny path. And with these breezes come drifts of fog curling over the mountains to the west.

For other walks along the Watershed ridge from Hallmark Park you can take the gravelled service roads of the San Francisco Water Department that follow the Watershed boundary. Good for walks in wet weather, these surfaced roads extend more than a mile west and southeast. Going west from Hallmark Park you will come to the upper entrance to the Sheep Camp Trail at the St. James Road Watershed gate.

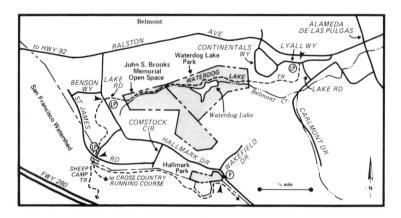

Waterdog Lake Trail

The trail through Belmont's wooded Diablo Canyon passes Waterdog Lake and comes out on the crest of the hill at the eastern boundary of the Watershed, where panoramic views of Crystal Springs Lakes and the Santa Cruz Mountains spread out before you.

Distance   3 miles round trip.

Time   1½ hours.

Elevation Gain   300'

Jurisdiction   City of Belmont.

Facilities   Trail for hikers, joggers. Lake for fishing and picnicking.

Rules   Open dawn to dusk. No swimming, no boating.

Maps   City of Belmont *Jogging Trails* and USGS topo *San Mateo*.

How To Get There   From Freeway 280 take Freeway 92 east and turn on Ralston Avenue to (1) East entrance: turn south on Lyall Way. Look for the gate and sign just beyond the Lake Road intersection. (2) West entrance: turn south on Hallmark Drive, go west on Benson Way, and then south on St. James Road. Find the trail entrance across the street from the gate to the Watershed, just past Rinconada Circle.

TRAIL NOTES

Enter the Waterdog Lake Trail through a narrow opening in a chain-link fence on the south side of Lyall Way at Lake Road. This trail was the old road over the hill to Laguna de Raimundo, now beneath the waters of Crystal Springs Lakes. In 1969 San Mateo County, using federal funds, rebuilt the road as an urban trail. Now, under the jurisdiction of the City of Belmont, it is maintained for recreational uses. Several signs invite users to picnic, hike, fish or jog, but strictly forbid swimming.

At first the trail winds up a hill past apartments; then, under a canopy of oaks you are in Cañada del Diablo, which the Spanish unaccountably called this lovely place. A walk of about ½ mile brings you to Waterdog Lake, a little reservoir that in earlier days was the water supply for Belmont, now a good stopping place for a rest, a picnic or even a morning of fishing.

From the dam at the end of the lake, the road climbs gently for another ½ mile to Hallmark Drive, with views across the wooded canyon, now rimmed with houses. In spring a roadside garden of blue lupine, yellow California poppies, scarlet Indian paintbrush and purple brodiaea graces your way.

When you emerge from the canyon at Hallmark Drive, cross the street to a gated easement, a steeper ½-mile stretch through oaks and behind backyards, to the highest point of the trail at St. James Road. Just across the street is a gate to the grassy slopes of the San Francisco Watershed.

Here you have several choices of other walks. You can follow the gravelled service road to the left along the upper boundary of the Watershed. Or the Cross Country Running Course to the southeast may tempt you to stretch your legs. A third choice takes you south for a 1-mile walk on the broad Sheep Camp Trail to join the Crystal Springs Trail beside Cañada Road.

Wide spreading canyon oaks shade the trail

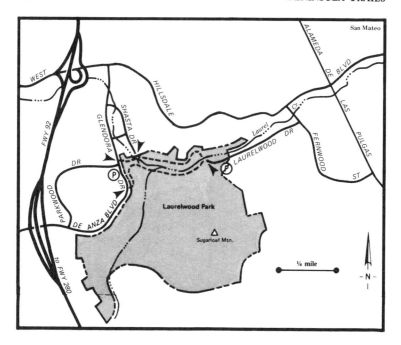

Laurelwood Park

Pleasant paths through the 40-acre park below Sugarloaf Mountain invite young and old to wander along the shaded canyon of Laurel Creek and climb its sunny hillsides. The City of San Mateo acquired Sugarloaf Mountain in 1988 and has plans for trails on its slopes.

Distance   1-mile loop.

Time   ½ hour.

Elevation Loss   150'

Jurisdiction   City of San Mateo.

Facilities   Trails for hikers, paved bike path, picnic tables and children's play area.

Park Rules   Open from sunrise to sunset.

Map   USGS topo *San Mateo.*

How To Get There   From Freeway 280 take Freeway 92 east to the De Anza Boulevard exit and go east on De Anza Boulevard to Glendora Drive. Parking is on the east side of Glendora Drive, where two paths enter the park.

TRAIL NOTES

Starting your walk down the paved path from Glendora Drive, you enter the upper canyon where it widens into a sunny natural amphitheater. An expanse of turf gives scope for games, and a small playground will keep young children busy. A few tables under widespreading oaks invite you to stay for a picnic.

As you continue on the main path, giant bay trees that gave the creek its name shade your way. On the north-facing, cool side of the canyon, ferns and iris thrive in the dampness under the trees. A short walk brings you to a flood-control dam at the lower end of the park. The path meets Laurelwood Drive downstream from the dam, where houses border the creek. Laurelwood Drive is used by bicyclists to enter the park.

You can retrace your steps from here or cross the dam to return by a footpath along the hillside. You will see the trail going up the grassy hill on the far side of the dam. On this open, sunny slope in spring a bright variety of wildflowers blooms in the grass—purple brodiaea, scarlet Indian paintbrush, blue lupine and orange poppies. Gray sage, pink-blossomed buckwheat and bush lupines flower in summer.

The trail contours around the hill above the oak-bordered creek. About halfway along you can find a path leading from this trail down to a picnic place beside the main paved path. However, continue along the hillside and descend to the Shasta Drive entrance to the park. Then go across Shasta Drive to the steps on the far side leading to paths through a handsome old grove of buckeyes. Follow the steps straight uphill to Glendora Drive.

Buckeye trees blossom on the hill below Glendora Drive.

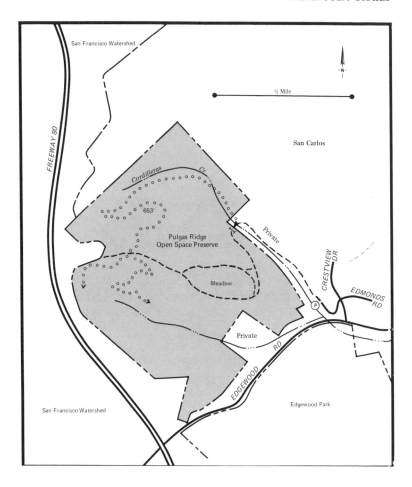

Pulgas Ridge Open Space Preserve

In the foothills west of San Carlos and just north of Edgewood Park is the 293-acre MROSD preserve featuring a broad central meadow flanked by two wooded canyons. Cordilleras Creek originates in the preserve's canyons and then flows east to the Bay, picking up volume from the streams in Edgewood Park.

Formerly the site of a tuberculosis hospital owned by the City of San Francisco, the area was purchased by MROSD in 1983. Residents of San Carlos approved a local tax on their assessed valuation to help fund the purchase.

A Loop Trip to High Meadowlands

This trip on a surfaced road takes hikers and bicyclists to a grassy meadow for picnicking, sketching or kite-flying.

Distance   3-mile loop.
Time   1½ hours.
Elevation Gain   400′
Jurisdiction   Midpeninsula Regional Open Space District.
Facilities   Trails for hikers, bicyclists and equestrians.
Preserve Rules   Open dawn to dusk.
Map   USGS topo *Woodside.*
How To Get There   From Freeway 280 take the Edgewood Road exit and go east 1 mile. Turn left on Crestview Drive and immediately left again on Edmonds Road. Around the first curve park at a roadside turnout.

TRAIL NOTES

From the roadside turnout walk 0.1 mile and turn right through a gate onto a paved 0.6-mile easement road through a valley owned by the San Francisco Water Department. This road curves left to reach the gated preserve entrance and then winds uphill to circle the high meadow, where once the hospital buildings stood.

This sloping meadow, capped by tall eucalyptus, rimmed with oak woodland and filled with wildflowers in spring, is a place to picnic and enjoy the views of San Francisco Bay through a notch in the foothills. South are Edgewood Park's grasslands and wooded hilltop; west are the forested Santa Cruz Mountains.

From the meadow walk farther along the paved road to the top of the preserve to look into the canyons on both sides of the ridge. Then turn back and follow the road down around the other side of the meadow to return to the preserve entrance.

An alternate route up to the ridgetop is proposed to leave the end of the valley just 200 feet before the entrance gate. An old trail, long overgrown, will be re-opened to ascend the tree-filled northeastern creek canyon. It will meet the road at the top of the preserve's high meadow, on which you can descend to make a 3.5-mile loop. The re-opened trail will join two proposed trails from the top of the preserve, one around the deep western canyon and another north to the San Francisco Watershed lands.

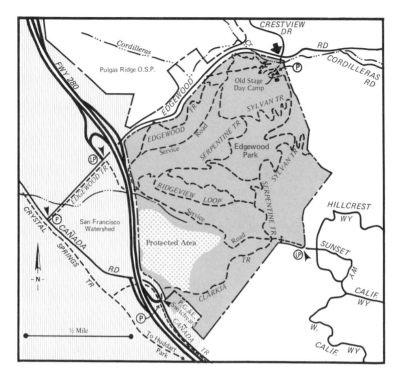

Edgewood Park

This San Mateo County park of hilltops, gentle meadows, oak groves and canyons faces the green expanse of the Skyline ridge to the west and looks out over the Bay plain to the east. It adjoins Pulgas Ridge Open Space Preserve just across Edgewood Road, and the southern San Francisco Watershed lands across Freeway 280. You can picnic here on a knoll listening to meadowlarks in the grass, climb a hill, or walk in cool, secluded glades.

Edgewood Park's 467 acres, crowned by a wooded hill rising steeply from the surrounding meadows, had been set aside for a state college. After years of negotiation the land was finally acquired for a park by San Mateo County and the Midpeninsula Regional Open Space District in 1980. The county planned a golf course on the park's serpentine grasslands and trails on the periphery. The proposed golf course, opposed by many biologists and botanists for its potential damage to endangered species of plants and butterflies, causes general concern, too, for the effect of tees and greens on nearby flower-filled meadows.

Despite the golf-course controversy, a well-designed trail system is in place. From the park's main entrance on Edgewood Road, more than 7 miles of trail lead through wooded, fern-filled canyons to the rolling grasslands that surround the central wooded ridge. Beyond the entrance near the trailhead are a day camp and an amphitheatre beside Cordilleras Creek. Close by are attractive picnic sites nestled on terraces under the shade of huge oaks and redwoods, open to the public except during summer day-camp periods. Other entrances also open onto trails that reach the flower fields, the wooded hilltop and the northern canyons of the park.

This is a park for all seasons. Its closeness to the hundreds of thousands who live in neighboring communities makes it a good choice for short outings. In winter, rain-washed air and north winds bring clear views and cold days for brisk hiking. In spring, the meadows underlain with serpentine are thick with goldfields, poppies, cream cups, lupines and owl's clover. On summer and fall days, shady oak groves provide good picnicking and inviting walks on the wooded northeast slopes.

Jurisdiction   San Mateo County.

Facilities   Picnic areas with barbecues, restrooms, day camp, amphitheatre. Trails for hikers and equestrians.

Park Rules   Open from 8 A.M. to sunset. No dogs or bicycles.

Maps   San Mateo County *Edgewood Park* and USGS topo *Woodside.*

How To Get There   From Freeway 280: (1) Main entrance on Edgewood Road at Old Stage Day Camp: Take the Edgewood Road exit and go east 1 mile; turn right at the *Edgewood Park and Day Camp* sign, cross bridge to park. Overflow parking uses the unpaved area beside Edgewood Road. (2) West of 280 on Edgewood Road: Take the Edgewood Road exit, go west under freeway. Park on south side of Edgewood Road near freeway or at Cañada and Edgewood roads. (3) Cañada Road: Take the Edgewood Road exit, go west under freeway, turn south on Cañada Road, go through the freeway underpass and park beside Cañada Road opposite the P.G.& E. switchyard. The Clarkia Trail entrance is immediately north of this installation. (4) Sunset Way: Follow directions for (3) above, but continue on Cañada Road 1.2 more miles and turn left on Jefferson Avenue. Turn left on California Way (not West California Way) and then right on Sunset Way to the park entrance at Hillcrest Way. Limited parking beside the road.

Three Trips from the Park's Main Entrance

Starting from the Old Stage Day Camp entrance, you enter the park across a narrow old bridge over Cordilleras Creek framed by spreading valley oaks. Just beyond the bridge a rustic brown sign points to Old Stage Road, a section of a mid-1800s route to lumber mills and camps in Woodside. Ahead is the parking area and the trailheads for the Edgewood and Sylvan trails.

Trip 1.   Loop Trip to the Wooded Hilltop That Crowns This Park

Take this trip across the park's wooded ridge for views over the Santa Cruz Mountains and out to the Bay.

Distance   5-mile loop.

Time   2½ hours.

Elevation Gain   600'

Start uphill on the Edgewood Trail to the right of the parking area, on switchbacks that take you up the north side of a steep canyon. Shading your way are woods of buckeye, madrone and oak, with an understory of toyon, snowberry and poison oak.

Skirting a sloping meadow accented by immense spreading oaks, you continue uphill, crossing a service road to stay on the shady, tree-lined Edgewood Trail. At the next juntion take the Serpentine Trail to your left.

Now you traverse the steep canyon's rim and look across it to the southern San Francisco Bay and the East Bay hills. From a rocky outcrop beside the trail you can see into the canyon where once stood a Victorian house, part of the 1915 San Francisco Panama Pacific Exposition. It was disassembled and barged down to Redwood City, then reassembled on this site. Only the foundations of the house and vestiges of the garden walls remain today, artfully used to support terraced areas of the day-camp and picnic areas.

Continue around the hillside on the Serpentine Trail to its first intersection with the Sylvan Trail. If you turn left here, you will return to the park entrance and make this a 1½-mile loop trip. But if you stay on the Serpentine Trail, you first cross a high grassy plateau, then pass a turnoff to the Ridgeview Loop Trail on the right and another Sylvan Trail turnoff on the left. Unseen in the tall grasses are the homes of gophers, field mice and other rodents that make up the diet of the hawks you may see soaring overhead.

After the second Sylvan Trail junction you round two bends, leave the Serpentine Trail and turn right onto the Ridgeview Loop

Trail. Under a canopy of live oaks and buckeyes you soon come to a fork in the trail. Take the right-hand fork and walk on over the wooded crown of this hill and out into the chaparral. From a wide clearing, views stretch up and down along fifty miles of the San Andreas rift zone.

Looking northwest you see a vista relatively unchanged from early times (disregarding the multilaned concrete ribbon by which you reached this idyllic spot). In San Francisco Watershed lands you see thousands of acres of unbroken forests, from the Skyline ridge to the lakes along the fault line.

To continue on your trip, follow the Ridgeview Loop Trail around the hill, bearing left at each trail intersection. Then, contouring around the south side of the hill, you look down on the serpentine grasslands, site of the proposed golf course.

At a saddle on the ridge you complete the Ridgeview Loop. Walk straight ahead for another 500 feet and turn left onto the Serpentine Trail at the junction where you left it. Along this short stretch of trail look for clumps of the low-growing blue-eyed grass, which blooms from early spring into summer.

Almost 3 miles from the beginning of your trip, you come to the Sylvan Trail on your right. Take it for a different way back. Around wide switchbacks you descend deep into a steep canyon. A spring high up the headwall feeds a perennial stream, which you cross and then follow along its fern-covered banks.

Emerging from the canyon, you pass the other leg of the Sylvan Trail on your left. Go straight ahead and downhill for 0.2 mile. Then pass to the right of the Old Stage Day Camp or take the left-hand trail, which curves around the camp's picnic tables and barbecues on the landscaped borders of Cordilleras Creek. The park entrance is just beyond the day camp.

Picnic tables at the Old Stage Day Camp

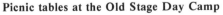

For a shorter route to the park's central ridge take the Edgewood Trail just below Edgewood Road on the west side of Freeway 280. This trail goes down the embankment to a fenced trail leading to a passageway under the freeway. After going through the passage, bear left at a service road. In 200 feet turn right and follow the trail to the Ridgeview Loop. Turn either left or right to circle the hilltop. This makes a 2¾-mile loop trip with an elevation gain of 430'.

Trip 2.   A Summer Supper Hike

Some warm summer evening, take the Edgewood Trail out to the grassy knolls northwest of the park's wooded hilltop.
Distance   2 miles round trip.
Time   1 hour.
Elevation Gain   400'

TRAIL NOTES

Starting from the trailhead at the main park entrance, just follow the Edgewood Trail past the Serpentine Trail junction. Then, for the next ½ mile, there is little change of elevation as the trail contours around several steep-sided ravines.

When you get out into the grasslands, choose a trailside picnic spot with a view of the western hills. If your picnic supper is accompanied by a flutelike bird call, it may be the meadowlark's song filling the evening air. These once-common, pale-yellow birds with a black cravat are becoming rare as development continues to diminish their grasslands habitat.

Rare, too, except in some protected grasslands, are the lemon-yellow blossoms of mariposa lilies, which dot these meadows in early summer. Their centers blotched with magenta, these delicate, bowl-shaped flowers bloom in surprising profusion for flowers of such elegance.

The rosy glow of the summer sun setting over the Skyline ridge will remind you to allow time for the 1-mile hike back to your car in the lowering light.

Trip 3.   A Shady Canyon Hike

Measured and marked as an exercise loop, the Sylvan Trail Loop circles the canyon south of the day camp. In shade for most of the way, it is a favorite warm-day trip for hikers and runners.
Distance   2-mile loop.
Time   1½ hours.
Elevation Gain   500'

TRAIL NOTES

This loop, closed to equestrians, starts by going straight ahead uphill from the parking area on the left of the greensward. In less than 0.2 mile you turn right on the Sylvan Trail and zigzag up the north side of the steep canyon. These switchbacks, at least 8 of them, take you through shady woodland to the edge of a high meadow, where you meet the Serpentine Trail. Turn left on it, and weave in and out of the woods for ½ mile.

Now pick up the Sylvan Trail on your left and follow its wide switchbacks downhill. This trail at first descends an exposed, south-facing slope, but soon drops into deep woods. In season, watch for some of spring's first flowers, the deep-red Indian warriors, blooming under patches of oaks. Watch too for the part of the Sylvan Trail that arcs far back into the canyon to a perennial stream crossing. If you linger for a moment here in the depths of this canyon on the urban fringe, the only sounds to break the stillness are those of flowing water and woodland birds.

Then, continuing on for a few minutes, you pass the other leg of the Sylvan Trail and go straight ahead to the park entrance.

Trip 4.   Trails to the Serpentine Meadows

For a spring wildflower pilgrimage take these short trails and glory in masses of colorful blossoms.

Distance   0.5 mile to 3½ miles round trip.
Time   1–2 hours, or linger as long as you can.
Elevation Gain   From 100′ to 400′

A serpentine meadow in Edgewood Park

TRAIL NOTES

Either the Edgewood or the Clarkia Trail leads to the park service road that crosses the main flower display. The quickest way to reach the flower fields is from the trail below Edgewood Road just west of Freeway 280. This trail goes abruptly down an embankment to connect with the trail from Cañada and Edgewood roads.

Take the fenced trail south to the passage under the freeway and thence to the service road on a grassy swale. Walk east for the best wildflower displays. Around the outcroppings of serpentine you will see goldfields, tidytips, cream cups, owl's clover, lupines and many more annuals. Where there is more moisture, look for blue larkspur. Bring your flower guide.

These serpentine meadows produce lovely carpets of flowers each spring. They are also home to the very rare checkerspot butterfly, found only here and on the extensions of this meadow west of the freeway, on San Bruno Mountain and on Jasper Ridge Biological Preserve. The presence of this butterfly, now on the federal list of threatened species, poses serious problems for the construction of a proposed golf course. Note on the accompanying map the protected area, the main habitat of the checkerspot, around which the course would have to be built. Threatened too are the flower-filled serpentine meadows that surround the park's central ridge, 150 acres of which would be used for the golf course.

If you have the time, walk the length of the service road and up on the Ridgeview Loop Trail, from where you can look down on the sea of color. In the shaded woodlands of this loop you will find different species, such as red Indian warriors, white milkmaids and blue hound's-tongue.

From Cañada Road the Clarkia Trail contours around a south-facing hillside past some large serpentine outcrops and through a scattering of oak trees to reach the east end of the service road. As its name implies, you will find a show of magenta-colored clarkias here in early summer. This 0.75-mile trail, closed to horses in winter, connects to the Serpentine Trail, and makes a good starting point for a trans-park trip.

Another entrance to the park's flower fields is from Sunset Way, but there is little parking there. For those with limited walking ability, this entrance offers a short route to an overlook of the colorful display.

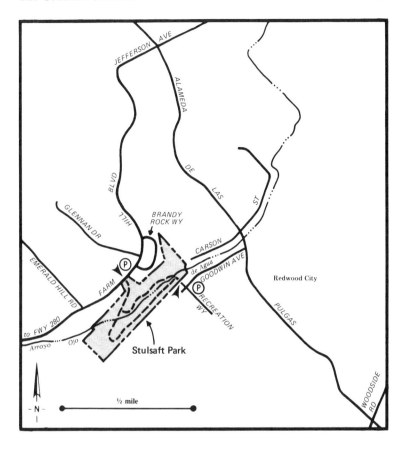

Stulsaft Park

Many paths wind through this park in a creek canyon where you can walk under the trees, picnic by the stream or bask in the sunshine by the playground at the upper canyon rim.

Distance   Round trips of 1–3 miles.

Time   Allow 1 or 2 hours to explore the park.

Elevation Gain   120′ from the Recreation Way entrance to the Farm Hill entrance.

Jurisdiction   Redwood City.

Facilities   Trails for hikers; playgrounds, picnic tables, barbecues and group picnic areas, playing field, restrooms and amphitheater.

Park Rules   Open 8 A.M. to sunset.

Maps   USGS topos *Palo Alto* and *Woodside*.

Great oaks make a shady entrance to the park.

How To Get There   From Freeway 280:   (1) Main entrance: Take
Woodside Road northeast to Alameda de Las Pulgas, turn northwest and at Goodwin Avenue turn left. Park on Recreation Way and
walk to park entrance. Parking lot is closed. (2) Farm Hill entrance:
Take Farm Hill Boulevard north 1.3 miles to the park entrance on the
right side. Limited parking on the street.

TRAIL NOTES

This 42-acre Redwood City park is in a cool, green canyon with
the Arroyo Ojo de Agua (Spring Pond Creek or Stulsaft Creek) in its
depths. Although the park is less than a mile long, in a few minutes
its paths can take you away from city streets and sounds into a quiet,
wooded retreat where you find bird songs, deer tracks and the music
of a running stream.

Formerly the J. B. Shroeder estate, dating back to the 1880's, the
land was later acquired by Martin Stulsaft and given to Redwood
City in 1951. Traces of the former estate can still be seen in the
bridge over the creek and the plantings of cultivated shrubs.

The many picnic tables and barbecues draw lively crowds on
summer weekends, but during the rest of the year you may have the
canyon almost to yourself. Even at the busiest times, the trails winding up the hillsides will take you to quiet, secluded places.

The wide, surfaced main trail from Recreation Way takes you to
the left, uphill, on the south side of the park, then down along the
stream. In a bend in the creek are picnic tables, barbecues,

restrooms and a little amphitheater. This is a popular spot for large gatherings.

Continue ten minutes farther along the trail to reach the west end of the park. If you are out for only a short amble in the woods, turn around here and retrace your steps. However, for a brisk climb, try exploring the side trails that wind around the south side of the canyon. Or cross an old bridge to the north side of the canyon and follow the trail uphill past a wide playing field and thence to the small tots' playground at the Farm Hill Boulevard entrance.

For still more creekside exploration and a scramble up the open north slope of the canyon, take the path straight down the hill from the Recreation Way parking lot. A bridge leads to more picnic tables and to informal trails up the hill on which you can make your way to the playgrounds and the entrance at Farm Hill Boulevard.

This is a delightful park on an early spring day when the grass is still green and leaf buds are just coming out on the buckeye trees. In autumn the bright red toyon berries sparkle in the sunlight glancing through the tall trees. In winter when the creek runs full and the foliage is fresh from recent rains, the surfaced paths make this a fine place to walk between showers. This is a park to linger in and enjoy, where you might perhaps share a leisurely midweek lunch with a few friends, or take children to enjoy the endless delights of the moving creek waters.

Arroyo Ojo de Agua flows through Stulsaft Park.

Mountainside Parks and Preserves on the Central Peninsula
Highway 92 to Highway 84

Forests cover most of the steep slopes on both sides of the Santa Cruz Mountains' crest. Those on the east slopes in the watersheds and in Huddart and Wunderlich parks are familiar to Baysiders as a backdrop of their communities.

Less familiar to Peninsula residents are the forests on the west slopes of the Santa Cruz Mountains in the seven thousand acres of preserves opened to the public in the late 1980s. And seldom seen are the spectacular views of the coastside and the ocean from high ridges in these preserves.

A century and a half ago majestic redwood forests extended from the valley floor over the ridge of the Santa Cruz Mountains and down the west slopes. In the forests on the east slopes, known to the Spanish as Pulgas Redwoods, Spanish soldiers, with the help of Indians, felled trees and dragged them by oxen to build missions in San Francisco and Santa Clara.

In 1840 the Mexican Governor of California, Luis Alvarado, granted to his friend John Coppinger the 12,545-acre Rancho Cañada de Raimundo, which included most of the Pulgas Redwoods, extending from the Woodside valley floor to the Skyline. During the decade in which Gold Rush San Francisco was built, the great trees were cut, and the lumber hauled down to the Embarcadero in Redwood City and sailed by schooner up the Bay to San Francisco.

By 1870 hardly a redwood tree remained uncut in the Pulgas Redwoods. Logging began then in the primeval forests along the Skyline and down the steep west slopes. Logging continued into this century until the old forests were almost completely cut over. In the years since, second-growth trees have been cut sporadically.

However, in the decade of the 1980s the Midpeninsula Regional Open Space District acquired much of these upper slopes west of the Skyline as preserves. The State of California purchased historic farmlands—the Burleigh Murray Ranch and lands extending to the Skyline ridge. And logging has ceased in Purisima Creek Redwoods, El Corte de Madera and La Honda preserves.

In these preserves and parklands extensive trail systems are being developed on old logging and farm roads. Trails in canyons and along creeks are now open to hikers, equestrians and bicyclists.

Important trail links join these western preserves and the parks and trail systems on the east slopes which reach down to cities on the Bayside. A long-distance ridge trail extending north and south along the Skyline is part of the Bay Area Ridge Trail initiated in 1987. In San Mateo County, many miles of this trail system are already in place, and a trail corridor has been designated to complete the gaps in the Ridge Trail through the county.

Future trail connections from Purisima Creek Redwoods and Burleigh Murray State Park may some day make it possible to walk from the Bay over the Santa Cruz Mountains to the ocean.

A fine old stone bridge arches over Mills Creek.

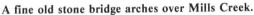

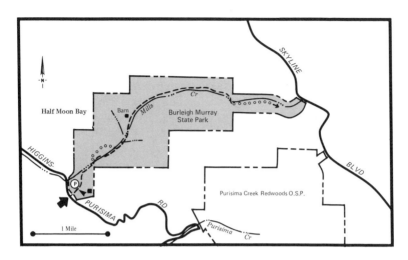

Burleigh Murray State Park

A historic ranch tucked away in a valley south of Half Moon Bay now belongs to the California State Park system. In the 1860s this was a working ranch, growing hay and grazing cattle. Perennial Mills Creek, named for the first owners of the ranch, flows through the narrow valley. An arched stone bridge crosses the creek to an old barn and a bunkhouse remaining from the ranching days. The State of California purchased the property in 1983 and later added a parcel known as Rancho Raymundo to extend the park to Skyline Boulevard.

The state may preserve the park for its historical interest, with an emphasis on interpreting early San Mateo County ranch life. The historic buildings, unparalleled on the north San Mateo County coast, will be restored—it is hoped—and the stone walls and the arch bridge preserved. Farming may be discontinued and the land restored to its natural state, with particular attention to protection of the sensitive riparian habitat.

Besides historic preservation, the major uses of the park will be day hiking and horseback riding. The park will provide an important trail corridor to link coastal trails with the Skyline route of the Bay Area Ridge Trail. An old farm road runs from the entrance on Higgins Purisima Road about 2 miles northeast, roughly following Mills Creek. This perennial stream rises near the Skyline ridge and flows through the heart of the park. A ½-mile loop trail on the north side of the creek is proposed for the future. Sometime during the next five years, the creek trail will be extended to the Skyline.

A small gravelled parking area just inside the park gate will be constructed in late 1988. Until this is accomplished, visitors may park along the edge of Higgins Purisima Road and walk into the park.

Jurisdiction   State of California.

Facilities   Trails for hikers, equestrians; parking in late 1988.

Park Rules   Open 8 A.M. to dusk.

Maps   USGS topos *Half Moon Bay* and *Woodside*.

How To Get There   From the Highway 1/92 intersection go south on Highway 1 1.2 miles to Higgins Purisima Road. Turn left (east) and go 1.7 miles to the park entrance on the left. Until the parking area is completed, park beside the road and cross the stile to enter the park.

A Hike on a Historic Ranch

Follow an old ranch road into a secluded coastal valley where an old barn and bridge remain from early San Mateo County ranching days.

Distance   4 miles round trip.

Time   2¼ hours.

Elevation Gain   680'

TRAIL NOTES

Leave the park entrance at the mouth of the valley on the farm road now used as a trail. As you near alder-bordered Mills Creek in the stillness of this secluded valley, you can hear the sounds of the stream accompanied by the songs of birds. Former farm fields border the trail and rounded hills rise on both sides of the canyon.

Upstream, where the valley narrows, you cross two bridges at a bend in the creek. Beyond in a semicircular meadow between the creek and the trail you find wildflowers blooming profusely in spring. On shady, north-facing road banks wild currant bushes blossom in winter.

One mile from the park entrance a small tributary enters the creek from the east and the trail veers left, following the creek into a broad flat near the old ranch headquarters. Past a 1930s bungalow that serves as a ranger's residence, you cross an old stone bridge arched over the creek. On the far side is a great wooden barn dating from the 1860s. Its roof now sags and its doors are wedged shut, but the state plans call for its restoration. A fine stone wall holds the

The handsome old barn was built in the 1860s.

bank beyond the barn, and moss-covered stone walls line the curve in the creek by the bridge.

Continuing on the road beyond the barn and its corrals, you pass a small wooden bunkhouse by the creek. In a tangle of blackberry bushes stand pumps, outbuildings, cattle chutes and gates, all no longer used.

The trail continues up the narrowing valley between steep, chaparral-covered hills to the east and high, overgrown hayfields to the west. Then, about a mile above the barn, the old road we have used as a trail becomes obliterated. However, in the future a trail will be continued up the steep ridge through the narrow Rancho Raymundo property to the Skyline. Heading back down the valley, we see the creek, rounded hills and valleys from a different perspective.

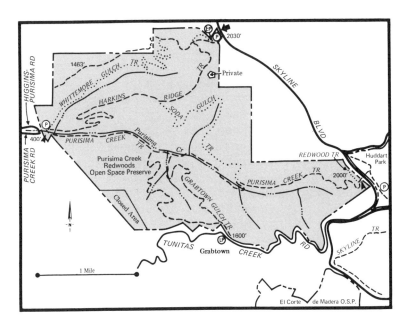

Purisima Creek Redwoods
Open-Space Preserve

This MROSD preserve is a 2511-acre treasure of redwood forests, clear-flowing streams, steep-sided canyons and long ridges. Its size and its rugged terrain make it a place to find both quiet seclusion and long trails for strenuous hiking trips. This northernmost redwood forest in San Mateo County is just minutes from the urban San Francisco Peninsula.

The preserve extends westward for 3 miles from the 2000-foot-high crest of the Santa Cruz Mountains. East across Skyline Boulevard are the San Francisco Watershed lands and Huddart Park. From the Skyline crest three ridges divide the preserve into two main canyons trending west. Between Harkins and Tunitas ridges flows Purisima Creek, the centerpiece of the preserve.

A beautiful, year-round stream fed by many tributaries, Purisima Creek rises along the Skyline ridge and flows west for 3 miles through the preserve. In the lower end of the preserve, large second-growth redwoods line its banks and side slopes. Leaving the preserve, Purisima Creek runs through rolling grasslands and the 2200-acre Cowell Ranch to reach the ocean in a waterfall over sandstone cliffs. The ranch, purchased in 1987 by the Peninsula Open Space Trust, includes some ocean front which will eventually become public open space.

Between Harkins Ridge and the next ridge north is Whittemore Gulch, where an intermittent creek flows through a lovely wooded canyon to join Purisima Creek at the preserve's west entrance.

In the 1860s, when redwoods were first cut here, the logs proved too large to drag up the steep canyons. Although the west end of the canyon was open, there was little need for lumber on the coastside and no port from which to ship it to San Francisco. Therefore, the trees were cut for shingles, which pack animals could haul out of the gulches over steep, winding trails. As many as eight shingle mills operated here during the late 1800s.

Logging was back-breaking, dangerous work, but some ingenious techniques were developed to hoist the heavy logs out of the canyon. One such device used a cable to operate a tramway rising one thousand feet from the creek to the ridgetop.

Lumbering ventures came and went in the narrow, steep canyon of the Purisima. Last logged in the 1970s, stands of second-growth redwoods now fill most of the canyon.

Then in 1982 MROSD bought 849 acres in Whittemore Gulch, and in 1984, assisted by the Save-the-Redwoods League, MROSD acquired an additional 1662 acres, including the headwaters of Purisima Creek. A few primeval redwoods remain; one is said to be 1200 years old.

Some of the most challenging hikes on the Peninsula are trips down Purisima's canyons and up its ridges. The old county road, now the Purisima Creek Trail, descends from Skyline Boulevard to follow the creek to the lower end of the canyon. New trails and old logging roads form a 17-mile trail network.

Some narrow trails are exclusively for hikers, others on logging roads are also open to horsemen and bicyclists. The ¼-mile Redwood Trail for the physically limited, funded by POST, meanders through tall redwoods along the Skyline ridge. From several turnouts for picnic tables one can look out toward the coast.

A short walk on an easy grade from the preserve's west entrance on Higgins Purisima Road reaches groves of the largest redwoods beside Purisima Creek. Starting long loop hikes from this entrance gives you the advantage of gaining altitude while you and day are fresh.

Trails in Purisima Creek Redwoods link with adjoining Huddart Park trails, making it possible to walk from Bayside cities over the

From Skyline Boulevard the Redwood Trail gives wheelchair users a trip through the forest.

Santa Cruz Mountains to the west end of the preserve, only a few miles from the ocean. With advance reservations, backpackers can camp in Huddart Park. This route has been suggested as a city-to-sea trail.

Be weather-wise when visiting Purisima Creek Redwoods Preserve. Because it is several miles back from the ocean, the preserve often has sun when fog hangs on the coast. However, on the days when fog sweeps in from the sea to reach the redwoods along the Skyline, condensed moisture falls from the tree branches like rain.

Jurisdiction   Midpeninsula Regional Open Space District.

Facilities   Trails for hikers, equestrians and bicyclists; one trail for the physically limited, with picnic tables, restroom and special parking. Equestrian parking.

Preserve Rules   Open from dawn to dusk.

Map   USGS topo *Woodside.*

How To Get There   The preserve's main entrance is on Skyline Boulevard 4.5 miles south of Highway 92. The Purisima Creek Trail entrance is 2.0 miles farther south. The Redwood Trail entrance and wheelchair parking are 0.2 mile south of the Purisima Creek Trail entrance. The west entrance is off Higgins Purisima Road, reached from Highway 1 just 1.2 mile south of its intersection with Highway 92 in Half Moon Bay.

Trip 1.   Purisima Creek Trail

Follow the old 19th century Purisima Creek Road down a deep canyon beside Purisima Creek to the preserve's west entrance. Today's travelers can enjoy tall trees, beautiful flowers and the sight and sound of a year-round stream.

Distance 8.4 miles round trip.
Time 5 hours.
Elevation Loss 1600'

TRAIL NOTES

A steady descent from the Skyline ridge, this trail could be a one-way trip with a shuttle or it could be combined with the Soda Gulch and Harkins Ridge trails to make a 10-mile loop trip.

Starting from the southern Skyline Boulevard entrance opposite Huddart Park, go over the hiker's stile and down the wide trail through a redwood-and-fir forest. Note to the left of the stile the wheelchair gate to the specially surfaced Redwood Trail. Before long you come to switchbacks, where logging operations cleared the trees to make level platforms or landings. Wild lilacs, spring-flowering in shades of blue and purple, and young tanoak trees are thriving in this clearing. The climax trees, Douglas fir and redwood, will eventually shade out these hardy early plants.

After about a mile down the trail you begin to hear Purisima Creek, and before long you see it through the trees. Soon you are walking close to it. At a sharp turn in the trail, the Soda Gulch Trail takes off to the right up a heavily wooded canyon to join the Harkins Ridge Trail. At the next turn you cross the ever-widening creek, where clear pools are edged with fern fronds and horsetails.

Around the next bend on the south side is the site of a mile-long cable tramway that in the 1870s lifted logs from Purdy Harris' shingle mill out of the canyon to a location near present-day Kings Mountain School. This ingenious device, a forerunner of modern cable-logging, had a short existence, but its location appeared on topographic maps for many years.

From here to the west entrance the old road is close to the creek, which stair-steps down the canyon over rocks and under bridges of fallen logs. Some logs, still rooted, are sprouting new shoots.

A heavy-timbered bridge crosses the creek to a trail leading to Grabtown, an old logging settlement on top of Tunitas Ridge. Where the canyon widens, two shingle mills operated in the early 1900s, some of the last in the canyon. This is an open, sunny place to stop for lunch and to speculate on the rugged life of those loggers, who had to deal with floods, fires and accidents.

The remaining 1.3 miles of your trip are less steep and more heavily wooded. Small streams trickle down the canyon sides, and flowers bloom at every season, from the deep red trillium of early spring to the lavender asters of fall. Soon your way is completely enclosed by forest.

Some immense redwoods remain near the creek at the lower end of the preserve. On the north side is a grove of memorial trees, dedicated by a contributor to the Save-the-Redwoods League which helped purchase this beautiful preserve.

Now you are near the preserve's west entrance. Before starting your return trip to Skyline Boulevard, find a log to sit on beside the creek to enjoy its clear waters and the light filtering through the redwood trees. You could shorten this hike by arranging a car shuttle at the west entrance.

Trip 2.   A Loop Hike from the North Ridge

This vigorous trip from the north ridgetop to the west entrance descends to Purisima Creek on the Harkins Ridge Trail and returns on the Whittemore Gulch Trail.

Distance   6.8-mile loop.

Time   4½ hours.

Elevation Loss   1630'

TRAIL NOTES

As you leave the north Skyline Boulevard parking area, go over the hiker's stile and watch for the foot-trail turnoff about 100 feet on the right, which bypasses the steep grade of the service road. The trail zigzags down the mountainside just below the ridgetop under Douglas firs, wide-spreading tanoaks, madrones, and a scattering of live oaks. If the day is clear, the views west present a sweep of the San Mateo Coast from Half Moon Bay north and south.

In 0.3 mile the trail again intersects the service road, which you cross onto the Harkins Ridge Trail. On a bench created by early landslides, this path traverses the hillside above a steep canyon among clumps of sizable redwood trees and a thick stand of Douglas firs. Abundant flowers brighten the trailside—iris in spring, lavender asters, a purple mint and apricot-colored sticky monkey flower in late summer.

After a 0.6-mile contour around the canyon headwall, the route turns right on the old fire road down the spine of Harkins Ridge and descends more than 1300 feet in 2.1 miles. The ridge is predominantly chaparral-covered, although some tanoaks and bay laurels grow on the steep mountainside. Small stands of firs and redwoods on the north side of Harkins Ridge give late afternoon shade. From here we look north down into Whittemore Gulch, the route of our climb back to the Skyline ridge.

In 0.3 mile down Harkins Ridge the Soda Gulch Trail takes off south to meet the Purisima Creek Trail in the canyon below. But you continue your descent on the Harkins Ridge Trail, passing knolls densely covered with ceanothus, which forms a showy blue cloud in spring.

After the trail arcs left off the open ridge, it makes 4 switchbacks into the cool shade of the Purisima Creek redwoods, then follows the creek downstream for ½ mile. Just a few steps before the bridge to the south side of the creek, you find the Whittemore Gulch Trail junction on the right. About 300 feet beyond the bridge is the preserve gate at Higgins Purisima Road. You could leave a car here and avoid the hike back up the mountain, or you could start the hike here and do the steep climb first. In any case, step down to the creek to see its pools and cascades at close range.

The Whittemore Gulch Trail offers a 3½-mile return to the Skyline ridge. In the lower gulch, redwoods deemed too small or irregular to cut in the logging days are now grown to handsome large trees. Alders and big-leaf maples fill openings among the redwoods and firs, and the canyon walls are lush with ferns. After crossing the creek, the trail passes close to the shell of a redwood tree, which we can estimate was at least 15 feet in diameter. There are venerable Douglas firs too. One old giant has sent out a branch that rises vertically after its first horizontal 8 feet, becoming an immense tree itself.

After 1½ miles, this well-designed trail leaves the canyon depths and zigzags more than a mile up the mountainside, crossing a thickly covered chaparral slope. Poison oak dominates the hillside, its fall colors brilliant reds and oranges. The southern exposure here is welcome on a winter's day, but can be hot in summer.

When you reach the old jeep trail on the ridge, turn right and follow it for ½ mile. Then watch for the trail junction where you turn left to enter the shade of the forested trail on which you started your trip.

Trip 3.   Grabtown Gulch Loop Trip

From the southern ridgetops of the preserve, this trip descends through the hardwood forests of Grabtown Gulch to the Purisima Creek Trail and then returns following another route.

Distance   4-mile loop.

Time   3 hours.

Elevation Loss   1200'

Spring-fed creeks flow through redwood groves.

TRAIL NOTES

To find the trail entrance, turn west off Skyline Boulevard on Tunitas Creek Road and go 2 miles to the familiar MROSD brown metal gate with its sign FIRE LANE, DO NOT BLOCK on the right side. There are several turnouts for limited parking on the road uphill from the entrance.

Grabtown Gulch takes its name from the settlement that sprang up on a small flat near the trail entrance. It was the first level spot that logging wagons reached on their three- or four-day trip to the embarcadero at Redwood City. According to legend, a boy named it Grabtown because settlers grabbed whatever lodging or garden space became available.

This trail starts off gently over a little rise, staying along the flank of the ridge (possibly the Grabtown site). When you reach the first little clearing, keep to the right and continue to a larger opening in the forest, a landing for logging operations. At this clearing trails take off left and right. You take the right-hand fork; you'll return up the left-hand trail.

You go down through Douglas firs and young redwoods that are beginning to overtake the tanoaks and madrones that sprang up after previous logging. At this stage of regrowth there is still plenty of space and light between trees for ceanothus, wild roses, toyon and honeysuckle. From openings in the trees it is possible to look out to the ocean—though it is often shrouded in fog.

Your trail continues downhill, cuts east across the ridge and then reverses direction to descend a very steep slope into Grabtown Gulch. You cross to its west side and follow a path lined with ferns and ocean spray, where the creek is well below the trail. After you cross to the east side, you walk right beside the creek. By the shady streamside in midsummer you can find 3-foot-tall orange tiger lilies.

Shortly, Grabtown Gulch Creek enters Purisima Creek, which you cross on an old logging bridge. You have reached the widest part of Purisima Canyon. Of the shingle mills that flourished here, no vestiges remain, but you can sit on the bridge to watch the water and listen to the birds at the confluence of these creeks.

To take the rest of the loop trip, hike down the canyon about ¼ mile to a trail on the left that climbs the ridge west of Grabtown Gulch and returns to the wide forest opening near Tunitas Creek Road.

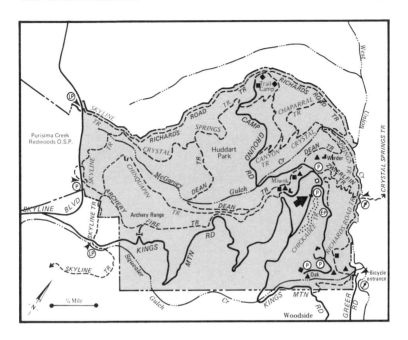

Huddart Park

In Huddart Park not only do stumps of the big redwood trees and vestiges of skid trails remind us of the early logging days, but many place names recall that era. Up on the mountain near the little logging town of Summit Springs, Frank King's Saloon flourished until the turn of the century, giving his name to the road that goes through the park. From Richards sawmill on the Skyline ridge, wagons carried lumber down a steep road that is now Richards Road Trail. Owen McGarvey had wood cutting rights on the gulch that traverses the park and now bears his name.

But a far more significant heritage for us is the handsome second growth redwood-and-fir forest and the woodland of oaks, madrones and California bay trees in this 973-acre park.

In addition to its picnic areas and playfields there are 18 miles of trails through its redwoods, along its creeks and up its mountain-sides. A disabilities access and a nature trail with special parking offer short, easy walks. A trail camp on the park's remote northern boundary is available by reservation.

Jurisdiction   San Mateo County.

Facilities   Trails for hikers, equestrians, and the physically limited.
Equestrian parking. Picnic grounds, trail camp.

Park Rules   Open from 8 A.M. to sunset. Group picnics and trail
camp by reservation only. Some trails open to hikers only. Trails may
be closed to equestrians in wet weather. No pets, no bicycles. Fees:
$3 per car; seniors free on week days.

Maps   San Mateo County *Huddart Park*. USGS topo *Woodside*.

How To Get There   Main Entrance: from Freeway 280 take
Woodside Road (Hwy 84) exit 1.5 miles west, then go right on Kings
Mountain Road 2 miles to main park entrance. Skyline Boulevard
entrance: turn right from Kings Mountain Road onto Skyline
Boulevard and go 0.3 mile. Use parking area on west side of Skyline
Boulevard, take short trail north and cross to Huddart Park entrance.

Connecting Trails   From the upper park: the Skyline Trail continues south to Wunderlich Park, and across Skyline Boulevard are
trails in Purisima Creek Redwoods O.S.P.; from the lower park: the
Crystal Springs Trail crosses West Union Creek to continue to
Highway 92.

Trip 1.   An All-Day Hike Circling the Park

This loop takes you from the Miwok picnic area down to West
Union Creek and up the magnificent Crystal Springs Trail to the
Skyline heights, ending with a downhill return on the Chinquapin
Trail west of McGarvey Gulch.

Distance   8.2-mile loop.

Time   5 to 6 hours.

Elevation Gain   1500'

TRAIL NOTES

Starting at the Miwok picnic area, pick up the Dean Trail heading
downhill. The trail swings down through redwoods for a little more
than ½ mile to McGarvey Gulch. Here West Union Creek is joined
by McGarvey Gulch Creek and you start up the Crystal Springs
Trail. This is the loveliest route up through the park and a part of the
County's north-south trail system.

At first in an oak-madrone woodland, you are soon in redwoods
on the far side of McGarvey Gulch. On wide switchbacks the trail
climbs past a sizable second-growth forest. Here and there are
immense stumps from the ancient forest.

In ⅓ mile the trail leaves the gulch canyon, passing the Chaparral Trail on the right and the Canyon Trail on the left, and then zig-
zagging up to the edge of the Trail Camp. If no camp is in session,

find a table on which to spread out your lunch. Otherwise, continue on the trail, which soon crosses the service road to begin a 2-mile climb to the Skyline.

Redwoods, firs and madrones cover the mountainside and birds fill the air with their songs. The trail winds in and out of small canyons and crosses grassy meadows, beguiling the hiker with new vistas around each bend. Springs dampen fern-covered ravines, and in spring wildflowers bloom where small clearings let in the sun.

Eventually the trail climbs steeply to meet the Dean Trail. At this point you could shorten the hike by returning to your starting point via the Dean Trail. But this trip continues up the ridge on comfortably-graded switchbacks through a glade of madrones. Their summer leaf fall makes a rustling carpet underfoot in a delicately colored pattern of lemon-yellow, pink and cream.

The trail levels off in a huckleberry flat under redwoods where the Crystal Springs and the Richards Road trails converge at the Skyline Trail. A bench at this crossing is a good place to pause before finishing the last ½ mile climb to the Skyline.

From this intersection take the Skyline Trail to the left and follow it toward Skyline Boulevard. The redwoods here have not been cut for over a century. Heavy winter rains (as much as 40 inches a season) and summer fog drip give these trees the moisture on which they thrive. Widely-spaced trees, many of them 4 feet in diameter, have a handsome understory of shiny-leaved huckleberry and a ground cover of wood fern and oxalis. In spring you will find yellow

A sunny meadow by West Union Creek draws summer picnickers.

violets, mauve mission bells and irises in many shades of blue and purple. For a short expedition to this part of the park, you can drive to the Skyline Boulevard entrance and get to this fine forest without the climb from below.

From the Skyline Trail a short connection cuts through to Skyline Boulevard opposite Purisima Creek Redwoods O.S.P. But to continue this trip, stay on the Skyline Trail ⅛ mile farther to meet the service road that the Skyline Trail follows east for another ¼ mile. From this point the Skyline Trail bears right to Kings Mountain Road, the service road (now the Archery Fire Trail) descends to park headquarters, and our route turns left onto the Chinquapin Trail.

Our return trip follows the 2-mile Chinquapin Trail, built in 1987, which veers north down a ridge in a handsome second-growth forest. A scattering of great stumps gives you a measure of the stately forest that grew on this mountainside until it was logged in the 1860s. The trail winds down a steep hillside into McGarvey Gulch, but before it reaches the creek it turns south to make a long traverse around the ridge and joins the Dean Trail a short ½ mile above the Miwok picnic area.

Trip 2.   A Loop Through the Center of the Park

A half-day hike takes you up McGarvey Gulch and down the other side.

Distance   4.3-mile loop.
Time   2½ hours.
Elevation Gain   400'

TRAIL NOTES

Find the Dean Trail west of the Miwok picnic area and head uphill. Less than a half-hour's walk along the side of McGarvey Gulch brings you to a bridge over the creek, a cool spot to linger on a hot day. In winter and early spring you can enjoy the creek waters cascading over mossy rocks. The logging road near the trail and the great redwood stumps remind us of past logging, but now second-growth trees reach high overhead. Where there is underground water near the creek, giant chain ferns are taking hold again and maples are growing on the bank.

Leaving the creek, the Dean Trail contours around a ridge on an easy grade. In a half hour a hiker should reach an intersection with the Crystal Springs Trail. Turn right on it, and after rounding another bend the trail turns downward through a handsome redwood forest.

From here the trip down repeats in reverse the journey up the

Crystal Springs Trail described in Trip 1. In 1.1 miles from the Dean Trail you come to the Trail Camp. After passing it, there are another 1.3 forested miles to the park's lower end. Turn up there on the other end of the Dean Trail to complete your trip to the Miwok picnic area.

Trip 3.   A Loop Trip In Lower McGarvey Gulch

Explore the forest and the chaparral-covered slope in the park's lower, northeastern corner to find tall forests, wide vistas and a walk down the old road from Richard's lumber mill.

Distance   3.5-mile loop.
Time   2 hours.
Elevation Loss   360′

TRAIL NOTES

This easy trip takes its one steep stretch going downhill. Start from Werder Flat on the Trail-Camp road (used only for service vehicles). On a slight rise in grade you go into and out of McGarvey Gulch. A little less than ¼ mile past the creek, turn right down the Canyon Trail. You switchback down the side of McGarvey Gulch in a transitional forest where redwoods are growing high enough to shade out the madrones and tanbark oaks that took over after these slopes were logged.

From the Canyon Trail join the Crystal Springs Trail and go downhill a few hundred feet to pick up the Chaparral Trail. At this

**A team of horses pulling tanbark oak logs
along Kings Mountain Road near the tollhouse**

point you leave the forest to traverse a ridge where scattered oaks, madrones and a few toyons cast light shade. Native bunchgrass covers open areas along with spring-blooming iris and snowberry. In ½ mile the trail approaches the park's northern boundary, beside which Richards Road Trail makes its steep way from what was Summit Road down to West Union Creek. In the 1850s this road carried logs down to Whipple's sawmill on the creek.

You start down Richards Road Trail on an open ridge among shrubby manzanita and blue-blossomed wild lilac. The view is toward Emerald Lake Hills, topped by a cross, and to the Bay plain beyond. To the right of the trail and paralleling it, the old skid road where oxen dragged logs to the mill is visible.

Below the chaparral, great canyon oaks meet above the trail. Then as you approach the creek you pass through groves of redwoods and the trail veers right to cross West Union Creek. After crossing the bridge and passing the Crystal Springs Trail, take the Dean Trail to the left and make a ½-mile easy climb through redwoods back to Werder Flat.

Trip 4.   A Shady Walk by West Union Creek

A warm summer day is a good time to explore these cool trails by the creek.

Distance   2-mile loop.
Time   1½ hours.
Elevation Gain   500'

TRAIL NOTES

The park's creekside trails, shaded by spreading big-leaf maples and tall redwoods, are a peaceful retreat. But over a century ago, in the 1850s, three sawmills operated along West Union Creek, handling logs cut from forests extending to the Skyline above.

For an easy, leisurely walk by the creek and a short loop up into the forest, start from the Redwood picnic area in the southeast corner of the park. Go down into the Meadow walk-in area through a pedestrian stile at the gate and past tables filled on weekends with groups of picnickers.

At the end of the meadow pick up the Richards Road Trail, which forms the southeast (and the north) boundary of the park. This trail, a broad service road, continues its nearly level way up the creek. Sounds from the picnic area begin to fade as you round the first bend and enter the quiet of the tall forest.

Picnic tables in the woods near the Dean Trail

This trip follows West Union Creek for 0.7 mile, then makes a loop on the Dean and Zwierlein trails to a flat and a picnic area 400 feet above, altogether 2.0 miles on easy grades.

West Union Creek runs year-round, though dry years leave the water level low. Ferns and lush shrubs line its banks. Here and there are inviting spots for a creekside picnic.

A half mile up the trail you come to a crossroads to which the Zwierlein Trail (which you take on the returning leg of the trip) descends from the flat above. At this point the Richards Road Trail is now called the Crystal Springs Trail. Along this part of the trail by the creek are some of the park's largest trees.

Another ½ mile on the Crystal Springs Trail brings you to McGarvey Gulch Creek. Fed by springs along the Skyline, it flows down a deep-sided canyon through the center of the park. The Crystal Springs Trail turns uphill at the creek crossing.

Take the Dean Trail left just before the crossing for a half-hour walk up through the redwoods to the vicinity of the Zwierlein group picnic grounds. Other tables are scattered under the trees just uphill.

For the return to West Union Creek, find the Zwierlein Trail below the restrooms and head downhill to complete your loop. For a few minutes you go along an oak-and-madrone-covered ridge, then on many switchbacks descend into a steep canyon. Ferns carpet the hillside and small streams flow down to join the creek below. An easy half-hour brings you to Richards Road Trail, another half-hour back to your starting place.

Trip 5.   Chickadee Trail into the Forest

This pleasant, nearly level trail goes through tall chaparral and oaks and past fern-lined banks to reach a redwood grove.

Distance   1-mile loop.

Time   ½ hour or more.

Elevation Gain   Nearly level.

TRAIL NOTES

This self-guiding nature trail, designed for wheelchair use, has a well-compacted surface and a grade of less than 5%. For the sight-impaired there is a guide wire. A brochure is available at the trail entrance.

From a level parking space in a corner of the main parking lot, the trail takes off around a hillside covered with wild lilac, coyote bush and toyon. A short bridge spans an old log chute left from early timber-cutting days. The path soon comes into the deep shade of redwoods. Here a bench awaits you for a rest before you retrace your steps or turn downhill for a return trip on a lower trail through oak woods to the parking lot.

Though suitably graded and surfaced for wheelchairs, this trail also provides a pleasant short walk for those who would enjoy an easy trip into the forest.

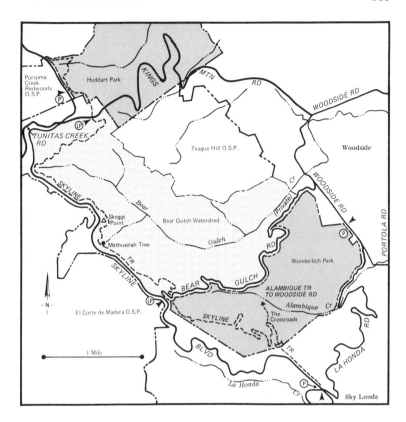

Skyline Trail

The Skyline trails of Huddart and Wunderlich parks are linked by a beautiful and varied trail through the Bear Gulch Watershed. This long trail follows the Skyline ridge, where frequent fogs make it a cool trip in hot weather.

Distance   8.5 miles one way.

Time   4–5 hours.

Elevation Loss   580′

Connecting Trails   Crystal Springs and Chinquapin trails east in Huddart Park, Purisima Creek Trail west in Purisima Creek Redwoods O.S.P., Alambique Trail east in Wunderlich Park, trails west in El Corte de Madera O.S.P.

Jurisdiction   San Mateo County.

Facilities   Trail for hikers and equestrians; last 0.6 mile restricted to equestrians.

Park Rules   Open from 8 A.M. to sunset. No dogs or bicycles.

Maps   San Mateo County *Huddart Park* and *Wunderlich Park,* USGS topo *Woodside.*

How To Get There   (1) Huddart Park entrances: On east side of Skyline Boulevard: (a) 1 mile north of Kings Mtn. Road, limited roadside parking; (b) ½ mile north of Kings Mtn. Road, limited roadside parking; and (c) on Kings Mtn. Road's north side 0.3 mile east of Skyline Boulevard, limited roadside parking.

(2) Bear Gulch Watershed entrances: enter on the south side of Kings Mtn. Road as in (c) above, or enter at Wunderlich Park (see below).

(3) Wunderlich Park entrance: At the intersection of Bear Gulch Road East (private, gated road), 3 miles north of the La Honda/Skyline Boulevard intersection. Limited parking across Skyline from the private road.

TRAIL NOTES

The Skyline Trail from the northwest corner of Huddart Park to Skylonda is a segment of the Bay Area Ridge Trail planned to encircle the 9-county Bay Area along its ridgetops. Following the crest of the Santa Cruz Mountains, the Skyline Trail passes under tall second-growth redwoods and Douglas firs, through two county parks and a watershed. A part of the old California Riding and Hiking Trail, it is also a segment of San Mateo County's north-south trail.

The segments of the Skyline Trail within Huddart and Wunderlich parks are described in those sections. Between these parks, the Skyline Trail runs through a fenced easement in the California Water Company's Bear Gulch Watershed, paralleling Skyline Boulevard for 4.7 miles. (The fencing is barely apparent and does not give a closed-in feeling.)

Starting on the south side of Kings Mountain Road (the first entrance 2 in the directions), we climb steeply under redwoods through low-growing huckleberries, then emerge at a sunny crossroads from which a watershed service road goes downhill. However, the Skyline Trail continues straight ahead beside a property-line fence. In spring and summer tall, yellow-flowered bush poppies brighten this spot.

Circling around a meadow you come to a spectacular view south to Monte Bello Ridge. Soon the trail enters a forest of redwoods, then one of Douglas-firs. As the trail contours around the ridges, you find redwoods growing especially tall in the deep, moist canyons below. Some of the Douglas-firs are huge trees of the old-growth forest, but an occasional thicket of younger trees has sprung up, perhaps after some past fire.

The trail roughly parallels Skyline Boulevard, but often goes out on the ridges some distance from the road. At times it brings you close enough to hear the sounds of traffic, but most of the way all you hear is the wind in the treetops, the call of birds and, in summer, the drip of fog.

At about the halfway point you come to a part of the forest where very large redwoods once grew. Note the size of some old stumps— 6–8 feet in diameter. Look for slots cut into the trees about 6 feet off the ground, signs of the early logging method. Loggers wedged boards in these slots to support the planks they stood on while sawing the trees. Uphill from the trail you may catch a glimpse of the "Methuselah" tree, one of the few surviving giants of the old forest on the east slope of the Santa Cruz Mountains. According to a sign at its base, it is 14 feet in diameter and 1800 years old. Its crown was lost in some long-ago storm, but its lower branches are still flourishing. You can picture the awesome size of the old forest as it was before the coming of the Anglos and lumbermen.

The "Methusaleh" tree

The trail continues in and out of canyons, here and there giving you a view out over the Bay. Wildflowers seen include many of the less common ones of the deep conifer forest. You can't miss the Clintonia in late spring, with its deep rosy-red blooms borne in clusters on 20-inch stalks above large basal leaves. Its unusual bright-blue berries glisten in the summer sun. But you will have to watch very closely for the rare coral-root orchid, a brownish plant bearing flowers on foot-high stalks without any green leaves. The cool, shaded forest environment prolongs the plentiful spring flower blooms into early summer.

In fall you will find the snowberry's inedible white balls on shrubs beside the trail, and the yellow leaves of the big-leaf maple reflect the light in golden hues. This trail is seldom dusty because the tall redwoods capture the fog, which then drips down to the forest floor.

Nearing Wunderlich Park the trail descends in switchbacks that takes it around a subdivision. After this detour, you climb back out of the canyon to reach Wunderlich Park at Bear Gulch Road. This is currently a private road, but the County has retained an easement for future trail use. From here the Skyline Trail goes 2.7 miles east, downhill, in Wunderlich Park to its southern boundary (described in reverse in Trip 3, Wunderlich Park). From the park boundary a 0.6-mile trail on an easement for equestrians reaches Skylonda.

With a car shuttle and a start at the north end, you will have fewer uphill climbs.

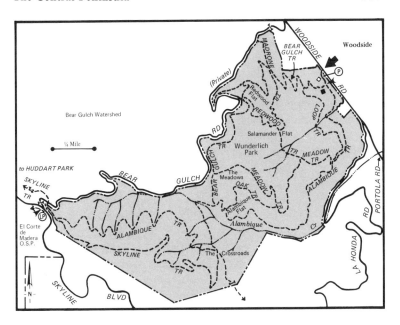

Wunderlich Park

The Pulgas Redwoods covered most of the mountainside of present-day Wunderlich Park. These forests, part of the Rancho Cañada de Raimundo, were heavily logged during the 1850s and 60s. After the timber was cut, some of the lower hills were cleared for farming, but on the steeper mountainsides redwoods began to grow again.

The upper reaches of Wunderlich Park extend along the Skyline ridge at an elevation of about 2200 feet. From the ridge the hillside falls away steeply, and the slope then flattens somewhat at the large meadow halfway down the mountainside. From this meadow smaller ridges and ravines descend to the lower park boundary along Woodside Road, making a total elevation change of nearly 1800 feet. Alambique Creek runs diagonally across the park, fed by streams in the precipitous wooded ravines to the north.

Alambique, which is the Spanish word for "still", reportedly was the site of a distillery in logging days. For a year the creek supplied water power for the Peninsula's first sawmill, until a steam boiler was installed. A plaque marks the site of the intersection of La Honda and Portola roads. Early residents drew their water from

Alambique Creek, eventually piping it to the reservoir at Salamander Flat.

In 1872 Simon Jones bought 1500 acres of the Rancho Cañada de Raimundo and turned some of the cutover land into a working ranch he named Hazelwood Farm. (You will see the graceful shrub, hazelnut, as an understory in the forests along the trails.) Vestiges of the orchards, vineyards and olive groves Jones planted remain on the lower slopes of the park.

For the next owner, James A. Folger II, who bought the farm in 1902, it became the site of excursions, carriage trips, and weekend campouts in the woods. He built the handsome stable near the park entrance and a mansion that still stands, though not within the park. This historic stable still retains the flavor of its former elegance. The graceful design, the redwood paneling and the marble fireplace in the tack room recall the days when well-cared-for horses and carriages provided the transportation to trains and to mountain retreats. An application has been made to register the stable as an historic building.

These lands changed hands again in 1956 when Martin Wunderlich acquired much of the Folger estate. In 1974 he generously gave 942 acres to San Mateo County for open space and park use.

The Trails

In 1978 San Mateo County completed the present extensive trail system, using the old ranch roads and logging roads and constructing a few new trails for loop trips, making this an outstanding park for hikers and equestrians. These 15 miles of trail, well laid out and clearly marked, lead through a mountainside wilderness of forest and meadow that can challenge hikers and horsemen with all-day trips to the Skyline or delight casual walkers with an hour or so of strolling under the trees.

It is possible to hike all day virtually without retracing any steps. A circle trip into the park from the main entrance on Woodside Road to "The Meadows" or from the Skyline Boulevard entrance down to "The Crossroads" and back is a good half-day's hike. Shady Alambique, Salamander and Redwood flats, 2 miles or less from the park office, are fine summer destinations. The Skyline Trail, crossing the upper park along the Skyline ridge is now a designated segment of the Bay Area Ridge Trail.

Once you have sampled some of these trails, you will want to return often to explore other routes. Following are more detailed descriptions of four suggested trips.

Wunderlich Park is popular with equestrians. When horses are passing, stand quietly on the upper side of the trail—sudden movements can startle horses.

Jurisdiction   San Mateo County.

Facilities   Trails for hikers and equestrians. At the parking area there is drinking water (none elsewhere, so carry your own) and a chemical toilet.

Park Rules   Open from 8 A.M. to sunset. No pets or bicycles allowed.

Maps   San Mateo County *Wunderlich Park* and USGS topo *Woodside.*

How To Get There   (1) Main entrance on Woodside Road: From Freeway 280 take Woodside Road (Highway 84) southwest for 2 miles. Look for the park sign on the right. (2) Upper entrance on Skyline Boulevard: Follow directions as above, but continue on Woodside Road to a right turn uphill on La Honda Road. Turn right off La Honda Road at Skyline Boulevard and go 3 miles to the park entrance on the east side of Skyline Boulevard near the entrance to Bear Gulch Road East (private). Limited parking on both sides of Skyline Boulevard.

Trip 1.   Figure-Eight Loop Trip to Skyline Ridge From Park Office

An ambitious all-day hike through the varied terrain and different ecosystems of the park includes sheltered, sunny meadows and cool streamsides. This hike follows the Alambique Trail to the Skyline ridge, then returns by the Skyline, Alambique and Bear Gulch trails.

Distance   10⅓ mile loop.

Time   6 to 7 hours.

Elevation Gain   1080'

Connecting Trails   Skyline Trail north to Huddart Park; trails west in El Corte de Madera O.S.P.

TRAIL NOTES

The Alambique Trail starts off just beyond the parking lot along a former ranch road. For the most part, it is an easy grade. For a short stretch you go up a hill through a redwood grove, but before long you note the invading "exotics"—eucalyptus, acacia, scotch broom, and other survivors of the ranch plantings, now gone wild. A project is underway to eradicate the eucalyptus and replant with redwoods, but you can see that that battle is far from won.

Rounding the hills and climbing, the Alambique Trail goes through open mixed woodland. Some deciduous black oaks and the familiar combination of toyons, canyon oaks and madrones are a friendly habitat for birds. Veteran birders will recognize many species, but even the novice will enjoy their songs and identify at least the insistent call of the scrub jay and the flash of his blue wings through the oaks.

The old road continues through the mixed woodland, where in late spring Douglas iris show their blue, purple or creamy blooms along the banks. After 2 miles from the start, the trail enters the redwoods above Alambique Creek, which forms the boundary of the park here.

The redwoods near the creek have grown again to a good size since the logging of a century ago, making Alambique Flat a cool, shady place to pause on a hot day. A side trip down to the creek over the soft duff shows you a sample of the redwood plant community. Note the size of the stumps of the old trees of the virgin forest cut in the 1850s. Huge trees (the largest some 8 feet or more in diameter where the water is most plentiful) were widely spaced but their high crowns nearly touched.

After leaving Alambique Flat you soon come to a junction with the Oak and then the Bear Gulch trails on the right, but you continue up the creek on the Alambique Trail. Soon you cross the creek and turn left to start a climb out of the canyon along the forested hillside to "The Crossroads,"where the Alambique and Skyline trails intersect.

You could take the Skyline Trail from here to the summit, but instead stay on the Alambique Trail, on which it's about 2 miles and a good hour's walk to the top. This part of the trail winds in and out of steep ravines, which support sword fern and woodwardia, the 4-foot-tall, feathery, giant chain fern. In the grove of big redwoods near the summit is an old loading platform from which logs were put on wagons for the mills below. Just ahead is the gate to Skyline Boulevard at Bear Gulch Road. Note the trail connection going north—the Skyline Trail.

Turn left (east) at the trail convergence and follow the Skyline Trail through a forest of the park's most magnificent Douglas-firs, which escaped the logger's saw of the last century. As the trail goes through the cuts for powerlines, you have fine views northward to San Bruno Mountain, the San Francisco skyline and Mt. Tamalpais.

Soon the trail borders a long meadow where bunchgrass mixes with sedges and imported oat grasses. In spring the meadow is thick

The Bear Gulch Trail leads to many places.

with flowers—baby blue eyes, rosy wild hollyhocks and blue and purple lupines. The sloping terrain faces southeast, a welcome warm exposure for winter morning hikes. As you look down the meadow, the Bay and East Bay hills are before you. There are fine spots here for eating the lunch you carried uphill.

Leaving the meadow, the trail leads again into fir forest, which is interspersed with huge specimens of madrone. Out from under the trees the trail emerges on a sunny ridge through a grove of chinquapin, a relative of the oak not commonly seen in San Mateo County but found in several of our hillside parks.

A hairpin turn brings you back into shady forest with an understory of buckeye, hazelnut and gooseberry. Just ahead is "The Crossroads." From here retrace you steps along the Alambique Trail to the Bear Gulch Trail, on which you turn left, uphill, to "The Meadows." Rolling acres of grasslands, fine views, shady or sunny resting spots, flowers in spring and hawks overhead all combine to make this an ideal place for a break in your hike. You will want to return to explore and enjoy this place on many another day.

Leaving "The Meadows" by the Bear Gulch Trail, you go along a narrow track under Douglas-firs. Some of the fallen trees give an idea of their great size at maturity, nearly 200 feet in height and 6 or more feet in diameter.

In early spring this trail segment is adorned with patches of the bold blue-flowered hound's tongue and a sprinkling of the little white blossoms of milkmaids. Hazelnut branches with pale green buds just showing make a lacelike tracery against the dark forest.

The trail soon crosses some old skid roads, those chutes where oxen dragged redwood logs down to the sawmills below. For a while the trail goes down the canyon close to Bear Gulch Road East on the northern boundary of the park, and then it veers away through Redwood Flat, a grove of tall second- and third-growth redwoods. Now the stump sprouts growing in circles around cut trees are as much as 100 feet tall, making a lofty redwood grove again.

From Redwood Flat the trail winds down ravines through a fir forest, crosses the Madrone Trail, zigzags downhill for ¾ mile, becomes the Loop Trail and then goes for another ¼ mile along brushy hillsides back to the stables and the parking lot.

Trip 2.   Loop Trip to the Meadows

This trip climbs gently to "The Meadows," the park's beautiful big grassland centerpiece, and returns by way of Salamander Flat, the site of a little reservoir in the redwoods.

Distance   5.5-mile loop.
Time   3 hours.
Elevation Gain   950'

TRAIL NOTES

After leaving the park office on the Loop Trail, you walk 0.2 mile along the lower slopes of the park through brush and oak woodlands. Then veer left on a gentle traverse to the Alambique Trail, which you follow for a very short distance before turning off to the right on the Meadow Trail. This is an old ranch road through the eucalyptus grove and orchards planted in Jones' farming days. After the Redwood Trail junction you are in a handsome stand of toyon and madrone, where flowers bloom beside the Meadow Trail. In spring look for purple shooting stars, yellow wood violets and magenta Indian warriors. Under a canopy of tall black oaks you go uphill for

½ mile. In summer the monkey flower's apricot blossoms brighten the banks and golden stars edge the trail.

At the next trail junction turn left on the broad Oak Trail, which is shaded by oak woodland for another ½ mile. Next you turn right on a very short stretch of the Alambique Trail. Follow the narrow track through a madrone, oak and fir woodland which filters the light falling on the ground cover of low-growing poison oak (fortunately kept away from the trail).

At the next junction, turn right on the Bear Gulch Trail, which goes through a small clearing and an oak glade before coming out in "The Meadows."

Bring along your binoculars, sketch book or paint box and enjoy this open space, so close to the cities, yet so remote. If you come here in the spring months—late March through May—it is bright with the blue of lupines and the gold of poppies, buttercups and cowslips. At any season you may see hawks wheeling overhead. It is in meadows like this that their proverbially sharp eyes can see the field mice, moles, gophers and other small burrowing creatures on which their survival depends.

At the top of the meadow, where perhaps there has been less plowing, you may find mounds where the grass grows in tufts, a sign that some of the ancient bunchgrass has survived here. This is one of the native perennial grasses that once covered the hills of California before being displaced by the annual European oat grass that now gives our state the famous golden look in summer.

Old clumps of bunchgrass are deep-rooted and may persist for

The trail to the hilltop above "The Meadows"

hundreds of years (some say even thousands), spreading outward in circles. Indians burned it off in the fall to improve hunting. Although the Spaniards found the native grass to be good forage, the oat grass they inadvertently brought with them thrived in the dry California summers and soon took over.

After exploring "The Meadows" leave on the Meadow Trail going east and stroll more than ½ mile through rolling grasslands bordered by large madrones and spreading oaks. Sweeping views to the southeast show the broad flanks of Black Mountain, with the bare slopes of Monte Bello Ridge on its northwest.

From the grasslands the trail makes a switchback bringing you back into oak woodlands, though eucalyptuses now have a good foothold here. You descend rapidly for ¼ mile to the Meadow/Oak Trail junction. Take the Meadow Trail left and retrace your steps downhill for ½ mile of the trail you took on your way up. This brings you to the intersection of the Redwood Trail, on which you turn left.

From the sunlight of the intersection of the Meadow and Redwood trails you enter the deep shade of redwood forest. The soft forest duff muffles your footsteps on the narrow trail and the air is cool on even the warmest day.

For ¾ mile the Redwood Trail crosses the park, contouring along the hillside at about the 1100-foot elevation line. It goes in and out of small ravines where moss-covered rocks line streams that cascade down the mountain after winter rains. After a ¼-mile walk you reach Salamander Flat, in a thick grove of big trees. An oval reservoir fed

Horses still occupy the handsome stable built in Wunderlich at the turn of the century.

by springs up the hill was once a water supply for the farm below; later it was reportedly used as a swimming pool. The deep shade of Salamander Flat is an inviting place to lunch on the stump of a giant redwood or pause for a while on a hot day.

To return to the park entrance from Salamander Flat, pick up the Madrone Trail going downhill. Keep the reservoir on your right. In wet weather the reservoir overflows its dam, creating rivulets along an old wagon road. The hiker takes the wagon road, too, passing fences and hand-fashioned gate posts left from the farming days of the park's past.

About ½ mile from Salamander Flat, the Madrone Trail intersects the Bear Gulch Trail and you turn right onto it, then descend the last ¾ mile to the park office and the parking lot.

Trip 3. Circle Trip to "The Crossroads" from the Skyline Entrance

You can swing down the Alambique Trail to "The Crossroads" and return by the Skyline Trail on a 4-mile loop through the heart of the upper park.

Distance 4-mile loop.

Time 2½ hours.

Elevation Loss 700'

TRAIL NOTES

Starting from Skyline Boulevard on the Alambique Trail, you can go downhill at a good clip around bend after bend on the old ranch road. On this, the remotest trail in the park, you may hear deer crashing through the brush, but no sounds of civilization reach you. For more details of these trails see Trip 1, above.

When you get to "The Crossroads," you are in one of the coolest canyons of the park, a delightful woodsy destination for a hot day. Here you pick up the Skyline Trail and start uphill. (The other segment of the Skyline Trail descends ¼ mile to the park's south boundary.) On the varied terrain of your uphill trip you will walk along a ridge covered with oaks and madrones, traverse the edge of a long, sloping meadow and then reach the upper park entrance under giant Douglas fir trees.

Trip 4.   A Short Loop Trip in the Lower Park to Salamander and Redwood Flats

This walk takes you to a small reservoir and shady redwood groves before circling back on the Bear Gulch Trail switchbacks.

Distance   3¼-mile loop.
Time   1¾ hours.
Elevation Gain   600′

TRAIL NOTES

This trip is in shade all the way, a delightful hot-weather walk. All the trail segments are described in earlier trips.

Starting from the park office, follow the Alambique Trail to the Meadow Trail junction and turn right. Follow the Meadow Trail for ⅓ mile, then turn right again on the Redwood Trail, which takes you on a gentle traverse at the 1100-foot elevation line. You pass through both Salamander and Redwood Flats, good stopping places for a leisurely lunch.

From the Bear Gulch Trail junction, the remainder of the trip is downhill, a quick 1.4 miles on easy switchbacks. At trail's end you might notice the handsome stone walls along the old roads and beside the stable, which attest to an early craftsman's art.

The shade of the Redwood Trail is most inviting on a hot summer day.

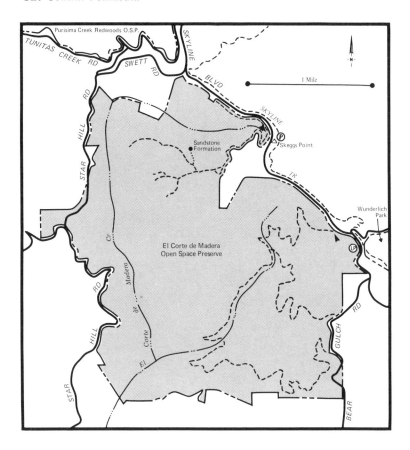

El Corte De Madera
Open Space Preserve

The El Corte de Madera Open Space Preserve's 2700 acres of forest, which include most of the drainage basin of El Corte de Madera Creek, lie west of Skyline Boulevard between Star Hill and Bear Gulch roads.

The creek rises from springs near the Skyline and flows between high ridges on the west side of the preserve, to be joined by its main (and nameless) tributary, which flows through the east side. The preserve, from its 2400-foot high point, Sierra Morena, to the canyon where the creek leaves the lower boundary at an elevation of 700 feet, is a place of high ridges and precipitously steep, deep canyons. From these high ridges views of coastside and ocean are breathtaking.

The primeval forests of El Corte de Madera's canyons and ridges were logged in the most accessible areas as early as the 1860s, starting first near the creek close to the Skyline. Logging of the old forest continued into this century, and second-growth forests have been cut sporadically since then.

The Midpeninsula Regional Open Space District acquired these lands in 1985, and logging has ceased except in a few limited areas where timber cutting will be completed in 1988. Although signs of logging are evident along certain roads, a handsome second-growth forest now covers the canyons and ridges.

An extensive network of old logging roads forms the basis for trails that are being designated for hikers, equestrians and bicyclists. Trails, as of this writing, are unmarked and should be used with great caution. Trails in timber cutting areas (Trip 3) will be closed until 1989.

Two entrances from the west side of Skyline Boulevard provide access to the preserve.

Jurisdiction   Midpeninsula Regional Open Space District.

Facilities   Trails for hikers, equestrians and bicyclists.

Preserve Rules   Open from dawn to dusk. No dogs.

Maps   USGS topo *Woodside*.

How To Get There   On Skyline Boulevard there are two entrances: (1) 2.5 miles north of Skyline Boulevard/Highway 84 intersection. Limited parking on west side of road near preserve gate. (2) Skeggs Point, 1 mile farther north, on east side of Skyline Boulevard. Park at Skeggs Point, walk 300 yards north and cross road to preserve entrance.

Trip 1.   Up the Ridge to the Sandstone Formation and Wide Vistas

A hike on a logging road brings you to a high plateau and new views of coast and ocean.

Distance   4.9 miles round trip.

Time   2½ hours.

Elevation Gain   300'

TRAIL NOTES

From the Skeggs Point entrance take the MROSD service road (not the paved private road to the left) which veers uphill and around a sharp bend. At this bend the road splits, its two branches being old logging roads that now serve as trails. Stay on the upper road for this trip. The lower road turns down to follow the creek (see Trip 2).

Our route continues around a hillside for 1½ miles, generally climbing, to reach a ridgetop, where there is a small clearing at an intersection of several trails. Here at an opening in the forest between a giant tanoak and a majestic Douglas fir is a view west down a canyon and out over the marine terrace to the sea.

To go to the Sandstone Formation from this vista point at the trail junction, take the trail to the right, downhill. In 200 yards, look on the right for a narrow footpath that leads down to the sandstone outcrops (hikers only on this path). You will soon see the picturesque cliffs jutting up some 25 feet above the wooded hillside. Erosion has given a honeycomb surface to the rocks and created some picturesque columnar structures.

For a longer walk along this ridge, retrace your steps on the narrow footpath to the trail you left and continue northwest along it for ¾ mile under oaks and firs to the end of the trail, then return to the ridgetop intersection.

For a stunning vista of the ocean, take the trail downhill southwest. Follow this old logging road for less than ½ mile to an open chaparral-covered area where ceanothus, scrub oak and manzanita grow on a rocky knoll. As you reach the point where the eroded road drops off sharply, you can look out over the panorama of coast and

District ranger at the Sandstone Formation

ocean from Pt. Reyes to Monterey Bay. It is worth picking one of our clear, bright days for this trip.

Turn back here, but watch for a path nearby turning westward (to your left). The path branches and either branch will take you in a few minutes to another ridgetop with still wider views of ocean and coastside to the west. From here retrace your steps to the ridgetop intersection and then back to the preserve entrance.

Trip 2.   Down El Corte de Madera Creek

After a short walk downstream you are in a redwood grove in a deep canyon beside the creek.

Distance   2 miles round trip.
Time   1 hour.
Elevation Loss   300'

TRAIL NOTES

From the Skeggs Point entrance take the MROSD service road (not the paved private road to the left) which veers uphill and around a sharp bend. At this bend where the road splits take the lower road downhill. This is the old El Corte de Madera Creek Road. At first, signs of past logging are around you. However, in a 10-minute walk you are down in a tall forest of redwoods and firs. The spring-fed creek beside you runs clear and ferns grow on its banks.

You soon come to a little flat where a side stream joins the creek from the left. This is probably the site of one of the earliest sawmills in the canyon, where Ambrose Saunders operated a water-powered mill in the 1860s.

Farther down the road ferns grow taller by the creek, which is lined here with brilliant red-blossomed monkey flowers. In July and August you find great clumps of orange tiger lilies. You can at this writing follow the creek as far as a gate at a bend in the road. Some day, we hope a trail will be opened down old El Corte de Madera Creek Road.

Trip 3.   A Loop Trip into the Preserve's Canyons

A long, challenging loop trip on the main haul road down the steep canyon of the main tributary of El Corte de Madera Creek returns by way of Bear Gulch Road.

Distance   9-mile loop.
Time   5 to 6 hours.
Elevation Loss   1600'

TRAIL NOTES

From the gated entrance on the west side of Skyline Boulevard 2.5 miles north of Highway 84 start down the road straight ahead and go through a second gate to the haul road. This day-long hike follows the broad, well-compacted old logging road for 2½ miles down the steep canyonside above the creek. After a mile down the haul road, we pass the junction of a road going left, downhill, the leg of our return trip.

Handsome second-growth redwoods and firs cover the ridges, in spite of extensive logging over the past century. However, as you go down the road, you pass areas of recent logging with fresh-cut stumps and an accumulation of branches on the ground. This accumulation, known as slash, is left to decompose to aid the regeneration of the forest.

Continue on the haul road in and out of ravines to the creek crossing at the lower end of the preserve. A highlight of the trip is the sight of this tributary of El Corte de Madera Creek as we cross over the bridge. Its clear waters cascade over mossy rocks and pause in pools above and below the bridge. Thimbleberries and huckleberries grow near its banks, and tiger lilies bloom here in late summer.

At the end of the bridge is the stump of an immense tree 6 feet in diameter, a remnant of the old forest. From the creek crossing you begin a long climb up the side of a ridge to Bear Gulch Road, a gain in elevation of more than 1000 feet.

Near Bear Gulch Road firs rather than redwoods dominate, some of great size and age. At the intersection with Bear Gulch Road 1 mile from its intersection with Skyline Boulevard there is parking for only two or three cars. To reach the last leg of this loop trip, walk up Bear Gulch Road for 10 minutes to another logging road (marked with a MROSD sign) which turns back into the canyon. There is no parking at all here.

The next mile is a delightful walk downhill through second-growth forest with a ground cover of sword fern and huckleberry. At little flats we have vistas across nearby canyons. As the road steepens, deep water bars across the road slow our descent.

In the canyon bottom we cross a creek where logging activities and grading for roads have disrupted the channel. But in ¼ mile we reach the main creek tributary that we followed down the canyon at the start of the trip. A few hundred yards uphill and we are back on the main haul road. From here it is little less than an hour's walk back to the entrance gate, after a day within the enclosing walls of this vast canyon.

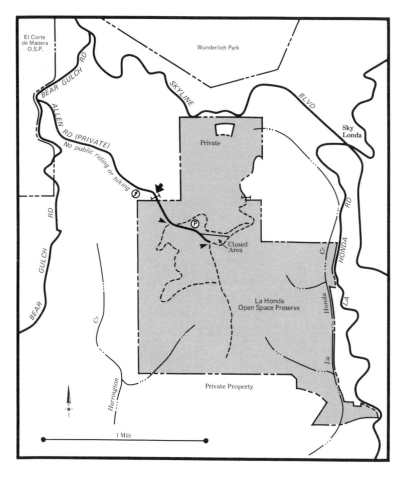

La Honda Creek Open Space Preserve

La Honda Creek Open Space Preserve includes nearly 600 acres of steep forest slopes and grasslands. At present the preserve takes in a sweep of meadow descending from private Allen Road to a plateau a mile below. To the west of the meadow are wooded hillsides. The east slopes of the preserve, heavily forested, fall off steeply to La Honda Creek. Magnificent views include much of the drainage basins of San Gregorio and Harrington creeks. Far to the west is the Pacific Ocean, and to the south rises ridge after forested ridge.

This preserve is now open only with special permit. Allen Road is not open to hikers, and no parking is permitted on it.

Only a few trails have been designated at this writing, and they are not yet signed. However, the loop trip described takes the visitor to remarkable vistas, lovely meadows and handsome forests in this preserve.

Jurisdiction   Midpeninsula Regional Open Space District.

Facilities   Trails for hikers, equestrians and bicyclists.

Preserve Rules   At this writing the preserve is open by permit only, which can be obtained from MROSD office (415-949-5500). No dogs permitted.

Maps   USGS topos *Woodside* and *La Honda.*

How To Get There   On Skyline Boulevard go 5 miles north of the Skyline Boulevard/Highway 84 intersection and turn south on Bear Gulch Road. Go 0.5 mile down this narrow, winding road, then turn left on private Allen Road and go 1 mile to a locked gate at the preserve boundary. Directions for entrance to this gate are included in the permit. A designated parking place is a short distance beyond the gate.

A Trip Down the Meadows
for a Bird's-Eye View of the Coastside

This trip descends the meadows to the lower end of the preserve and returns across the pasture and through the woods on the west side of the preserve.

Distance   3-mile loop.

Time   1½ hours.

Elevation Loss   300'

TRAIL NOTES

From the designated parking area walk east on the paved road up a rise through a redwood grove and past a little clearing edged with a few Douglas firs of magnificent proportions. The road soon veers south to a barn and caretaker's cottage. An enclave of private property is uphill from the road. Leave the paved road and go right down a ranch road between the barn and a corral, then go up through a wooden gate to a meadow beyond.

A few steps from the gate along the ranch road one of the dramatic vistas of the coastside ranches and ridges opens up. A sloping pasture is edged on the east by tall, dark oaks, firs and redwoods. You can see the hills along San Gregorio Creek and forested Butano ridge. Far west are the gleam of white surf and the blue ocean beyond.

In less than a mile the ranch-road trail enters a patch of forest at the foot of the meadow. Here are a few towering old redwoods passed by in early logging. You emerge quickly into a lower meadow and to more views. In spring these grasslands are bright with wild-flowers and the woods are bordered with blue irises. There are no trails here, and you will on the one side be stopped by a dense forest, or on the other by a precipitously steep hillside that falls off into the canyon of Harrington Creek. You will find any number of good picnic sites in the meadow.

Retrace your steps to the upper meadow, where you turn left on a path crossing to a service road on the west side of the preserve. Watch for the path across the pasture about halfway up to the hill-top. The path heads west, descending gradually down a ridge to pick up a service road, which you take uphill.

This winding road through a pleasant succession of woods and clearings gives you a chance to enjoy the variety of oaks, madrones, firs and redwoods along the way. You can see the 4- and 5-foot stumps of redwoods cut in early logging and compare them with the sizable second growth.

In a half hour you come out on a hillside clearing below a ridge and above a wooded canyon that drains into Harrington Creek. Around a bend is the parking area and your car.

From La Honda's open meadows you have sweeping views of the west slope of the Skyline ridge.

The Southern Peninsula
Mountainside Preserves and Parks on the Skyline Ridge

Highway 84 to Highway 85/9

A vast complex of public land in parks and preserves now encompasses much of the Skyline area of the Santa Cruz Mountains from Skylonda/Highway 84 south to Saratoga Gap/Highway 9 and down the eastern and western slopes. Altogether, 9000 acres of conifer forests, oak/madrone woodlands, grasslands and streamsides are open to trail users.

Public lands and trails now reach east to the urban Bay plain, south beyond Saratoga Gap to Sanborn Park and Castle Rock State Park and west to the forest parks along Pescadero Canyon (Portola State Park and Pescadero, Memorial and Sam McDonald county parks). This edition of *Peninsula Trails* covers Skyline parks and preserves as far south as Saratoga Gap. *South Bay Trails* includes parks from Saratoga Gap to Sanborn Park and on south to Mt. Madonna.

Hikers can now follow nearly 30 miles of trails along the crest of the Santa Cruz Mountains from Skylonda to Saratoga Gap. Such a Skyline Trail fits the concept of a Bay Area Ridge Trail, initiated in 1987 by the Bay Area Trail Council and being carried forward with the support of the National Park Service, the Association of Bay Area Governments, and other regional and local public agencies and private organizations. Trail-users can look forward to the establishment of an unbroken trail along the Peninsula Skyline.

A network of trails in these mountainside preserves and parks now offers a variety of trips, from an hour's walk along a ridgetop to an invigorating day-long hike in deep canyons. Hostels in the foothills, a backpack camp on Monte Bello Ridge and a planned trail link to park campgrounds in Pescadero Canyon make possible vacation-sized expeditions through the Santa Cruz Mountains from trailheads only a half hour from the Peninsula's urban plain.

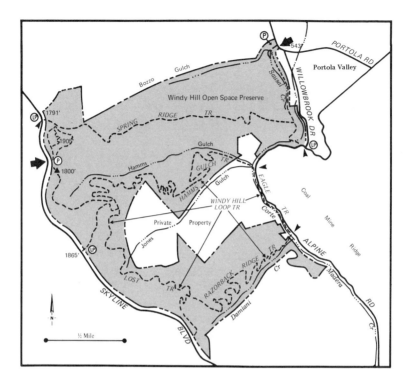

Windy Hill Open Space Preserve

This 1131-acre preserve includes the two bald knobs of Windy
Hill and the long, grassy ridge extending from the Skyline to the floor
of Portola Valley. The upper grasslands of Windy Hill, familiar landmarks on the midpeninsula mountains, stand out against the adjacent
forested slopes. We watch Windy Hill from the Bay plain as it turns
green in spring and as it is occasionally whitened by winter snows. In
summer the wind and fog from the ocean sweep over this bare hill to
give it the name it has been known by for 50 years or more.

Once part of an early Mexican land grant belonging to Maximo
Martinez, known as El Corte de Madera ("the wood-cutting place"),
these lands were also used for cattle grazing and hayfields. The
Brown Ranch stood on the site of today's picnic area on Skyline
Boulevard, and the Orton Ranch was located north at the head of
Spring Ridge. Beautiful second-growth forests now clothe many
slopes and fill the canyons of the preserve.

The first 537 acres of this preserve were donated to the Peninsula Open Space Trust in December 1979 and were later sold to the
Midpeninsula Regional Open Space District. Additional purchases
include the 429 acres of Spring Ridge, acquired in 1987. Located
between clusters of county parks and MROSD preserves north and
south along the Skyline ridge, Windy Hill Open Space Preserve is
part of an expanding chain of public ridgelands on the Peninsula.

Approximately 14 miles of trails traverse Windy Hill's grassy
slopes, climb its steep ridges and follow its stream canyons. From
the main entrance on Skyline Boulevard, where a rustic fence
encloses a picnic area, you can climb to the summit of Windy Hill
for a 360° view—ocean, Bay, cities and distant mountains. Or you
can take one of three long ridge trails that descend to Portola Valley,
and return on a trail up another ridge.

Fund-raising headed by the Peninsula Open Space Trust (POST)
brought donations from local citizens to the Windy Hill Endowment
Fund to build the 8.4-mile Windy Hill Loop Trail and to endow its
maintenance. These funds also helped construct the new trail up and
around the Windy Hill knobs. The Windy Hill Loop Trail, one of the
longest trails on the Peninsula, was laid out and constructed by
volunteers, MROSD staff and the California Conservation Corps.

Kite-flying on Windy Hill is superb, though the wind will test the
sturdiness of your kite. Others who take advantage of the ridgetop
breezes include members of the South Bay Soaring Society, who
operate their nonmotorized model gliders on Windy Hill.

Jurisdiction   Midpeninsula Regional Open Space District.
Facilities   Trails for hikers and equestrians; bicycles on Spring
Ridge Trail only. Picnic area.
Preserve Rules   Open dawn to dusk. Dogs on leash in north
Skyline area and on the Spring Ridge and Eagle trails only.
Maps   MROSD brochure *Windy Hill*, USGS topo *Mindego Hill.*
How To Get There   (1) Take Woodside/La Honda Road (Highway
84) or Page Mill Road to Skyline Boulevard. The main entrance is on
the east side of Skyline Boulevard 2.1 miles south of La Honda
Road. Two other entrances north and south of the main entrance are
marked by brown pipe gates and hiking stiles. (2) Take Alpine or
Sand Hill Road to Portola Road. The preserve entrance is on the
west side of Portola Road, ½ mile south of the Portola Valley Town
Center. (3) Alpine Road entrances: Take Alpine Road south past
Portola Road to the corner of Alpine and Willowbrook roads. Park
on the north side of Alpine Road and walk up the road to trail
entrances on the right side; (a) Spring Ridge Trail entrance (south

end) 0.1 mile beyond parking area; (b) Hamms Gulch Trail entrance, 0.3 mile farther; (c) Razorback Ridge Trail entrance, 0.6 mile still farther up the road.

Trip 1. The Windy Hill Loop Trail

A leg-stretching loop around the preserve starts from the Skyline ridge, descends 1120' to Corte Madera Creek and then climbs back up to the ridge on the Hamms Gulch Trail.

Distance 8.4-mile loop.
Time 5½ hours.
Elevation Loss 1120'
Connecting Trails Toyon and Old Spanish trails southwest on Coal Mine Ridge.

TRAIL NOTES

This spectacular trip starts from the picnic area at the main Skyline Boulevard entrance. Take the signed 0.6-mile connector trail on the right and contour around the knoll to the Loop Trail junction. Bear right there to cross a chaparral-covered shoulder of the ridge. Then, on an old road re-named the Lost Trail, you go around bends and into hollows below the crest of the Santa Cruz Mountains. Under madrones and oaks and across rivulets, this trail continues for 1.7 miles to the top of the ridge between Fitzpatrick and Damiani creeks.

Then, turning left, you begin a series of downhill zigzags on the well-graded 2.5-mile Razorback Ridge Trail. Along the sides of small ravines and out onto shoulders of the ridge, the trail drops steadily downward under a high oak-and-madrone canopy. Hikers often find deer quietly making their way over the leafy forest floor.

At the lower end of the trail you join a dirt road and cross a bridge to Alpine Road. Paralleling the road beside Corte Madera Creek is the Eagle Trail, which you follow for 0.6 mile downstream. Cool and shaded in summer, it leads to a bridge over Corte Madera Creek at the stone-pillared, gated entrance to Rancho Corte Madera, a private inholding.

Go left across the old bridge with the moss-covered stone railing, then immediately go right between another set of stone pillars and step onto the Hamms Gulch Trail. In a few feet you cross a wooden bridge over Jones Gulch and start uphill. This trail, built on the alignment of the old Brown Ranch Road, takes today's trail users through magnificent oak, madrone and fir forests.

About a mile up the trail, at a break in the forest, you'll find a bench erected by MROSD rangers. From here you look across the wooded canyon of Hamms Gulch to the grasslands of Spring Ridge. Continuing uphill, the trail then climbs the south side of Hamms Gulch. On the side of this gulch grow immense Douglas firs. Some at least 6 feet in diameter must have escaped logging early in this century.

The trail skirts around the trees and out of the forest, and then beyond a few bends you turn right on the trail that leads back to your starting point at the picnic area, the old Brown Ranch site.

Trip 2.   Spring Ridge Hike

Climb up Spring Ridge to the Windy Hill Preserve heights, a 7-mile round trip. Or make it a 9-mile loop by returning on the Hamms Gulch Trail.

Distance   7 miles round trip on Spring Ridge Trail, 9 miles loop trip returning on Hamms Gulch Trail.

Time   4 hours round trip on Spring Ridge Trail; 5 hours on loop trip.

Elevation Gain   1260′

The Spring Ridge Trail is the only one open to bicyclists in Windy Hill Preserve.

TRAIL NOTES

The long, grassy ridge rising to Windy Hill's summit provides delightful short hikes to large, tree-bordered meadows, and serves as one leg of a long loop trip from the valley floor to the Skyline ridge and back. The trail follows an old ranch road right up the spine of bald Spring Ridge. The views from this expanse of high grasslands are superb. Start this uphill hike early and carry plenty of water on hot days.

From the main Portola Road entrance follow the tree-lined road to a left turn beside the little reservoir where Sausal Creek is impounded. If you want just a short outing, here is a pleasant site for a picnic in the shade of old eucalyptus trees near the water's edge.

Past the lake's marshy borders you find a weathered cattle chute on your left and occasional oaks arching over the trail. Where a side trail comes in from Alpine Road on the left, note it for your return, if you come back down the Hamms Gulch Trail. At this trail intersection, your route up the ridge turns right and begins a series of steep rises and short, flat stretches. Curving left, then right, and ever upward, this old road keeps to the open slope. At the edges of wide meadows, clumps of oaks interspersed with maples and spring-flowering buckeyes fill the ravines.

After about 2 miles, the trail arcs right and levels off. Here a wide track goes left, but you follow the narrower path to the right, leading to an oak-bordered lane at the edge of Bozzo Gulch. Thickets of berries, poison oak and willows cover the gulch's steep sides. Along this shady lane you could stop to enjoy the view. Framed by the oak branches, the Stanford campus lies beyond the low Portola Valley hills.

After you leave the lane and are again in open grasslands, you pass through a line of weathered fence posts. Uphill is a clump of Monterey cypresses that sheltered the Orton ranchhouse. Only a few old fruit trees and a jumble of fallen logs remain to remind today's trail users of these early settlers.

Several paths take off from here straight up to Windy Hill. But the wide trail curving around north above the ranch site follows a better route. It makes a last gentle ascent and then levels off north of the hill to reach Skyline Boulevard.

To return to the valley floor, the shortest route is back down the Spring Ridge Trail. However, if you want a gentler grade and a different way back, follow the short trail south from here around the Windy Hill knobs to the picnic area (see Trip 3). From there a 0.6-mile trail leads east to the Windy Hill Loop Trail. At the first junction turn left and drop down into Douglas fir forest on the Hamms Gulch Trail, which you will follow for 2.4 miles back to the valley.

After crossing the bridge at the lower end of the trail, walk left along Alpine Road for 0.3 mile to another trail entrance, just west of Willowbrook Drive. Cross the creek and go up the rise under magnificent spreading white oaks. Bear right to meet the trail along Sausal Creek, which leads back to the parking area from which you started. It is 1.5 miles from the creek crossing to the parking area. See Trip 1 for more Hamms Gulch Trail description.

Trip 3.   A Short Hike to the Preserve's Summit

Take this trail for a top-of-the-world view of the Bay Area from Windy Hill's bald knobs.

Distance   ¾-mile loop.
Time   ½ hour.
Elevation Gain   127'

TRAIL NOTES

Leave the left (north) side of the Skyline Boulevard picnic area on the trail that goes around and up the Windy Hill knobs. This is an ideal place to take your out-of-town visitors, if the day is clear. A climb to the top will orient them with fixes on some Bay Area peaks—Black Mountain, Mt. Hamilton, Mt. Diablo and Mt. Tamalpais. West lies the Pacific Ocean; north, east and south are San Francisco Bay and its surrounding cities. A map will help you pick out local landmarks.

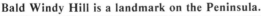
Bald Windy Hill is a landmark on the Peninsula.

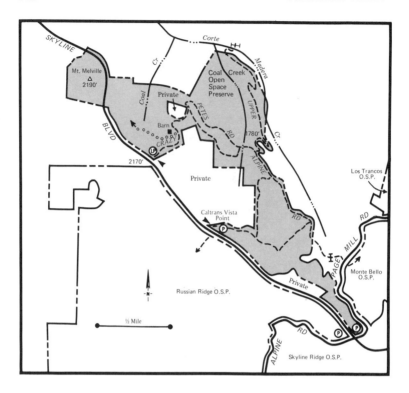

Coal Creek Open Space Preserve

Along the east side of Skyline Boulevard, crescent-shaped 476-acre Coal Creek Open Space Preserve is almost surrounded by other Midpeninsula Regional Open Space Preserves—Russian Ridge west across the Skyline, Monte Bello and Skyline Ridge south, and Windy Hill just a few miles north.

Three lovely meadows lying just below the Skyline ridge are central attractions of this preserve. Their flowery slopes invite springtime outings. Groves of handsome oaks and madrones fringing their grasslands are right for summertime picnics—easy, short walks from Skyline parking. Birds, deer and cottontail rabbits flourish in these meadows and forests.

These meadows, one in the north and two in the south, are linked by two old roads, now part of the preserve's trail system. Historic Crazy Petes Road drops down from Skyline Boulevard and traverses oak-and-madrone woodlands above the preserve's steep, forested lower hillsides to join Upper Alpine Road, which forms the preserve's northeast boundary.

Trails through the southern meadows also connect with Upper Alpine Road, making a much-needed off-road hiking, riding and bicycling route from Skyline Boulevard to Portola Valley.

Jurisdiction   Midpeninsula Regional Open Space District.

Facilities   Trails for hikers, horsemen and bicyclists.

Preserve Rules   Open dawn to dusk.

Maps   USGS topo *Mindego Hill.*

How To Get There   Take Woodside/La Honda Road (Highway 84) or Page Mill Road to Skyline Boulevard. On the east side of Skyline Boulevard are: (1) the north entrance at Crazy Petes Road, 6.1 miles south of Woodside/La Honda Road—limited parking, stay clear of the mailboxes; (2) the south entrance at the Caltrans Vista Point, 8.9 miles south of Woodside/La Honda Road, 1.0 mile north of Page Mill Road.

Trip 1.   Over the Meadow and Through the Woods

This loop trip traverses the southernmost meadow and follows Upper Alpine and Crazy Petes roads to the other end of the preserve. A leafy streamside and a sunny knoll make pleasant picnic destinations.

Distance   4-mile loop.

Time   2 hours.

Elevation Loss   400'

Connecting Trail   Upper Alpine Road north and south.

TRAIL NOTES

Starting from the Caltrans Vista Point on Skyline Boulevard, walk north along the road 200 yards to the first driveway on the right. This unpaved road goes downhill to the preserve entrance, identified by MROSD signs.

Under wide-spreading live-oak trees you descend past two private driveways to the top of a broad grassy meadow surmounted by a grove of immense madrone trees. In springtime this meadow is a beautiful swath of green, flecked with blues of lupines, gold of poppies and pinks of checker bloom. On an autumn day the authors saw a four-point buck standing in this meadow. Although such a sight is rare, you often see does along preserve trails.

From the trail junction at the top of the meadow, a trail descends to the left, the return route on this loop trip. Now, however, you go

straight ahead and slightly uphill from this junction through a forest
of moss-covered madrones and oaks growing among large sandstone
outcrops. At this writing the trail through the forest is badly eroded
from past motorcycle use, but you follow it for only about 5 minutes.
Then the trail veers left and emerges in another large ridgetop
meadow surrounded by oaks, both deciduous and evergreen,
Douglas firs and big-leaf maples. In spring big, yellow-blossomed
daisies, called mule ears, brighten these grasslands, and late into
summer poppies bloom here.

Your path goes east across the length of the meadow, and then
enters a grove of madrones and oaks. From a clearing in the middle
of this grove, take the narrow path that drops off abruptly to the
right, terminating at unpaved Upper Alpine Road, where you turn
left. You follow this old road, which we now call a trail, for the next
¾ mile downhill along the west edge of Corte Madera Creek Canyon.
The trail passes under a canopy of deciduous black oaks where you
find shade in summer and brightly colored leaves in fall.

About ½ mile down the canyon on the left is the gate to Coal
Creek Preserve's middle entrance. Note it for the return trip, but go
nearly ¼ mile farther, watching for Crazy Petes Road uphill on your
left, marked with an MROSD sign.

Leave Upper Alpine Road here and step over the stile to this
historic road now used as a trail. In 200 yards you cross a bridge
over a boulder-strewn creek. Ferns, moss and moisture-loving dogwood line the banks of pools on either side of this bridge.

Beyond the bridge beneath wide-spreading madrones is a
veritable thimbleberry terrace extending to a Y-shaped trail junction. Here Crazy Petes Road goes right and a dirt service road arcs
left. This trip continues to the right on Crazy Petes Road and returns
on the service road. In woods of live oak and madrone the old road
narrows and curves around the mountain, with views north and east
over the canyon of Corte Madera Creek. In about 15 minutes you
come to a little knoll in a clearing that catches the sun in midday.

Gaining altitude now, the trail becomes a narrow, uneven path
trending left through a miniature forest of long-leaved, lavender-
flowered yerba santa. Shortly you reach a gate across Crazy Petes
Road. Turn left at this gate on a dirt service road for the start of the
return leg of your loop trip.

The service road climbs through oak woodlands where vistas,
framed by the trees, open up over a succession of ridges on the far
side of Corte Madera Canyon. Passing an open hillside, where a few
private homes sit outside the preserve, you now descend around a

Ancient oaks in the woods rimming the upper meadow

big curve and into the shade of the madrone woods. At the **Y**-shaped junction you are back on Crazy Petes Road, going right to cross the bridge, and then down to Upper Alpine Road.

To finish this loop trip, first bear right here for ¼ mile to the next trail entrance on the right. Then go through the gate and begin a steady climb to the high grasslands. The trail, eroded at this writing, may have been a construction road for the powerlines you pass under at the lower edge of the meadow. Beside the trail in spring blue irises and purple lupines bloom, and later wild roses flower.

At the top of the meadow turn right on the unpaved road through the woods on which you started this trip, and return uphill to your car at the Vista Point. From here, looking beyond the meadows and forests of your hike, you see the midpeninsula cities below, less than 10 miles from the preserves along the Skyline ridge greenbelt.

Trip 2.   A Short Hike to a Protected Meadow

Starting from Skyline Boulevard, hike ½ mile to sheltered grasslands above the urban scene.

Distance   1 mile round trip to meadow; 2½ miles round trip to knoll.

Time   ½ hour round trip to meadow; 1¼ hours round trip to knoll.

Elevation Loss   200′ to meadow; 370′ to knoll.

TRAIL NOTES

With a sketch book, your favorite flower guide or bird book, and a snack in your daypack, start at the northern entrance to Coal Creek Preserve, ½ mile north of the Vista Point. There is limited parking where Crazy Petes Road intersects Skyline Boulevard.

Walk along Crazy Petes Road less than ½ mile to a point on your left where you can get down into the pasture near the big old barn. In the 1990s a trail will cross this meadow and extend north to Mt. Melville. In the meantime, there are pleasant places to enjoy your picnic in these sloping grasslands where Coal Creek originates.

You can walk another ¾ mile down Crazy Petes Road to the protected knoll described in Trip 1, where the only sounds are those of birds in the trees, or possibly deer in the forest.

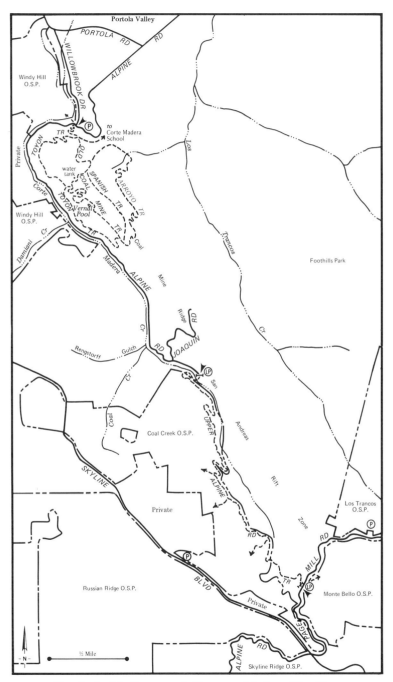

Portola Valley and Upper Alpine Trails

Upper Alpine Road

(Map on page 147)

A tree-shaded walk follows an old road from Corte Madera Creek to a ridge that extends to Page Mill Road near Skyline Boulevard. This section of Alpine Road, now closed to motorized vehicles, is a quiet winding way up a wooded mountainside where no houses or traffic intrude.

Distance   2½ miles one way.

Time   1¾ hours.

Elevation Gain   1000'

Connecting Trails   Monte Bello O.S.P. trails ½ mile east on Page Mill Road and Coal Creek O.S.P. trails to the west.

Jurisdiction   San Mateo County, Midpeninsula Regional Open Space District.

Map   USGS topo *Mindego Hill.*

How To Get There   (1) Lower entrance: From Freeway 280 take the Alpine Road exit south toward Portola Valley. Stay on Alpine Road for about 3 miles past the Portola Road junction, until your way is blocked by a green metal gate. There is limited parking; keep the gate clear. (2) Upper entrance: Gated section of Upper Alpine Road intersects Page Mill Road about ½ mile north of Skyline Boulevard.

TRAIL NOTES

Alpine Road gets its name not from the heights of the Santa Cruz Range but from a pine tree, *El Pino,* which grew beside the Pescadero Trail to the coast. The area near the intersection of the present Alpine Road and Portola State Park Road (3.1 miles southwest of Skyline Boulevard), called "El Pino" by native Californians, became "Alpine." The name was first attached to the road west of Skyline, built in 1879. The part of the road we are walking on, built in 1894, was for some time called the Martinez grade, after the owner of Rancho Corte de Madera.

Before you start out on foot, you have a scenic drive up Corte Madera canyon, as Alpine Road leaves the open valley. The road beside the creek looks down into one of our loveliest streams. Maples, alders and bays shade its winding course, and wood ferns clothe its steep banks. In the late fall and early winter, when the maples turn golden, this is an enchanting drive.

About 3 miles from the Alpine/Portola Road intersection, just past Joaquin Road, you come to a fork in the road where a heavy metal gate bars the righthand side. Park at one of several turnouts, crawl through the gate and start up the unpaved road.

The bridge over the creek at the first bend is washed out and, at this writing, not repaired. However, when the creek is low, you can follow informal paths down into the creekbed and scramble up the other side. A little farther uphill at another washout the road is reduced to a narrow path, but from there to the upper entrance this is a wide trail for hiking, bicycling and horseback riding.

On the opposite side of the road from the creek, the steep canyon wall rises to Coal Mine Ridge, where you may glimpse thin veins of coal along the road cuts. Low-grade coal was once mined from this ridge.

Whether you take this road in winter after the first rains freshen the foliage and the cold turns leaves to gold, in the spring with the burst of pale new leaves and flowers along the way, or at some less dramatic time of year, this is a fine, quiet old road where tall trees meet overhead and new views open up at each turn.

Hiking here in late fall or early winter, you will find that the shrubby willows that line the creek have turned yellow. The tall maples along the creek are golden, and other maples make bright splashes of color here and there on the hillsides where they mark springs that give them the moisture they need.

From the canyon the road climbs to a flat on a ridge covered with deciduous black oaks. Under the umbrella of this grove the light takes on a golden hue in the fall from the tawny yellow of their leaves. Many deer inhabit these woods, as you can see from their tracks on the road. In fall and winter, bucks, does and the fawns born the preceding spring stay together, and you can see the hoof prints of these family groups where they cross the road to the creek below. Occasionally you glimpse them as you round a bend.

From this flat the road continues up the ridge on an easy grade. In late fall and early winter madrones on the hills are heavy with red berries, and thick-clustered toyon berries are accented against their dark-green leaves. Black-headed Oregon juncos feast on wild cherries hanging down below shiny leaves.

The MROSD's Coal Creek Open Space Preserve borders Upper Alpine Road to the west almost up to the Page Mill Road intersection. Trails from Upper Alpine Road into the preserve make a good loop trip through woods and across meadows to destinations for hillside picnics. The first of these trails, Crazy Petes Road, turns off

Upper Alpine Road just beyond this flat and another trail turns off ¼ mile beyond. For descriptions of this trip see the section on Coal Creek O.S.P. on page 142.

On the hill across the canyon, scattered houses of a subdivision come into view, and only the faint sound of a dog's bark or the chopping of wood reaches the road. As you near the top of the hill, the road winds in and out of a forest of great live oaks and bays. Streams in the ravines and lush ferns and moss are signs that you are now high in the Santa Cruz Range, where rainfall is twice what it is in the valley below. In shady bends in the road, the first cold weather turns the deciduous snowberry, hazelnut and thimbleberry bushes into delicate golden patterns set against the dark woods.

The ridge you have been seeing to the east and the canyons on either side of it are in the San Andreas Rift Zone. The canyon of Corte Madera Creek below follows an old line of broken rock within the zone. You are close to the upper entrance to Alpine Road, and from the gate at the junction of Page Mill Road you can walk across the road to an entrance to Monte Bello Open Space Preserve.

However, if you turn around at the upper gate you can be back at your car in less than an hour. On the way down take time to look out from the observation points at the switchbacks. You can see far to the northwest.

For a contrasting scene come this way again in early spring, when the willows by the creek will be soft yellow-green as the catkins bloom and new leaves appear. Pinkish buds show on the maples, and new growth on the deciduous oaks is rosy. White blossoms of milk maids are sprinkled in the grass and a few hound's tongues will be in bloom. Here and there by the road wild currant bushes are covered with pink tassels. By April, Douglas iris will be blooming on the road banks.

The sights of spring will compensate for the mud your boots pick up on the road. It is encouraging to know that this section of the road is included in the trail and bikeway plans of both San Mateo and Santa Clara counties.

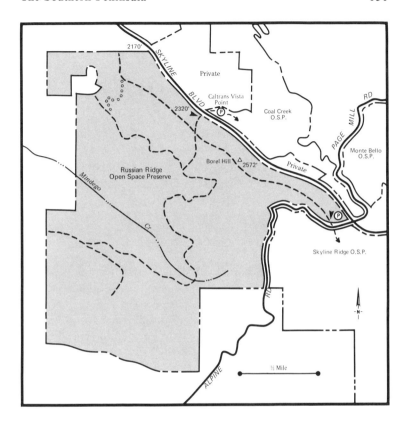

Russian Ridge Open Space Preserve

Russian Ridge Open Space Preserve's 835 acres lie along the west side of Skyline Boulevard for about 2 miles north from the Page Mill/Alpine Road intersection, extending southwest into the deep canyons of Mindego Creek. Trails run along the ridgetop parallel to Skyline Boulevard, and ranch roads lead down the west slopes. Views are spectacular of the Bay and beyond to the East Bay hills, and to the west over an expanse of ridges to the ocean.

Jurisdiction   Midpeninsula Regional Open Space District.

Facilities   Trails for hikers, equestrians, bicyclists.

Preserve Rules   Open dawn to dusk. No dogs permitted.

Maps   USGS topo *Mindego Hill.*

How To Get There   Take Highway 84 from Woodside, Page Mill Road from Palo Alto or Highway 9 from Saratoga to two preserve entrances: (1) at the Skyline Boulevard/Alpine Road intersection, with parking on the northwest corner, and (2) at the Caltrans Vista Point 1 mile north of this intersection.

Trip 1.   A Ridgetop Walk for Those Clear Days When You Can See Forever

A trail along Russian Ridge for the length of the preserve has views out to the Pacific Ocean across ranchlands and forests little changed since American settlers moved to California over a century ago.

Distance   4 miles round trip.
Time   2 hours.
Elevation Gain   300'

TRAIL NOTES

From the northwest corner of Skyline Boulevard and Alpine Road, step over the stile and make a switchback on the steep rise to the ridge. In ¼ mile up the grassy slopes you reach the high plateau of 2572-foot Borel Hill. Few spots can beat this ridge for views that take in the Peninsula from Bay to ocean. If you can go on a still, fogless evening in early summer when daylight lingers, this is a spectacular supper picnic site. Among the scattered rock outcrops are many places to spread out an evening meal and watch the sunset over the Pacific Ocean.

If you are out for a longer walk, follow the ridge to the saddle at its midpoint and continue up the north part of the ridge. In early spring poppies, red maids, Johnny-jump-ups and lupines are in bloom and, by April, a profusion of goldfields covers the grasslands.

To complete this ridge walk, go on to the fenced radio facility near the north end of the preserve. From here you can return the way you came.

Trip 2.   A Loop Trip from the Top of the North Ridge

A walk up the northern part of Russian Ridge for the views and a steep descent across old pasturelands brings you to an old ranch road for an easy return.

Distance   2½-mile loop.
Time   1½ hours.
Elevation Loss   400'
Connecting Trails   East to Coal Creek Preserve and Crazy Petes Trail; south to trails in Skyline Ridge Preserve.

TRAIL NOTES

From the Caltrans Vista Point on Skyline Boulevard cross the road to the stile and enter the preserve on the ranch road straight ahead. Trails lead north and south along the ridge, and a ranch road heads west down the slopes. Turn right from the ranch road on the trail beyond the vestiges of an old corral. As the trail climbs the ridge along the rock-strewn crest, you have sweeping views of the Bay plain and beyond to the East Bay hills. To the west stretch ranchlands, creek canyons and ridges, and the ocean lies beyond. In morning light mists often hide the ocean, but late in the day the ocean waters glisten as they reflect the light of the late afternoon sun.

Southwest before you is Mindego Hill. In spring its green bulk and flattened top stand out against dark ridges beyond. Mindego Hill is of volcanic origin, probably formed more than 135 million years ago. At that time it was submerged below the ocean as part of a range of mountains at the edge of the Pacific Plate. These mountains, which we now know as the Santa Cruz Mountains, have been moving northwest along the San Andreas Fault. In today's time frame, we walk over the eroded, worn down remnants of these mountains little changed over the last century of cattle ranching.

Continue along the ridge toward the radio facility's antenna, near the north preserve boundary. Far below is the old ranch road you will take on your return. A proposed trail will make a long switchback downhill from the ridge near the boundary to pick up this road. Instead of walking straight down the hill, you can try to approximate this route. As you descend you look down into the deep, heavily wooded canyon of a branch of Mindego Creek that flows down the north side of Mindego Hill to join Alpine Creek and then San Gregorio Creek.

On the way watch for deer herds, which often come out of the woods by the road below to forage. When they get wind of you, they will soon disappear into the cover of the woods. Less retiring are meadowlarks, whose exuberant songs fill the air.

When you reach the lower ranch road, turn left for a winding, mile-long trip back. About halfway along, as the road turns into a wooded ravine, it crosses one of the spring-fed tributaries of Mindego Creek. Farther along, among great lichen-encrusted rock outcrops, grow old, wind-topped fir trees. Beyond these trees, you enter a little tree-bordered meadow, sheltered from wind and secluded—a fine place for a long, leisurely lunch before walking the last ¼ mile back to the preserve entrance.

Trip 3.   Down to Mindego Creek and to the Slopes of Mindego Hill

A ranch road descends southwest, traversing pasturelands and winding in and out of canyons to reach one of Mindego Creek's main branches and approach Mindego Hill.

Distance   6 miles round trip.
Time   3½ hours.
Elevation Loss   400'

TRAIL NOTES

Park at the Caltrans Vista Point, cross Skyline Boulevard, and step over the hikers' stile onto the old ranch road that heads downhill. It passes both trails on the right that we took in Trip 2 and turns southeast. It descends through grasslands and soon turns into a canyon shaded by oaks, madrones and Douglas firs. In half an hour you emerge into open pasture again, looking out across forests toward Mindego Hill's truncated summit.

Groves of buckeyes and oaks bordering the grassland below the road are tempting sites for a picnic stop or a welcome pause on the trip back up.

A few minutes' walk farther down the trail brings you to a little flat beside a tributary of Mindego Creek. On one side of the flat, pasturelands furrowed by a century of grazing cattle rise steeply. On the other side, huge canyon oaks and tall laurels edge the creek, making a cool lunch spot for a hot day or a good place to turn around for a shortened trip. But to continue, cross the creek and go up over a little ridge and down to another branch of the creek. From here you make a brief climb to another ridge overlooking the canyon of Alpine Creek and the ridges to the south. A private road on the left leads out to Alpine Road. However, you follow the road northwest on the narrow ridge toward Mindego Hill.

Immense canyon oaks line one side of the road. A mile walk along the ridge brings you to the fenced boundary of the preserve on the lower slopes of Mindego Hill. Turn back at the fence to retrace your steps to the Skyline.

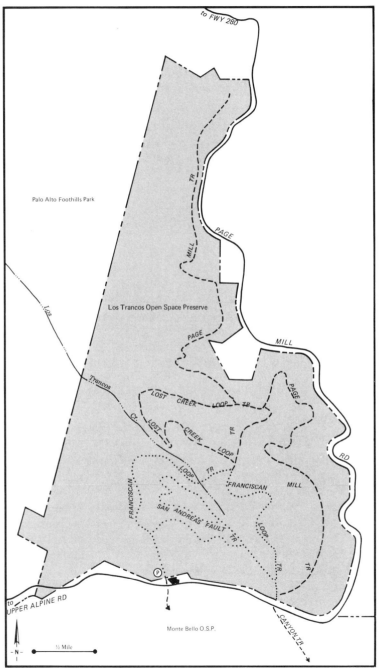

to FWY 280

Palo Alto Foothills Park

Los Trancos Open Space Preserve

TR

MILL

PAGE

Los

Trancos

PAGE

MILL

LOST CREEK LOOP TR

Ct.

LOST CREEK LOOP

TR

PAGE

RD

LOOP TR

FRANCISCAN

FRANCISCAN

MILL

SAN ANDREAS FAULT TR

LOOP TR

TR

P

to UPPER ALPINE RD

Monte Bello O.S.P.

CANYON TR

N

½ Mile

Los Trancos Open Space Preserve

Los Trancos Open Space Preserve
(Map on page 155)

Here is an enticing variety of trails over meadows and into canyons. A self-guiding fault trail explains earthquake phenomena, and a hike out to the far end of the preserve offers magnificent Bay views. Docents lead walks along the San Andreas Fault Trail Sundays at 2 P.M.—no reservations necessary.

Jurisdiction Midpeninsula Regional Open Space District.

Facilities Self-guiding earthquake-fault trail and trails for hikers, equestrians and bicyclists.

Preserve Rules Open dawn to dusk. No dogs. Some trails for hikers only.

Maps MROSD brochure *San Andreas Fault Trail.* USGS topo *Mindego Hill.*

How To Get There From Freeway 280 take Page Mill Road south for 7 miles and park at the preserve entrance on the right.

Trip 1.   San Andreas Fault Trail

Distance 0.6-mile loop.
Time 1 hour.
Elevation Loss 240'

TRAIL NOTES

A self-guiding trail through a section of the fault zone shows you many signs of the violent movements of the earth in quakes of past centuries.

With the District's information-packed brochure in hand, follow the yellow markers and learn all about plate movements, sag ponds, benches and scarps. Though it is only a short walk, you will want to spend at least an hour on this fascinating loop trail learning how the grinding action along the fault line affects the land.

Trip 2.   Loop Trip on Franciscan and Lost Creek Trails

Descending into the cool, shady forest of the preserve's north-facing slope, this trip combines the Franciscan and Lost Creek Loop trails.

Distance   2.5-mile loop.
Time   1½ hours.
Elevation Loss   400'

TRAIL NOTES

Start from the parking lot on the San Andreas Fault Trail, then turn left onto the Franciscan Loop Trail. As you cross the meadow on a clear day, you can see straight up the San Andreas Fault Zone to the Crystal Springs Lakes. Your trail soon descends into the woods under massive canyon oaks. In the fall deciduous oaks and big-leaf maples brighten the forest as their leaves turn golden.

You round the hill to cross a bridge over Los Trancos Creek, and then a short climb brings you to an open flat and a trail junction. Here you leave the Franciscan Loop Trail and begin the Lost Creek Loop. Keep to the left and go up a little rise through the woods. At the top of the rise the trail turns down to follow a ridge into the canyon of Los Trancos Creek.

Here and there firs tower above the oaks and you can see a scattering of these tall trees across the canyon as the trail descends toward Los Trancos Creek, mossy and fern-lined. Wild currant bushes show their pink blossoms very early in spring; later, mission bells, false Solomon's seal, star flower, trillium and wood fern grace the hillside.

As the creek drops into a narrow gorge, the trail veers away, traversing the hillside to follow a minor tributary. In the shade of large bays and oaks our trail climbs to a ridgetop. For a short stretch we join the Page Mill Trail on its way to the north meadow, then we turn right (west) on the Lost Creek Loop Trail up to the flat where it completes its loop.

From the flat take the Franciscan Trail. Bear right, following the trail down into a glade of bay trees. As you circle a low hill you pass a scattering of great craggy limestone outcrops and some ancient oaks that probably lost limbs in the violent shaking of the 1906 earthquake.

Ascending gradually to more open county, we reach the grasslands near the start of our trip and turn right on the Fault Trail to return to the parking lot. From early spring to summer this upper meadow is a bright exuberance of flowers. By fall the meadow has dried, leaving pale beige, gauzy-textured grasses with accents of dark seed pods from the small lavender and pink flowers of dwarf flax.

Trip 3.   Page Mill Trail to the North Meadow

An easy trail along open countryside parallels Page Mill Road.
Distance   3½ miles round trip.
Time   1¾ hours.
Elevation Gain   200′

TRAIL NOTES

On the north side of Page Mill Road east of the main parking lot
and across from Monte Bello Preserve's Canyon Trail is a stile for
hiker, equestrian and bicycle access to this trail. In a minute turn
right on this 1¾-mile trail, which keeps high above the canyon but
below Page Mill Road. Our trail turns briefly down into the woods,
touching the Lost Creek Loop Trail, then climbs to a meadow
above.

Curving right around a hill, the trail comes out of the trees and
emerges onto a series of rolling, grassy meadows that overlook the
Bay. Canyon oaks and madrones rim these hilltop meadows, their
dark foliage contrasting with the new light green grass in spring and
the golden dry grass of summer and fall.

Continuing to the farthest north edge of the preserve, you will be
looking for just the right spot to enjoy the view and watch hawks sail
on the updrafts. While you won't see the small meadow creatures—
mice, gophers and ground squirrels—you can see their myriad holes
riddling the meadows.

In the northwest you will see the distant, dark shape of Mt.
Tamalpais in Marin County. After taking in the exhilarating vistas
and enjoying your knapsack lunch in the sun, retrace your steps at
your leisure.

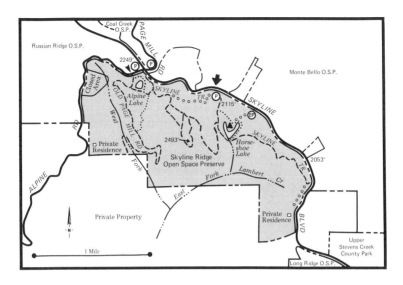

Skyline Ridge Open Space Preserve

Skyline Ridge Open Space Preserve lies along the western crest of the Santa Cruz Mountains in the heart of thousands of acres of public open space. Monte Bello, Coal Creek, Russian Ridge and Long Ridge open space preserves and Upper Stevens Creek County Park surround Skyline Ridge Preserve. From its highest point, one can see west to the forests of state and county parks nearby.

Known to many Peninsula residents for its Christmas-tree farm, Skyline Ridge's 1200 acres also include the two small reservoirs that lie in the valleys flanking a high central 2493-foot unnamed knoll. Rolling grasslands cover the preserve's upper reaches and evergreen forests clothe its steep lower slopes.

Indians gathered acorns from oak forests on the ridge and ground them on bedrock grinding stones that have been found here. As early as 1850, settlers built ranchhouses and raised cattle, hogs, horses and hay along the crest of the Skyline ridge. In 1868 William Page built Old Page Mill Road across the northwest corner of the preserve to link his mill in present-day Portola State Park with the embarcadero in Palo Alto.

The most famous previous owner of the land was Governor James Rolph, who used the modest farmhouse at Skyline Ranch as an occasional summer capital in the 1930s. Today a chestnut orchard and the Christmas tree farm occupy many acres of the site.

Skyline Ridge Open Space Preserve is rich in history, varied in landscape and easily accessible to a million Peninsula residents. The Midpeninsula Regional Open Space District plans to make it the focus of their development on the crest of the Santa Cruz Mountains. By 1989 the northern area will be used for environmental education and historic interpretation, centering on Alpine Lake and the old ranch buildings. The main entrance ¾ mile south along Skyline Boulevard will feature recreational activities—at Horseshoe Lake there will be picnic areas, piers and multi-use trails. Parking and related facilities will accommodate the physically limited. There will also be an equestrian parking area.

The Skyline Trail, due to be completed by 1989, will join these two activity areas. Open for hikers, equestrians and bicyclists, it will close one gap of the Bay Area Ridge Trail in the Santa Cruz Mountains. With only a few missing links, this trail is already open between Huddart Park in the north and Sanborn Park in the south. Plans are now underway to complete such a trail on ridges all the way around the Bay.

In the meantime, Skyline Ridge Preserve is open to the public. Many miles of trail include the one on Old Page Mill Road and several on the former ranch roads that lead to the high central knoll, reach Horseshoe Lake and extend down to the south end of the preserve.

Jurisdiction   Midpeninsula Regional Open Space District.
Facilities   Picnic areas, observation decks, miles of trails for hikers, equestrians, bicyclists and the physically limited.
Preserve Rules   Open from dawn to dusk.
Maps   USGS topo *Mindego Hill.*
How To Get There   Take Highway 84 from Woodside, Page Mill Road from Palo Alto or Highway 9 from Saratoga to two preserve entrances: (1) At the Skyline Boulevard/Alpine Road intersection.

Park on the northwest corner of this intersection and cross Skyline Boulevard to two trail entrances: (a) one at the corner leading to the ranch area and (b) the other 400' down Alpine Road on the left. A new parking area is planned for the northwest corner of this intersection. (2) On Skyline Boulevard ¾ mile southeast of this intersection. Park beside the road until the new parking area is completed.

Trip 1.   A Trip Down Historic Old Page Mill Road

Hike down to Lambert Creek on the early logging route to Page's Mill.

Distance   5 miles round trip.
Time   2½ hours.
Elevation Loss   650'

TRAIL NOTES

From the preserve's north entrance at the corner of Skyline Boulevard and Alpine Road walk 400 feet down Alpine Road to the trail entrance on the left. Take this trail, which passes west of Alpine Lake, to its intersection with paved Old Page Mill Road. Turn right here, heading downhill under tall old firs and past some sculptured sandstone outcrops. You are soon in a clearing with splendid views southeast over a succession of forested ridges.

At this clearing the now unpaved road arcs left, winding around the forested east side of west Lambert Creek canyon. On the way it crosses Lambert Creek tributaries cascading over sandstone boulders on the steep mountainside. About a mile downhill the road goes through some chaparral on a south-facing slope. Blooming at road's edge in summer are yellow bush poppies and magenta chaparral-peas. Around a sharp switchback look to your left to see the site of the former Glass Ranch. Said to be a stagecoach stop on this route to the Bayside, nothing of it remains today.

Back into the forest, now dominated by tall Douglas firs, you engage several more switchbacks to reach a bridge over the creek near the preserve boundary. Old Page Mill Road, long closed to the public, continues on to present-day Portola State Park, where Mr. Page milled logs and then transported the lumber up this canyon and on to Palo Alto's embarcadero.

To begin your upward trip, retrace your same route to the chaparral area and watch for an opening on the right from where a trail, as yet unsigned, climbs steeply up over exposed sandstone. Take this to an oak-surrounded meadow on the hill above. Horses are sometimes pastured in the meadow, so be sure to leave the gates closed. From here take the foot trail left, uphill, to join Old Page Mill Road at the ranch area. After the interpretive displays are installed here in the old barn, you can pause to learn more about the historic and natural features of the preserve. To return to your parking area, walk downhill, north, past the barns.

Trip 2.   A Loop Around Alpine Lake

A trail circling the lake leads to observation points from which to enjoy birds, fish, frogs and insects.

Distance   ½-mile loop.
Time   ½ hour.
Elevation Change   Nearly level.

TRAIL NOTES

From the preserve's north entrance at the corner of Skyline Boulevard and Alpine Road, walk 400 feet down Alpine Road to a trail entrance on the left. Just a few steps inside the preserve take the trail that goes left and follow it through a meadow which is filled with yellow buttercup blossoms in spring. At breaks in the lake's cattail-and-willow border on your right are several places where visitors can get close to the water and look for fish, frogs and waterskeeters.

Reed-rimmed Alpine Lake

You can watch for red-wing blackbirds, barn swallows and marsh wrens from the shore, and look for raccoon and deer tracks in the mud at lakeside. Later you may want to picnic in the meadow or harvest blackberries in a nearby thicket.

By the end of 1989 you will be able to walk out on observation platforms built over the lake to get a closer look at its aquatic life.

Trip 3.   The Skyline Trail

Hike the length of the preserve on a trail that connects to miles of trail along the crest of the Santa Cruz Mountains.

Distance   6 miles round trip.

Time   3½ hours.

Elevation Gain   250' to Vista Point; **Elevation Loss**   90' to south end of preserve.

Connecting Trails   Russian Ridge trails north, Monte Bello trails east.

TRAIL NOTES

This trail will be rerouted in 1989 for all trail users, but in the meantime hikers can go from one end of the preserve to the other on old farm roads. Passing through a lovely oak, madrone and maple forest, the new, hard-surfaced trail will join the ranch and the Horseshoe Lake areas.

Starting from the preserve's north parking area, take the preserve road at the corner of Skyline Boulevard and Alpine Road. Walk uphill past the old ranch buildings and take the road going off to the left. Beyond the tennis courts, installed by the last ranch owner and a surprise in this rural environment, curve right, uphill. When the new Skyline Trail is built, it will go left into the forest just past this curve.

To reach the vista point and the park's summit, keep right at the next two junctions. At the first, the surfaced farm road leads left to reach the Horseshoe Lake area. At the second, a dirt farm road branches to encircle the hilltop. Staying right at the second junction, you ascend the west side of the hill past a wooden water tank and the terraces where Christmas trees once grew.

Then, the farm road you have been following veers east and you make a short, steep climb on it. Dramatic views open up across the canyon to the south. Almost to the park's summit you meet a foot trail to its tree-topped crown. For better views however, turn right on a road sometimes closed to vehicles, and head south to a butte that overlooks miles of forested ridges and rolling grasslands stretching from here to the Pacific Ocean. Many of the forested lands you see are in the public domain—southwest is the canyon of Pescadero Creek where Portola State Park and Pescadero and Memorial county parks lie. Southeast on a clear day you can see all the way to the Monterey Peninsula.

A hike to this vista point makes a 2-mile round trip with an elevation gain of 250 feet. Linger as long as you like in the shade of gnarled oak trees here, knowing that the return trip will take less than half an hour.

If you want to hike to the south end of the preserve, continue around the butte to the surfaced farm road and turn right, descending east on it to the shores of Horseshoe Lake. This little reservoir impounds the waters of East Lambert Creek, currently used for farming operations on Skyline Ranch.

To continue on the Skyline Trail, follow a dirt farm road uphill around the east side of Horseshoe Lake and then go southeast into the forest, avoiding the Christmas-tree plantings. Set out in straight rows across the hillside, these formal plantings contrast markedly with the casual elegance of white oaks dotting the grasslands.

The farm road, winding around small knolls and crossing gullies, then makes a last rise to the southeast entrance of the preserve at Skyline Boulevard. Someday a trail will go another ½ mile to the chestnut orchard at the extreme southeast preserve boundary. From there it is less than ¼ mile south to Long Ridge Open Space Preserve and the start of a 4-mile trail to Saratoga Gap.

On your return to the parking area at Alpine Road, you could bypass the vista point and the park's summit by keeping to the surfaced farm road.

Trip 4.   Loop Hike Around the Shores of Horseshoe Lake

A short downhill trip from the ridge brings you to vistas of a forested canyon and to picnic sites beside the lake.

Distance   1½-mile loop.
Time   ¾ hour.
Elevation Loss   115′

TRAIL NOTES

From the preserve's entrance on Skyline Boulevard ¾ mile southeast of Alpine Road, pick up the farm road and head downhill into a valley surmounted on the west by the steep flanks of the preserve's summit. As you descend through this upper watershed of East Lambert Creek, the **U**-shaped lake comes into view, wrapped around a tree-topped knoll.

In ½ mile from the parking area you are at the south end of the lake, where you walk across the earthen dam on a farm road, then take a footpath along the lake's marshy southeast rim. In the quiet of early morning or late on a summer day, you may catch sight of the deer, raccoons or foxes that inhabit the woods and meadows of this preserve. At any time of day you can watch the birds swooping down to the lake for insects.

Continuing on the footpath around the lake, you reach the knoll where picnic tables will be installed sometime in 1989. Also planned is a trail to this picnic area for the physically limited. Now you can sit here and enjoy your daypack refreshments and look into the vast forested canyon of the Pescadero Basin below you.

To return to the parking area, make your way on the footpath around the north side of the knoll and back to the trail from which you started.

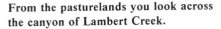

From the pasturelands you look across the canyon of Lambert Creek.

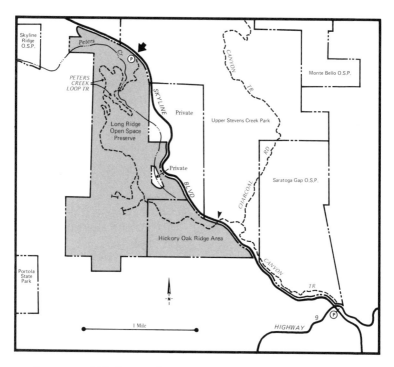

Long Ridge Open Space Preserve and Hickory Oak Ridge Area

Long Ridge Preserve and the adjoining Hickory Oak Ridge Area extend along the heights of the Santa Cruz Mountains for 3 miles just west of Skyline Boulevard. Trails through 735 acres of wooded hillside and open grasslands lead to dramatic vistas westward.

Peters Creek runs through Long Ridge Preserve, from its headwaters to the start of its descent into Devils Canyon. Firs, oaks and madrones cover the eastern slopes, and magnificent spreading canyon oaks, known also as hickory oaks, dot the hillsides.

A trail from the main entrance on Skyline Boulevard leads down to Peters Creek and up Long Ridge. From there the main Long Ridge Trail traverses open slopes into the Hickory Oak Ridge Area.

Jurisdiction Midpeninsula Regional Open Space District. The Hickory Oak Ridge Area is owned by the Sempervirens Fund, but managed by MROSD.

Facilities More than 6 miles of trail for hikers, equestrians and bicyclists. Area for dogs on leash.

Preserve Rules   Open dawn to dusk.
Maps   USGS topo *Mindego Hill.*
Connecting Trails   The Grizzly Flat Trail and Charcoal Road in Upper Stevens Creek Park connect with the Canyon Trail going north in Monte Bello Preserve. Charcoal Road connects to a trail going southeast to Saratoga Gap. A proposed trail will join this preserve to Skyline Ridge Preserve to the northwest.
How To Get There   Take Skyline Boulevard south from Page Mill Road 3 miles or north from Saratoga Gap 3 miles to parking on the west side.

Trip 1.   To the Ridge via the Peters Creek Loop

From the saddle on Long Ridge Road there are spectacular views westward to the coast.

Distance   4 miles round trip to the saddle; 2 additional miles round trip to Hickory Oak Ridge.
Time   2 hours to the saddle; 1 additional hour to Hickory Oak Ridge.
Elevation Gain   400′

TRAIL NOTES

The trail heads across a grassy slope to a little valley where Peters Creek emerges from a narrow canyon. The trail soon enters woods of oak and fir trees. Peters Creek at this point is a small stream you can easily cross on rocks in summer and in fall.

Shortly after the crossing you will see a trail turning right (north). This is one part of the Peters Creek Loop Trail, which you can take on the return trip. Continue now along the creek upstream as it passes through a narrow, steep canyon. Huge moss-covered boulders lie in the creek bed; laurels, firs and oaks meet overhead, and ferns line the banks.

You soon emerge from the canyon into a sunny little valley where the trail rises gently and the creek disappears beneath tall willows. An apple orchard, part of an old farm, grows between the willow-bordered creek and the hillside to the west. The trees are thriving in spite of neglect, and you may find a few apples in the fall.

As you continue along the trail by the orchard, watch for the sign marking a sharp right turn uphill. Here you take an old road leading toward Long Ridge's summit. On an easy grade the trail takes you up a hillside under live oaks, madrones and tanoaks. From the tree-tops you will hear the calls of blue-black crested Steller jays, less raucous than the canyon jays of the foothills.

After a 20-minute climb you come to a crossroads in a small clearing where the trail branches left and right. You will note that across the clearing another trail leads to a private road through the preserve, closed to hikers. The Peters Creek Loop Trail turns right (north) here to circle the hill, returning to the creek below near the crossing you made on the way up. You can take this trail on the way back.

But to reach the ridgetop, turn left and wind your way uphill— about a 20-minute walk. Rock outcrops punctuate the steep hillside, and great canyon oaks and firs cast heavy shade. Then suddenly you step out onto open grasslands at the ridgetop—before you stretches ridge after forested ridge to the Pacific Ocean.

Grassy hills fall away precipitously from the ranch road-trail you now follow along the crest of the ridge. Clumps of spreading canyon oaks dot the hilltop, making good sites for laying out your picnic.

As you lunch you will have time to orient yourself to the ridges and canyons before you. Due west in the great redwood canyon of Pescadero Creek is Portola State Park. Its east boundary is only 3 or 4 miles below this preserve, and a trail connection to the park is planned. Downstream are Pescadero Park and adjoining Memorial Park. Butano Ridge crosses the southwest horizon. Directly east below the ridge is a little reservoir by the headwaters of Peters Creek (in an enclave of private property).

The trail ahead along the west side of the ridge leads to the adjoining Hickory Oak Ridge Area. The trail crosses a rolling, grassy slope to enter an oak forest and reach the Hickory Oak Ridge entrance on Skyline Boulevard.

On your return trip, retrace your steps along the crest of Long Ridge, and then take the path back downhill through the woods. At the crossroads take the north leg of the Peters Creek Loop Trail. This trail makes one short switchback uphill before it circles west around and down through the woods. Watch for an opening in the trees by a patch of manzanita along the trail for a dramatic view down Devils Canyon and out to the sea.

In 20 minutes you will be back at the creek. Turn left to cross the creek and climb the short hill back to the preserve entrance.

Trip 2.   Hike Through an Oak Forest to Long Ridge

A short, easy walk takes you through a fine hickory-oak forest and across handsome meadows.

Distance   2 miles round trip.

Time   1 hour.

Elevation Gain   100'

Connecting Trail   Across Skyline Boulevard in Upper Stevens Creek Park, Charcoal Road leads north to the Canyon Trail in Monte Bello Preserve and it leads to a trail going southeast to Saratoga Gap. An 8-mile loop trip takes Charcoal Road, turns northwest on the Canyon Trail, turns south on the Grizzly Flat Trail and then crosses Skyline Boulevard to follow the Long Ridge trails back to this preserve entrance.

TRAIL NOTES

One and nine-tenths miles south on Skyline Boulevard from the main Long Ridge Preserve entrance there is limited parking for the Hickory Oak Ridge Area. Take the hikers' stile around the gated fire road to pick up the ranch road-trail through the woods.

In 100 yards our road turns right under wide-spreading hickory oaks. From their massive, clear trunks, sometimes up to 5 feet in diameter, grow huge horizontal and often contorted limbs. This oak, *Quercus chrysolepis,* also called canyon, gold cup and maul oak, has fine-grained hardwood which was prized for wagon wheels and farm implements.

Beyond the grove and uphill to the left (west) a parklike meadow opens up, rimmed with handsome trees and dotted with rock outcrops. Views down Oil Creek from the top of the meadow are worth the short side trip. Returning to the road, you continue for a pleasant 15-minute walk under more oaks before you come out onto the grasslands. The road climbs over rolling pasturelands that fall off to the forested canyons below.

In ¼ mile you approach the preserve boundary, from where a trail leads uphill into Long Ridge Preserve. From the preserve boundary you can retrace your steps or continue on the trails in Long Ridge Preserve.

Another trail at the boundary leads down meadows and woodlands not yet open to trail users. We can look forward to a time when a trail will be open through this area of Long Ridge Preserve into Portola State Park in the canyons below.

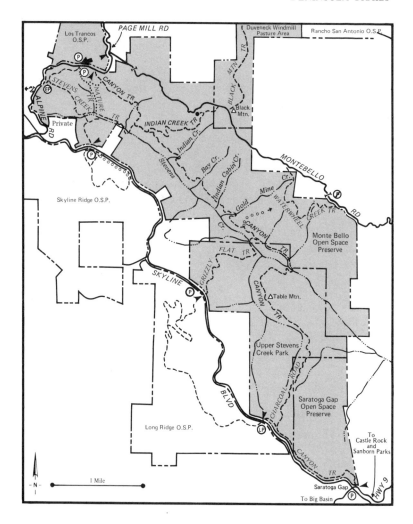

Monte Bello and Saratoga Gap
Open Space Preserves and
Upper Stevens Creek County Park

These 4500 acres of open space preserves and county park encompass most of Stevens Creek Canyon from Page Mill Road to Saratoga Gap and from Skyline Boulevard on the west to Monte Bello Ridge on the east. This aggregation of woodlands, streams and grasslands is a magnificent near-wilderness treasure close to Peninsula cities.

Trails into the vast canyon of upper Stevens Creek invite you to explore its depths and to climb the heights of Monte Bello Ridge.

Monte Bello Open Space Preserve's 2700 acres include the upper reaches of Stevens Creek, the west flanks of Black Mountain and the densely forested east side of the Skyline ridge. One of the first preserves acquired by the Midpeninsula Regional Open Space District, Monte Bello is just across Skyline Boulevard from Skyline Ridge and Long Ridge open space preserves and immediately southeast of Los Trancos and Coal Creek preserves. Monte Bello's nearly 12 miles of trails serve as links between the parks and preserves north and south along the Skyline ridge and those east near urban areas.

Upper Stevens Creek County Park lies along the Skyline between Monte Bello and Saratoga Gap open space preserves. Its steep, rugged terrain is covered with dense woods of old-growth Douglas fir, madrone and big-leaf maple. Two trails through the park from Stevens Creek to the Skyline form links with trails in the adjoining Long Ridge and Hickory Oak preserves to the west.

Saratoga Gap Open Space Preserve extends northwest from Saratoga Gap on the east flank of the Skyline ridge. A 1-mile segment of the Canyon Trail and a short section of Charcoal Road cross the preserve. Notable along the Canyon Trail are great outcrops of lichen-covered wind- and rain-carved sandstone. The preserve's steep wooded hillsides indented by stream canyons are a cool environment for summer hiking.

Jurisdictions Midpeninsula Regional Open Space District and Santa Clara County.

Facilities A nature trail for hiking only, accessible for ⅛ mile to the physically limited. Most other trails open to equestrians and bicyclists. Restroom at the Page Mill parking area. Equestrian parking by reservation at special parking area on Page Mill Road.

Rules Open from dawn to dusk. No dogs allowed. No bicycles or horses on the Nature Trail.

Maps MROSD brochures *Stevens Creek Nature Trail* and *Saratoga Gap Open Space Preserve,* Santa Clara County *Upper Stevens Creek Park* and USGS topos *Mindego Hill* and *Cupertino.*

How To Get There There are 4 access points: (1) At Monte Bello O.S.P. main entrance on south side of Page Mill Road 7 miles south of Freeway 280; (2) on east side of Skyline Boulevard 0.7 mile southeast of Page Mill Road, limited roadside parking; (3) at Grizzly

The west side of Monte Bello Ridge

Flat in Upper Stevens Creek Park on east side of Skyline Boulevard 3.1 miles from either Page Mill Road or Highway 9; and (4) at Saratoga Gap on southeast corner of intersection of Highways 9 and 35 (Skyline Boulevard).

Trip 1.   The Canyon Trail

This long trail, best done with a car shuttle, follows the San Andreas Rift Zone from Saratoga Gap to Page Mill Road. After dropping down to Stevens Creek, it leads up the quiet valley where the creek originates.

Distance 7.6 miles one way.
Time 5-6 hours.
Elevation Loss to Stevens Canyon 1400'
Elevation Gain to Page Mill Road 800'
Connecting Trails Skyline-to-the-Sea Trail from Saratoga Gap southwest to Castle Rock and Big Basin state parks; Skyline Trail southeast to Sanborn-Skyline County Park; Los Trancos Preserve trails and Upper Alpine Road north across Page Mill Road; Skyline

Ridge and Long Ridge open-space preserve trails west across Skyline Boulevard.

TRAIL NOTES

By starting at Saratoga Gap, the trip's highest point, you walk the steep, exposed grade of Charcoal Road going downhill. For a car shuttle, leave one car at the Page Mill entrance and take another to the Saratoga Gap entrance.

From the parking area, cross Highway 9 to the northeast corner of the intersection, where you'll find the signed entrance to Saratoga Gap Preserve. A stile in the wooden fence leads to the trail, which at first closely parallels Skyline Boulevard through a mixed woodland of firs, madrones, bays and oaks. These lands, too steep even for grazing, have remained virtually as they were before the coming of the Spaniards.

After about a mile through a fragrant forest, the trail emerges in a clearing where the old Charcoal Road comes in from Skyline Boulevard. Across this opening a new trail takes off west through the woods to reach Skyline Boulevard opposite the Hickory Oak Ridge Area of Long Ridge Preserve. From this clearing too, a new footpath going north of Charcoal Road, when completed, will reach Table Mountain.

However, for this trip into Stevens Creek Canyon, bear to the right at the clearing, taking Charcoal Road, a broad old farm road, leading north, downhill, into an oak woodland. After a steep descent of more than a mile, you leave Charcoal Road on a trail up Table Mountain. On its flat top an abandoned Christmas-tree farm still has a large variety of exotic conifers, from Sierra redwoods to the spruces of the northern forests.

The trail then leads east around the mountain and zigzags steeply down to Stevens Creek through a forest carpeted with ferns. In spring it blooms with the flowers of the damp woods—purple trillium, lavender iris, and checkered mission bells. Standing in this remote canyon, you can believe reports that a few mountain lions still survive here.

When the creek is running full in spring, it is a challenge to cross without getting wet. On the far side a small flat makes an inviting picnic place where you can lunch to the sounds of the creek.

In less than ½ mile the Canyon Trail meets the Grizzly Flat Trail taking off to the left. As described in Trip 4, this route climbs 2 miles out of the canyon to Skyline Boulevard, where you could leave a car for a shuttle back to Saratoga Gap.

Continuing beyond this junction the Canyon Trail follows a former ranch road for about 3 miles, all the way to Page Mill Road. This tree-canopied route crosses the little watercourses that furrow Monte Bello Ridge—Gold Mine, Indian Cabin, Bay and Indian creeks. The canyon gradually widens into more open, grassy slopes and a few meadows shaded by valley oaks. You go by occasional fragments of old orchards. The Canyon Trail passes the Indian Creek Trail, which turns right to Monte Bello Ridge. This is the only marked trail junction to the east as you come up Stevens Creek Canyon.

Shortly past this trail intersection look for the left turnoff to the Stevens Creek Nature Trail. Here is another route to Skyline Boulevard, about 1 mile away. This trail comes out across the road from Skyline Ridge Open Space Preserve and is described in Trip 3.

From this junction, the Canyon Trail continues through an area of sag ponds, which provide evidence that you are walking in the San Andreas Fault Zone. Earth movements during several severe quakes in the 19th century which were centered here created benches that interrupted watercourses, leaving the small, linear ponds that are one of the signs of a rift zone.

The knolls rising west of the trail beckon you to clamber up for a view of your hike along the earthquake valley to Saratoga Gap, where you started. Beyond, you see where the San Andreas Fault goes west of Loma Prieta Mountain and Mt. Umunhum.

As you near Page Mill Road, there are remnants of former ranching—orchards and fenced fields. Finally, after a day spent in the remote canyons and forests of Stevens Creek's headwaters, you are at the preserve entrance.

Trip 2.   Loop Hike to Black Mountain on Indian Creek Trail

A hike from the Page Mill Road entrance descends into the canyon, then climbs steeply up the Indian Creek Trail to Black Mountain for spectacular views and wildflowers in season. You return on Monte Bello Road through the grasslands along the high ridge.

Distance   4-mile loop.

Time   2½ hours.

Elevation Gain   840'

Connecting Trails   Black Mountain Trail north to Duveneck Windmill Pasture Area of Rancho San Antonio Open Space Preserve, Page Mill Trail west in Los Trancos Creek Open Space Preserve.

TRAIL NOTES

Bring your wildflower guide and binoculars and choose a cool day or an early start. The Indian Creek Trail up the ridge has no shade for much of its length, so it can be very hot. From Page Mill Road take the Canyon Trail toward Saratoga Gap. After 1.2 miles turn left on the Indian Creek Trail. This old ranch road goes uphill, for a while shaded by oak trees. Soon the trees are widely spaced, with only an occasional one for shade when you pause for breath. Then, for the rest of the trip to the top, the trail passes through treeless chaparral and grasslands.

As you pause on your climb to the top, look back west at the series of mountain ridges stretching to the ocean. In ever-paler hues of blue and purple, their tops seem like small waves on the horizon. At times, the fog hangs in the valleys between the ridges; often fog blankets them. To the south you can see all the way to Mt. Umunhum, and to the north to San Bruno Mountain.

In spring a brilliant succession of flowers blooms through the grass. In early summer yellow and black butterflies flutter about the purple blossoms of the shrubby, sticky-leaved yerba santa. On the open hillsides are patches of chia, its whorls of lavender flowers forming little globes on stiff stems. Its fine seeds were a delicacy of the Indian diet, ground for their pinole (seed cakes) and considered medicinally valuable.

On the Canyon Trail from Page Mill Road to Saratoga Gap

Near the summit a poplar by the road marks an old spring. Around the bend sits the old red barn of the mountaintop cattle ranch and the houses that belonged to the Morrell family.

You are now on Monte Bello Road, the old route from Cupertino to Page Mill Road. It starts at Stevens Canyon Road, and winds up the northeast side of Monte Bello Ridge. No longer open to through traffic, it follows the ridgetop, then makes a short descent to Page Mill Road. It provides access to several residences near Page Mill Road and to MROSD lands, and serves primarily as a fire road.

The road is open to hikers, and makes a breath-taking, top-of-the-world walk over the high grasslands above Santa Clara Valley. In late June the deep magenta blossoms of farewell-to-spring that carpet the hilltop and the songs of meadowlarks in the grass are rewards for your climb.

If you have time, explore along the road to the southeast. In about ½ mile you reach the 2800-foot summit of Black Mountain, where an airway beacon and telephone relays stand. A 3-mile trail north down the mountainside connects with the Duveneck Windmill Pasture Area.

After retracing your steps to the ranchhouse, walk a few steps farther to the MROSD backpack camp. With advance reservations you can spend the night here under the stars.

Then continue straight ahead on Monte Bello Road. Here and there clumps of oaks shade the trail, but it is open most of the way, with views up the San Mateo County skyline. In June brilliant lemon-yellow Mariposa lilies fill small meadows by the roadside. At the locked gate that marks the end of the MROSD lands, climb the stile, pass the side roads to the water tank and residences, and you are at Page Mill Road. Turn left (southwest) for a 0.7-mile walk along the preserve boundary back to the parking area. Or walk 200 yards north on Page Mill Road to a gate into Los Trancos Preserve and follow the Page Mill Trail southwest to the parking area across Page Mill Road.

New trails planned for this preserve include a trail from the east end of Monte Bello Road to join the Canyon Trail in the vicinity of Gold Mine Creek.

Trip 3.   Stevens Creek Nature Trail

Explore the headwaters of Stevens Creek with a self-guiding pamphlet that explains ladybug wintering sites, creekside vegetation and the manifestations of movement along the San Andreas Fault Zone.

Distance   3-mile loop.
Time   3 hours.
Elevation Loss   450′

TRAIL NOTES

More than the usual walking time is listed, to allow leisure to experience all the sights, sounds and smells of this delightful walk down the canyon by this lovely creek. Spring-fed, it flows year-round, unusual for these dry hills and most welcome in summer and fall.

At the parking area pick up the trail brochure and head out to the viewpoint above the canyon. Here on a bench commemorating Frances Brenner, a public figure who did much to preserve these open-space lands, you can sit and appreciate the vastness of the near-wilderness below. Spread out before you is the watershed of Stevens Creek, and in fall the gold of big-leaf maples marks the course of the creek down the canyon. Firs of great height grow thickly on the eastern side of the canyon and oaks of immense breadth flourish on the warmer west-facing hills.

Four marked stations on the route tell salient facts about the linear valleys, sag ponds and pressure ridges created when San Andreas Fault pressures were released by earthquakes. Other stations describe the intricate process of wood decomposition by beetles and ants, and the life cycle of the ladybug.

From the bottom of the canyon a marked trail climbs on a pleasant grade to Skyline Boulevard. Directly across the road a stile leads to hiking and horse trails in the 1200-acre Skyline Ridge Preserve. However the Nature Trail Loop turns left after the last creek crossing and completes the loop on the Canyon Trail, passing oak-topped knolls, sag ponds and walnut orchards.

If you want to learn more about this area's natural history, come back on the third Sunday of the month at 10 A.M. for a docent-led hike or call the MROSD office to arrange a special tour for your own group of five or more.

Trip 4.   Hike to Grizzly Flat in Upper Stevens Creek Park

An easy trip on an old jeep road takes you 2 miles down through woods to a stately fir forest and a lovely creekside picnic spot in Upper Stevens Creek County Park.

Distance   4 miles round trip.
Time   2½ hours.

Elevation Loss   900'
Connecting Trail   Canyon Trail in Monte Bello Preserve.

TRAIL NOTES

Follow directions to the Grizzly Flat parking area, access point 3, and go over the stile in the fence. As you enter the park, stay on the broad jeep road a little to the left of the stile. Don't take the foot trail that goes off along the ridgetop to the right; it soon disappears in a maze of deer trails and brush. The jeep trail goes down through oak and madrone woods where in summer the madrone leaves crunch pleasantly underfoot. About halfway down, the steep grassy slopes of Monte Bello Ridge come into sight on the far side of the canyon.

Black oaks and canyon oaks form a dense woodland here, but as you descend farther into the canyon you see increasing numbers of Douglas firs. Near the creek you find yourself in a forest of large firs and maples. Although some wood cutting has occurred in the past in the upper part of this park, the lower canyon's great firs, 5 or 6 feet in diameter, are a fragment of virgin forest. Big-leaf maples filter the light at the bottom of the canyon, and a mosaic of the large, deeply lobed leaves of colts foot edges the stream. Here you will find choice sites for a picnic.

If you veer left at Grizzly Flat, a narrow path through a thimbleberry thicket takes you to a crossing over Stevens Creek. Several sandy flats under maples and tanoaks edge clear pools in the creek protected by a high south wall clothed with five-finger ferns. This trail continues 0.4 mile uphill on many switchbacks to meet the Canyon Trail in Monte Bello Open Space Preserve.

For an 8-mile loop trip starting on the west side of the Grizzly Flat parking area in Long Ridge, use the trails in Long Ridge and Hickory Oak Ridge, crossing Skyline Boulevard to pick up Charcoal Road and follow it down to the Canyon Trail, then climbing back uphill on this Grizzly Flat Trail.

This cool creekside is a fine destination for an early supper expedition in summer, but allow plenty of time for your return trip before dusk. At a leisurely pace you will take an hour and a half to get back up to Skyline Boulevard, a delightful trip in the shade of the hills. As you climb out of the canyon in the early evening, you will want to pause often to look out between the dark firs at tawny Monte Bello Ridge glowing in the setting sun.

Town of Portola Valley Trails
(Map on page 147)

Thoughtfully designed wooded trails follow Coal Mine Ridge, which rises to the Skyline between Corte Madera and Los Trancos creeks. The Old Spanish, Coal Mine and Toyon trails are three of the town's many neighborhood trails that are particularly inviting. Coal Mine Ridge is owned by the Portola Valley Ranch Homeowner's Association and is dedicated to the town as an open-space preserve.

A FEW WORDS TO TRAIL USERS

Remember you are going through private property. Although the trails are unfenced, it is your responsibility to stay on the trail and to comply with trail rules. Hard-working volunteers spend weekends constructing and maintaining these trails.

Do not disturb vegetation, rocks or wildlife. No smoking or fires. Carry out your garbage and pick up a little after others. Leave your dog at home; even dogs on a leash are not permitted because of wildlife disturbance. Go quietly and respect the prior rights of wildlife.

Jurisdiction   Town of Portola Valley.

Facilities   Trails for hikers and equestrians, trailside benches.

Trail Rules   Hikers only on Toyon Trail. No dogs, no bicycles. Open dawn to dusk.

Maps   USGS topo *Mindego Hill;* trail maps available from Portola Valley Town Hall.

How To Get There   From Freeway 280 take the Alpine Road exit south. Continue on Alpine Road past the Portola Road junction to the intersection of Willowbrook Drive, where there is limited parking on the north side of Alpine Road.

Trip 1.   A Loop Trip on Coal Mine Ridge

A delightful trip at any time, this walk tours a flowery garden in spring. The Coal Mine Trail up the ridge of its name and the Toyon Trail, which follows along the west side of the ridge, join at a big meadow by a water tank about halfway up and again at the upper end of these trails. Described here is a loop trip combining these trails.

Distance   3.75-mile loop.

Time   2½ hours.

Elevation Gain   360′

TRAIL NOTES

The Old Spanish Trail starts up through the woods opposite the parking area at Willowbrook Drive. In less than 10 minutes up some switchbacks you reach a junction where the Toyon Trail turns right. A few steps farther the Old Spanish Trail turns right, up the hill, under oaks and past small meadows. (The trail straight ahead goes to Corte Madera School.)

Beside the trail in April and May are great clumps of Douglas iris. The particular strain of these orchidlike flowers found on the ridge has pale buff blossoms with a delicate veining of violet, rather than the more usual lavender or purple blooms. Blue hound's tongues, magenta Indian warriors, white milkmaids and rose-purple shooting stars are among the flowers you will see along this wooded part of the trail.

As you come out of the woods, the Old Spanish Trail turns right, paralleling the service road going uphill to a water tank. Soon the Old Spanish Trail turns left and you step onto the Coal Mine Trail, which continues across the meadow to the left of the big water tank. On the opposite ridge you can see the homes of Portola Valley Ranch, whose owners dedicated this open space to the town.

Beyond the water tank, the trail goes into the woods and you reach another trail junction. Keep left on the Coal Mine Trail. To the right is a connector to the Toyon Trail, which circles around the ridge below. If you want to cut your trip short, you can turn back here and follow the Toyon Trail.

From the junction, the Coal Mine Trail zigzags southeast up under oaks and bays. At an opening in the trees you will find the Vernal Pool, perhaps a sag pond, a sign of past earthquakes and land movements. Circle it carefully to avoid disturbing the pond plants at its edges. By summer the water will have evaporated, yet the plants have adapted to the dry summers and they return each year.

Another ½ hour through the woods takes you to the high point of the trip. From the meadow here you can see the Bay and across to the eastern foothills (unless it's smoggy). In the foreground to the east the brush-covered ridge on the far side of Los Trancos Creek rises to join Monte Bello Ridge. Its 2800-foot Black Mountain summit is just out of sight from here.

As you enter this meadow look for the upper end of the Toyon Trail on your right. On your left is an ancient, wide-spreading live oak, a good, shady resting place. In spring you will be glad you made the final climb to this ridgetop meadow to see the carpet of lupine, pink mallow, forget-me-nots, dandelions, buttercups, cowslips and

Ancient oaks arch over the Old Spanish Trail.

poppies. The edge of the woods has a fringe of bush lupine and iris.

You can return the way you came, which is somewhat shorter, or take the 2¼-mile Toyon Trail back on the west side of the ridge. This is a narrow trail for hikers only (horses may use the Old Spanish and Coal Mine trails). Cut into the steep side of the ridge, it descends through an oak forest on a very gentle grade down into the canyon of Corte Madera Creek.

In about a mile along the Toyon Trail you come to a junction where the short connector to the lower water-tank meadow takes off. Continue straight ahead at this junction. You soon cross two wooden-plank bridges over little streams. Though the streams run only after a rain, there is moisture enough for a garden of maidenhair ferns lining their banks. The trail continues past a couple of sunny chaparral-covered slopes, then turns back into the woods of oaks, bays and buckeyes. Benches along the way invite you to sit and enjoy the view of grassy Windy Hill through the trees and the heavily forested ridges across the canyon. As you listen to the calls of birds, you may also hear the sounds of Corte Madera Creek below.

This trail is particularly appealing in a gentle drizzle on mild days in February when the pale leaves of new growth are beginning to appear on the trees and the delicate pinkish-white blossoms of milk-maids herald another spring. As the seasons progress you will find new interest along the way. In March you see blue-blossomed hound's tongue and yellow buttercups, by April patches of deep-purple larkspur, in May the buckeye's pinkish-white flower spikes, and from April through July the deep-pink blossoms of farewell-to-spring. The warm days of late summer and fall bring out the pungence of chaparral and from late fall through winter the red berries of toyon are abundant on the trail. And all through the year you have the pleasure of walking in the beauty of Corte Madera Canyon.

Trip 2.   A Hike up the Old Spanish Trail and down the East Slopes of Coal Mine Ridge

From the top of the ridge you descend on the Arroyo Trail.
Distance 5-mile loop.
Time 3 hours.
Elevation Gain 360'

TRAIL NOTES

Start up the Old Spanish Trail as in Trip 1, but keep left (east) where the Coal Mine Trail goes uphill past the water tank.

Our route on a service road goes through an oak glade on a gentle grade, then turns up through chaparral and oak woodland. In ½ mile we reach the hilltop meadow and meet the Coal Mine and Toyon trails.

After a pause to catch your breath, or in spring to admire the flowers in the meadow, start down the Arroyo Trail. Under spreading canyon oaks the trail heads down switchbacks on the east side of the ridge. You cross grasslands, then go through a eucalyptus grove before heading down through the woods. Under the shade of oaks and madrones you descend a fern-clad north slope to reach a bridge across a tributary of Los Trancos Creek.

Shortly beyond the bridge, the trail forks. Bear left and continue along the hillside for ½ mile to gravel-surfaced Bay Laurel service road. Cross it, turn left, uphill, on the trail beside the road, and go ¼ mile to an intersection where you rejoin the Old Spanish Trail. Turn downhill here and retrace your steps back to Willowbrook Drive.

Trip 3.   The Larry Lane Trail

This trail climbs from the floor of the valley halfway to Skyline Boulevard.

Distance   1¾-mile loop.

Time   1 hour.

Elevation Gain   500'

How To Get There   From Portola Road ¼-mile south of Old La Honda Road, turn west, uphill, on Hayfields Road and park at the first roadside pullout.

TRAIL NOTES

This public riding and hiking trail is dedicated as a memorial to Laurence W. Lane, who loved to ride these hills with his family and friends.

The trail begins at Hayfields Road where there is limited parking ¼ block above Portola Road. On switchbacks the trail climbs past some homes along the way, so trail users are asked to stay on the trail at all times except at trailside rest areas. Locked gates in the upper part of the trail lead into Woodside Trails Club paths for equestrians only.

As the trail emerges from the woods it splits east and west, and then the branches meet on a traverse at the top of the hill. Here a magnificent oak spreads its ancient limbs over the trail. Benches along the way give you a rest on your climb and a place to enjoy the mountainside scene.

Looking north from Coal Mine Ridge

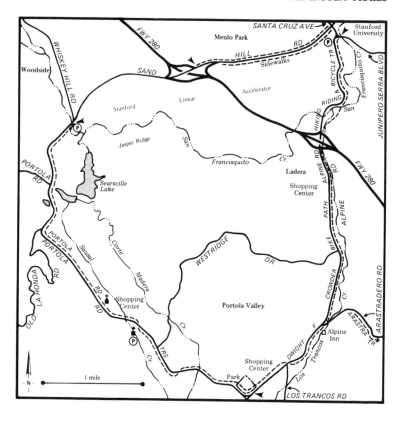

"The Loop"—Alpine, Portola and Sand Hill Road Trails

A roadside loop trail of nearly 12 miles goes past the community of Ladera, through Portola Valley and along the outskirts of Woodside. It includes off-the-road paved paths, unsurfaced horse and hiking trails and continuous bike lanes on road shoulders.

Trip 1.   Alpine Road Hiking, Riding and Bicycle Trail—Dwight F. Crowder Memorial Bike Path

These two paved trails follow the route of Alpine Road, at times wandering along the woodlands bordering San Francisquito and Los Trancos creeks, past open pasturelands and rolling, oak-studded hills from the Stanford Golf Course to the Alpine/Portola Road intersection. The stands of tall oaks, alders and bays and the small meadows within the creek bends make this parklike route a favorite of joggers, bicyclists, equestrians and casual walkers.

Distance   5 miles one way.

Time   2½ hours. Many convenient entry points allow walks of different lengths. Gentle uphill grade.

Jurisdiction   San Mateo County, Town of Portola Valley.

Maps   USGS topos *Palo Alto* and *Mindego Hill.*

How To Get There   From Freeway 280 take the Alpine Road exit. Go right or left to parking areas at trail access points: (1) beside Alpine Road at the Santa Cruz Avenue/Junipero Serra Boulevard/Alpine Road intersection; (2) near the San Francisquito Creek bridge opposite the rear entrance to the Linear Accelerator.

TRAIL NOTES

The trail was built in 1969 by San Mateo County under a federal program to encourage trail building in urban areas. This trail skirts the Stanford Golf Course and curves onto the old road fronting a small settlement formerly known as Stanford Weekend Acres, once summer cottages in the woods, now filled with new subdivisions. Opposite the Linear Accelerator, the trail leaves the road and crosses a bridge over San Francisquito Creek on the old road alignment.

San Francisquito Creek drains the area from Huddart Park to the San Mateo County boundary. Just upstream from the bridge it is joined by smaller Los Trancos Creek.

As the path comes back to Alpine Road it goes under Freeway 280 and dips down toward the creek, where it has its own underpass below the on-ramp of southbound Freeway 280.

The trail passes the Ladera community and a swim and tennis club, then enters the Portola Valley town limits and becomes the Dwight F. Crowder Memorial Bicycle Path. This trail honors a Portola Valley planning commissioner, conservationist and bicycling enthusiast who worked long and successfully to get this bicycle trail underway. In Portola Valley the path veers away from the road to skirt a meadow shaded by immense valley oaks, the memorial Dorothy Ford Park. Adjoining it is Kelley Park, with its baseball diamond, the site of Little League games in the valley.

Again the path comes close to the road, but it is shielded from it by trees and tall chaparral. This sunny stretch is welcome on winter walks.

Crossing Arastradero Road, you come to California's oldest roadhouse, the Alpine Inn, formerly Rossotti's, now a registered historical landmark. The bronze plaque embedded in a boulder by the entrance tells that the structure was built in the 1850s as a gambling retreat and a meeting place for Mexican Californios. It was strategically located on the earliest trail used by rancheros and American settlers crossing to the coast. It has continued to serve as a roadhouse and saloon to this day. On sunny days at any time of the year, hikers, bikers and horsemen mingle with groups of Stanford students and men in business suits at the picnic tables. Join the crowd with an order of one of "Zot's" big treats and watch the local scene.

Once past the adjoining soccer field, you are headed straight toward the mountains. The weather on the dark-forested Skyline ridge ahead often gives early warning of changing weather in the valley—gathering clouds signal impending rain, blue haze heralds a smoggy day ahead and fog falls announce the coming of cooler temperatures.

At the intersection of Los Trancos Woods Road, the path crosses to the other side of Alpine Road. By the redwood at the path's edge is a historical marker noting the home of Maximo Martinez, who received the grant of Rancho Corte de Madera, the first in San Mateo County. Three generations of Martinezes lived here in the house that remained until 1940. The path continues along Alpine Road to its intersection with Portola Road, where it ends in a charming little park planted by the garden club. Furnished with benches and graced by a fanciful iron deer, this park is a good place to picnic or to wait for the bus that stops at the adjoining shopping center.

Trip 2.   Portola Road Trails

An unpaved footpath and equestrian trail continues around The Loop, separated from the road by bushes and trees so that traffic is heard but not always seen. Although better known to horsemen than

**The landmark Alpine Inn has refreshed its guests
for over 100 years.**

hikers, this part of the route is inviting for short walks through
Portola Valley.

Distance   From the Alpine/Portola Road junction to the Whiskey
Hill/Sand Hill Road junction 4 miles one way.

Time   2 hours.

Elevation Change   Relatively level.

Connecting Trails   Spring Ridge Trail in Windy Hill O.S.P.; Larry
Lane Trail in Town of Portola Valley.

Jurisdiction   Town of Portola Valley.

Maps   USGS topos *Palo Alto* and *Mindego Hill.*

How To Get There   Use same directions as for previous trip, continuing to the Alpine/Portola road intersection.

TRAIL NOTES

Go west from the park at the corner of Alpine and Portola roads
on the trail along the northeast side of Portola Road. After passing
playing fields and orchards, the trail crosses the road at the stone
gatehouse of the former Willow Brook Farm. Built in 1912 of wood
faced with stones from Corte Madera Creek, this is the only structure left of the estate which with its mansion once dominated the
valley.

Here Portola Valley widens and before you lie fields and
orchards on the valley floor and unbroken views of the Santa Cruz
Mountains. Going through the valley on foot allows you to appre-

ciate the charm of this quiet rural scene. Right below your feet, nevertheless, is one of the most active earthquake faults in the country. Because of this seismic hazard, much of the valley floor is still planted to hay and fruit trees or used for riding rings. In the great earthquake of 1906 the land displacement in some places nearby was as much as 16 feet.

At the Jelich orchards you can buy fresh fruit in season. And farther on is the little red Portola Valley schoolhouse, built in 1912. An interesting example of the mission-revival style popular at the turn of the century, it is now a historical landmark. The modern school buildings next to it, built before earthquake hazards were fully recognized, currently house the Town Center, library and meeting rooms.

At the Village Square Shopping Center the path returns to the northeast side of the road. Beyond is the charming California mission-style Church of Our Lady of the Wayside. Built in 1912, it is a favorite subject of local art classes. For the next mile the trail follows along the fences of tree farms, orchards and estates.

Where Portola Road turns north at Old La Honda Road, you can see Searsville Marsh. Bordered by willows and cattails, it is a favorite resting place for ducks and other migrating waterfowl.

Beyond the marsh Portola Road turns west but the path continues straight ahead along Sand Hill Road. At this junction you may want to cross the road to read the historic marker noting the lumber-

The little red Portola Valley School no longer houses students, but it still intrigues architectural historians with its mission-revival style executed in redwood.

man's village that once stood here. John Sears, the first settler, came here in 1832. His hotel, a store, school and dwellings were removed as the water rose behind a new dam which created the lake we know as Searsville.

From here to the junction of Whiskey Hill Road the path follows the fence of Stanford University's Jasper Ridge Biological Preserve. Somewhat removed from the road and its traffic, the path goes gently up and down through the trees.

Trip 3.   Sand Hill Road—Paths, Bike Lanes and Sidewalks

There is no formal off-road path for 1.3 miles on Sand Hill Road between Whiskey Hill Road and Freeway 280. Many hikers and joggers use the unpaved road shoulder. It is a favorite stretch for bicyclists because it is uninterrupted by side roads and the bike lanes are wide. The sidewalks on both sides of Sand Hill Road from the freeway to Santa Cruz Avenue are good cool-weather walks, with vistas of the rolling foothills and their forested mountain backdrop.

Distance   Whiskey Hill/Sand Hill Road junction to Freeway 280 1.3 miles one way; Freeway 280 to Santa Cruz Avenue 1.5 miles one way.

Time   1½ hours.

Elevation Change   Very gentle grade.

Jurisdiction   San Mateo County and Menlo Park.

Map   USGS topo *Palo Alto.*

TRAIL NOTES

The mile-long linear accelerator lies on the south side of the road beginning opposite the Whiskey Hill Road junction. Rising beyond is the rocky promontory of Jasper Ridge, Stanford's Biological Preserve, a protected treasure of unique flora and fauna. (Docent-led walks through the preserve may be arranged by calling Jasper Ridge Tours at 415-327-2277.)

In summer and fall the pale gold fields of oat grass on both sides of the road are accented by dark-green valley oaks. This once-common kind of grassland scene, cherished by Californians, is fast disappearing.

Before reaching the freeway, cross to the north side of Sand Hill Road because sidewalks and pedestrian crosswalks are only on this side of the interchange. You will have to cross several freeway ramps. When you are beyond the interchange, for the best views cross Sand Hill Road to its south side. From here to Santa Cruz

Avenue you walk on paved paths over knolls where office buildings
and their parking lots are interspersed with open fields and stately
oaks. This section makes a good walk from Santa Cruz Avenue going
west toward the hills, especially on a sunny winter day.

Near the Santa Cruz Avenue intersection you pass the tree-filled
Buck estate, now willed to Stanford University. At the corner go east
across the intersection with the traffic lights and take the paved path
on the right to the bridge. Using the pedestrian crossing there, you
reach the Alpine Road Hiking, Riding and Bicycle Trail entry—The
Loop's starting point.

Whether taken in sections or in its entirety, this easily accessible
and varied loop is an asset to Peninsula hikers, bicyclists and
equestrians.

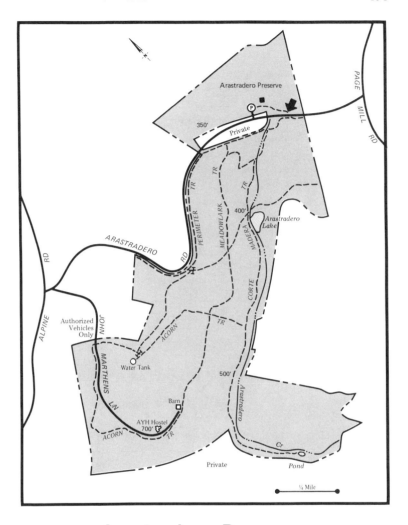

Arastradero Preserve

For a glimpse of the rolling grasslands and magnificent oaks of foothill ranchlands, visit the City of Palo Alto's Arastradero Preserve. On the south side of Arastradero Road between Alpine and Page Mill roads, this 600-acre preserve is open daily to the general public. The preserve adjoins two large open-space areas—Palo Alto's Foothills Park on the south and Stanford lands west of Freeway 280 on the north, although neither is accessible from the preserve.

More than 6 miles of trails, mostly former ranch roads, traverse the gentle hills and valleys of the preserve. Just minutes away from midpeninsula cities, it is easy to find quiet and solitude on a hike to nearby Arastradero Lake or to the oak-studded ridge at the south end of the preserve. Equestrians, especially, use the Perimeter Trail to make connections between Portola Valley and Los Altos Hills trails. Proposals for a trail from Arastradero Preserve through Foothills Park to Los Trancos Open Space Preserve have been considered.

The American Youth Hostel Association plans to convert a large house near the Acorn Trail to a hostel for hikers and other travelers. Proposed trails would link it to Hidden Villa and Sanborn Park hostels in neighboring foothill open space.

Jurisdiction   City of Palo Alto.

Facilities   Trails for hikers, equestrians, and bicyclists; restroom.

Preserve Rules   Open 8 A.M. until dusk. Dogs not allowed on weekends; permitted on leash only, Monday through Friday. No boating or swimming in the lake. Bicycles not permitted on the Perimeter Trail.

Maps   City of Palo Alto *Arastradero Preserve* and USGS topo *Palo Alto*.

How To Get There   From Freeway 280 take Page Mill Road south, turn right on Arastradero Road and go ½ mile to the preserve parking lot on the north side of the road. Take the gravelled path

Mallard ducks nest at little Arastradero Lake.

from the parking area and cross Arastradero Road to reach the preserve entrance. The area surrounding the fenced parking lot is not dedicated parkland.

Trip 1.   Hike along Arastradero Creek to the Lake and up the Canyon to Its Headwaters

Try this hike in the early morning when ducks are paddling on the lake and birds are singing in the willows by the creek.

Distance   3½ miles round trip.
Time   2 hours.
Elevation Gain   350'

TRAIL NOTES

Start on the Corte Madera Trail, which leaves the preserve entrance beside Arastradero Creek. In late winter and in spring this can be a rushing stream, but by summer it is reduced to a trickle. The huge tree stumps on the far side of the creek are remnants of giant eucalyptuses that bordered an old ranch road, damaged during a serious fire here in 1985. Palo Alto is eliminating these trees from the preserve.

Beyond the creek crossing, a well-worn trail climbs up a short hill where brilliant orange poppies and blue lupines bloom profusely in spring. Stately white oaks with wide-spreading limbs dot the grasslands. As you approach the lake a gravelled road takes off left, and almost immediately you come to the tree-shaded, reed-bordered lake. The slanting light of the morning sun streams through the trees, picking up the iridescent green of mallard ducks and the glossy shoulder patches of red-wing blackbirds. If you are a fisherman, you may want to try your skill on the fish in this little lake.

Continuing on the Corte Madera Trail, you follow Arastradero Creek upstream along its willow-bordered course. Dense stands of trees clothe the hillsides east of the creek. Occasional oaks and some stands of buckeyes offer shade on the grassy slope west of the trail, and in spring flowers bloom in abundance. A haze of magenta clarkia covers the hillside in late June. As the creek bends east, so does the trail, until you come to a pond probably built for watering cattle.

A bit farther on in the ever-narrowing, moist canyon, a California dogwood thrives. Soon the trail ends, and your route becomes a rutted utility service road, to be repaired late in 1989. For now, it is time to retrace your steps for a downhill return to the preserve entrance.

Trip 2.   Sample-All-the-Trails Loop

From creekside to topside this trip offers wide views and a stop in a quiet, wooded dell.

Distance   4-mile loop.
Time   2½ hours.
Elevation Gain   400'

TRAIL NOTES

Begin on the Corte Madera Trail, as in Trip 1, until you reach the gravelled road that takes off to the right near Arastradero Lake. Take this road through wide meadows, which in spring are filled with flowers. Shortly you meet the Meadowlark Trail and turn left (uphill) on it. Out on top of the rolling grasslands you may see red-tailed hawks, black-shouldered kites or northern harriers in their endless sky patrol for rodents and snakes. An occasional great blue heron wings overhead on its way to fish in the lake.

Crossing the Acorn Trail and still climbing the hill, you soon reach a barn at the crest of the hill. Past this handsome barn, the trail becomes a gated, gravelled road. Just beyond is the entrance to the planned Arastradero Hostel.

The trail changes its name at the gate, becoming the Acorn Trail, and turns off to the left side of the road. On it you descend past fields of oat grass dotted with ancient oaks and accented with bright flowers through spring and early summer. Just before a white-rail boundary fence the Acorn Trail goes right. Under a light forest cover you drop down to a grassy valley beside a little watercourse, where there is a remote dell for your knapsack lunch.

From this quiet place it takes only a few minutes continuing downhill to reach a gravelled road. Instead of taking this road, you go right, through an opening in a nearby fence, and then immediately turn left, uphill, still on the Acorn Trail. Now you traverse a tree-shaded hillside where ferns and horsetails thrive and in spring deep-pink shooting stars bloom.

In a few minutes you reach the wide central plateau of the preserve. Southeast lies the dark shape of Black Mountain and north are the cities by the Bay's shore. On this plateau you may hear the meadowlark's call, even before you meet the Meadowlark Trail. Turn left on this trail and walk down the plateau past one trail junction to the Perimeter Trail. Then, bearing right on it, you pass the area where barns and buildings were lost in the same fire that destroyed the eucalyptus trees. In ¼ mile on the Perimeter Trail you are back at the preserve entrance.

Foothills Park

The fifteen miles of trail through the woodlands, grasslands and chaparral-covered hills of this park are restricted to residents of the City of Palo Alto and their accompanied guests.

Jurisdiction   City of Palo Alto (Residents Only).

Maps   USGS topo *Mindego Hill* and maps available at park entrance.

How To Get There   From Freeway 280 take Page Mill Road south about 3 miles to the park entrance.

The park, as stated in its brochure, "preserves 1,400 acres of serenity and beauty on the fringes of a vast metropolitan area. Quiet oak-woodland, rolling grassland, rugged fields of chaparral and cool hollows studded with ferns and scented with bay comprise a diverse and inspiring natural scene. Superb vistas punctuate the park's picturesque setting between baylands and redwood forests."

Foothills Park is popular with Palo Alto residents, whose frequent visits number in the hundreds of thousands each year. Understandably, it arouses some envious thoughts in those living in neighboring communities, who may visit the park only as guests. However, the park, to quote the Palo Alto Municipal Code, "has been established as a nature preserve in order to conserve for the residents of the City the natural features and scenic values within the City boundaries, to protect and maintain the ecology of the area . . . The fire hazard in Foothills Park is extreme and the population load in Foothills Park must be restricted and said park must be subject to reasonable closing hours and open only to residents of the City of Palo Alto . . ."

The Arastradero/Foothill Expressway Hub

Three paved paths radiate out from this busy intersection to quiet rural scenes. Though school children and commuters hurry along these convenient routes, you can enjoy a leisurely stroll on each and find creeks and beautiful trees along the way. Combining two of these trails provides an off-the-road route from Los Altos Hills or Los Altos to Palo Alto.

Facilities   Paved paths for pedestrians and bicyclists.

Trail Rules   Open daylight hours. No motorcycles.

Maps   USGS topos *Palo Alto* and *Mountain View.*

How To Get There   From El Camino Real or Foothill Expressway in Palo Alto, take Arastradero Road to Gunn High School. Parking limited during school hours.

Trip 1.   Varian/Bol Park Path

On the west side of Gunn High School a path winds gently north along a wide, abandoned railroad easement, reaching charming, secluded Bol Park and Hanover Street in Stanford Industrial Park. Tree-shaded paths that skirt the east side of Bol Park and Gunn High School offer alternate routes.

Distance   2.8 miles round trip.
Time   1½ hours.
Elevation Change   Level.
Jurisdiction   City of Palo Alto.

TRAIL NOTES

Starting from Arastradero Road in front of Gunn High School, go west around the corner to Miranda Way. Take the path that follows the school's western edge, passing playing fields and tennis courts on your right. This winding path in a wide old railroad easement is the former route of the Southern Pacific Railroad and the Peninsular Electric Railway on their runs to Los Gatos and San Jose. Though houses, industry and heavy traffic are now nearby, the City of Palo Alto has used this easement in a way that retains the feel of the open countryside that the early trains used to travel through.

Views to the west are dominated by ever-changing light patterns on the Peninsula foothills. Crossing the sturdy wooden bridge over Matadero Creek, you come down into the green lawns of Bol Park. Magnificent oaks, benches and playground equipment invite you to stop in this little park dedicated to Cornelis Bol. Tree-bordered Matadero Creek, which runs the length of the park on its east side, and the gentle rise known as Roble Ridge on the west side shelter this peaceful dell.

On leaving the park, cross Matadero Avenue and continue on the path to Hanover Street, three blocks ahead. Many pedestrians and bicyclists take this pathway to their jobs in the adjacent industrial park.

When you return, you can take the path along the east side of Bol Park and admire the big valley oaks there and on Roble Ridge. *Los robles* was the Spanish name for the deciduous valley oaks, while *encina* was their word for live oak.

Then you can take the path skirting the school's east side or return the way you came. In either case you can look up to Black Mountain, magnificent in every season. A crystal-clear day reveals every canyon and ridge on its flank; a stormy one finds big billowy clouds hanging on its upper slopes.

Motorcycle ban allows hikers and cyclists to pass.

Back at the Miranda Way entrance, you turn left at the corner to the Gunn High School entrance, your starting point.

Trip 2.   Palo Alto/Los Altos Bike Path

A wide, paved path winds through the landscaped right of way for the City of San Francisco's Hetch Hetchy aqueduct. This is a good path for a winter stroll in midday.

Distance   1½ miles round trip.
Time   ¾ hour.
Elevation Change   Level.
Jurisdiction   Cities of Palo Alto and Los Altos.

TRAIL NOTES

The path starts from Arastradero Road opposite and just east of Gunn High School. A sign "Bike Path, Los Altos" marks the entrance. Passing between the old trees and well-kept lawns of Alta Mesa Cemetery on the right and the expansive playing fields on the left, the path continues toward Los Altos. Much used by children on their way to school and by families on short strolls near their homes, this path also serves as a shortcut for commuters going to their jobs.

A handsome bridge crosses Adobe Creek, which forms the boundary between Palo Alto and Los Altos. The path meanders past backyard gardens as an occasional apricot tree, lonely remnant from Los Altos' former vast orchards, stands beside it.

The path ends at a cross street, although city streets will take you to El Camino Real or San Antonio Road. Turn around at the cross street and retrace your steps to Gunn High School.

Trip 3.   Arastradero Bike Path

A third walk follows Arastradero Road westward along the route of the Spanish timber haulers on a paved bike path to Purisima Road in Los Altos Hills.

Distance   3½ miles round trip.
Time   1¾ hours.
Elevation Gain   100′
Jurisdiction   City of Palo Alto.

TRAIL NOTES

This path follows the route of one of the earliest roads on the Peninsula. Its name recalls the days when the Spanish hauled trees, cut in the forests of present-day Portola Valley, down this route to build the Santa Clara Mission. *Arrastradero* (the correct Spanish spelling uses a double "r") signifies a place where something is dragged along. Cars now speed along Arastradero on a divided road, but once again there is a place for those on foot.

For 1½ miles from the expressway the path goes past landscaped industrial buildings and parking lots on the north side of the road. However, beyond the industrial park, the path is routed away from Arastradero Road into the ravine beside the creek, where there is a peaceful scene of grassy hills, valley oaks and grazing horses. This is a short, pleasant walk for the rainy season, when it is good to have paving underfoot.

Remember, this is a path for bikes. They move silently and swiftly, so be alert.

Horses graze the hillside above the trail.

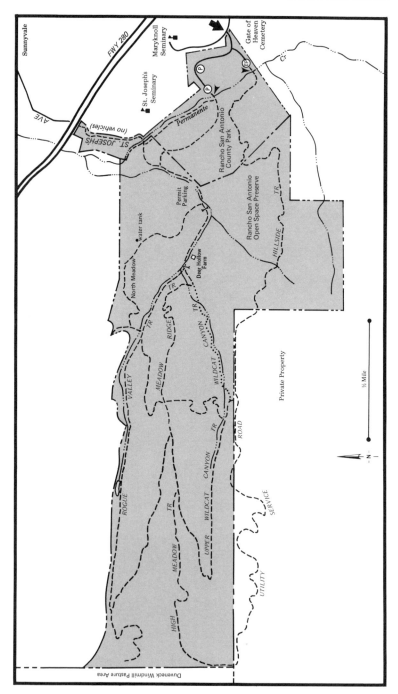

Rancho San Antonio
Open Space Preserve and
Rancho San Antonio County Park

A 1100-acre foothill retreat consists of a Santa Clara County park and a Midpeninsula Regional Open Space District Preserve. A diversity of trail environments, from spreading oaks and cool creeksides of the valley floor to dry chaparral and oak-madrone forests on the slopes of Black Mountain, makes this a place of endless interest.

Most of these lands were part of Rancho San Antonio, a Mexican land grant deeded to Juan Prado Mesa in 1839, whose boundaries ran from Adobe Creek to Stevens Creek. In 1860 the Grant brothers purchased much of the land included in the preserve site for a cattle ranch. Many of the original ranch buildings remain, adding to the pleasure of walks through the preserve.

The County Park entrance from Cristo Rey Drive off Foothill Boulevard just west of Freeway 280 is the main entrance to the preserve. The park provides a paved bicycle path and trails for hikers and equestrians, parking for cars and horse trailers, and restrooms. At this writing, Santa Clara County is preparing a plan for further development of this park.

The City of Mountain View's Department of Parks and Recreation operates Deer Hollow Farm, using some of the old ranch buildings, and conducts programs for children. MROSD has occasional docent-led tours.

The accessibility and variety of the preserve's trails make them some of the most popular on the Peninsula for hikers, runners and equestrians.

Jurisdiction Midpeninsula Regional Open Space District and Santa Clara County.

Facilities Trails for hikers and equestrians; parking for cars and horse trailers; restrooms; environmental education programs.

Park and Preserve Rules Open from dawn to dusk. Bicycles allowed only on paved path in County Park and on service road to Deer Hollow Farm. No dogs.

Maps   MROSD brochure and USGS topos *Cupertino* and *Mindego Hill.*

How To Get There   From Freeway 280 take Foothill Boulevard south. Immediately turn right on Cristo Rey Drive and go 1 mile to the County Park entrance. For trips in the Open Space Preserve use the northwest parking area and take the hiking or bicycle path to Deer Hollow Farm and the preserve trails.

Trip 1.   Deer Hollow Farm

A walk through Deer Hollow Farm gives children (and adults too) a chance to see farm animals and some of the Grant brothers' barns.

Distance   2.2 miles round trip.
Time   1½ hours.
Elevation Change   Nearly level.

TRAIL NOTES

The farm buildings go back to the days of the Grant Ranch that thrived here over a hundred years ago. From the cattle chutes visible at the entrance to the preserve, to the barns and outbuildings at the farm, we have an opportunity to see a ranch complex now rare but once common in Santa Clara County. The board-and-batten whitewashed redwood construction and functional design have a classic simplicity that delights the eye and appeals to photographers and

The feed barn at Deer Hollow Farm is the center for the children's programs of the Mountain View Park and Rec. Dept.

painters. The high, airy feed barn at the far end of the farm is a fine example of the uncontrived grace of ranch architecture so characteristic of the county's rural past.

Although the Deer Hollow Farm is closed to visitors except for the programs of the Mountain View Parks Department, from the pathway through the farm one can see the goats, pigs, chickens and other farm creatures.

For school-group environmental-education programs run by the City of Mountain View, contact the Department of Parks and Recreation at 415-966-6331.

Trip 2.   Wildcat Canyon, Meadow Ridge, Rogue Valley Loop

This loop along the canyons and over Meadow Ridge is popular with hikers and runners.

Distance   4.7-mile loop.
Time   2½ hours.
Elevation Gain   620'

TRAIL NOTES

Past the last barn at Deer Hollow Farm take the trail to the left at a junction for Wildcat Canyon (a trail for hikers only). You enter a cool, fern-walled, narrow canyon under the arching branches of dark bay trees, a quiet place remote from the suburban world only a mile or so away. After ½ mile the canyon widens and the path rises gently to reach a junction with the trail to the meadow above, and you bear right.

A few easy switchbacks take you up a sunny, chaparral-covered slope where quail call from the cover of sagebrush and mountain mahogany beside the path. Soon the path levels off as it reaches Meadow Ridge above. Spring is a time to linger here to enjoy the flowers dotting the rounded grassy hills—bold yellow daisies of mule ears, orange poppies, purple brodiaea, dark-blue lupine and patches of blue-eyed grass. You will find good views and fine places for lunch.

Although you could cut the trip short and return 1.1 miles down the Meadow Ridge Trail from here, to continue this loop take the trail north down to Rogue Valley. The shady trail descends on long switchbacks through the woods, a pleasant route for a hot day. Oaks meet overhead and in the dampness of spring maidenhair ferns cover the banks. Each turn offers new glimpses of the valley below.

In ½ hour you are down in Rogue Valley, and bearing right you go past the farm to the parking area.

Trip 3.   Up Rogue Valley and back over the Ridge to Upper Wildcat Canyon.

Explore the upper valley and the canyons on either side of the ridge.

Distance   7¾-mile loop.

Time   4 hours.

Elevation Gain   600′

TRAIL NOTES

From the farm you have the choice of starting either up Rogue Valley or up Wildcat Canyon. However, from Rogue Valley you have a shady climb to the crest of Meadow Ridge, rather than climbing a sunny south slope.

Going west up the valley by the creek, you soon come to tall bay trees, alders and maples. A dam impounds the creek to create a small reservoir. Farther upstream the maples are even taller, and like the others they turn satisfyingly golden in fall. In less than a mile you come to a junction with an old ranch road, which turns left up to Meadow Ridge, and you turn onto it.

As you climb the mile up an easy grade, you begin to see across the canyon and beyond to the East Bay hills. At the ridgetop trail junction the ranch road turns downhill back to the farm, but this trip continues uphill along the ridge. You look up toward Black Mountain and across Wildcat Canyon to the dark, wooded flank of Permanente Ridge. In ½ mile you come to another junction, where you leave the ridge and the road that continues to the top of the preserve. You then bear left along another old ranch road down into Upper Wildcat Canyon.

It is an easy descent into the tight canyon of Wildcat Creek. Thick stands of bays and oaks darken this steep canyon, making it a good route on warm summer days.

The creek and the trail beside it drop rapidly for nearly a mile to a junction with the trail on the south side of Meadow Ridge.

Near the junction, in late winter and early spring, the trail is brightened by the tiny, bright yellow blossoms of the uncommon shrub, leatherwood (*Dirca occidentalis*). Masses of this shrub along the canyon have the effect of a sprinkling of flecks of gold against the dark bay laurels. Where the canyon widens there are the pink blooms of wild currant. From the junction it is only 1 ½ miles back to the parking area.

Trip 4. Up Meadow Ridge to the Shoulder of Black Mountain

A dramatic hike up the Meadow Ridge Trail to the 1600′ heights of the preserve returns down the side of Permanente Ridge.

Distance 8 miles round trip.
Time 4½ hours.
Elevation Gain 1200′

TRAIL NOTES

Park in the southernmost parking lot in the County park and go past the preserve entrance to start the climb beyond Deer Hollow Farm, taking the Meadow Ridge Trail. A few turns up the buckeye-, oak- and madrone-covered slope bring you to the grassy expanse of Meadow Ridge, green and flower-covered in spring or golden as the season turns.

From these 1000′ heights you look down on densely settled Santa Clara Valley. In the other direction are the wooded slopes of Permanente Ridge, which rise to Black Mountain's 2800′ summit.

Continue up the ridgetop, past junctions with the trails to Rogue Valley and Wildcat Canyon. Our trail up the mountain continues around bend after bend as it climbs. Views become more sweeping with each turn in the road. Across Wildcat Canyon you can see the utility service road which you take on the return trip.

After another mile's climb you leave the grassy slopes as the road makes a sharp turn into oak woods before circling a knoll at 1400′. Crowning the little knoll above the road are a few spreading oaks and a madrone. This is a dramatic place to pause or picnic. You can take in the whole Peninsula from here. Looking far north, beyond San Bruno Mountain you see the unmistakable outline of Mt. Tamalpais. Black Mountain's summit, marked with antennas, is just visible above Permanente Ridge. Southwest lies the Santa Clara Valley.

After another ½ mile up the mountain, the trail turns east at the boundary of the preserve. Here you pick up the utility service road and start the return trip. From this vantage point you look straight down the wilderness of Wildcat Canyon. The road here is outside the preserve's boundaries, but it is used by hikers and equestrians.

Downhill all the way from here you wind in and out of wooded ravines along the south edge of the preserve. The road banks are furrowed by so many deer trails that you know that a great number of these wild creatures live on Black Mountain. However, unless you are here in the early morning or evening you will see only the tracks they make on their way to water in the creeks below. Bobcats and mountain lions share this mountain too, but are too shy to make their presence known.

Stay on the utility road back to the County park and your parking place there.

The High Meadow Trail to the shoulder of Black Mountain is popular with runners.

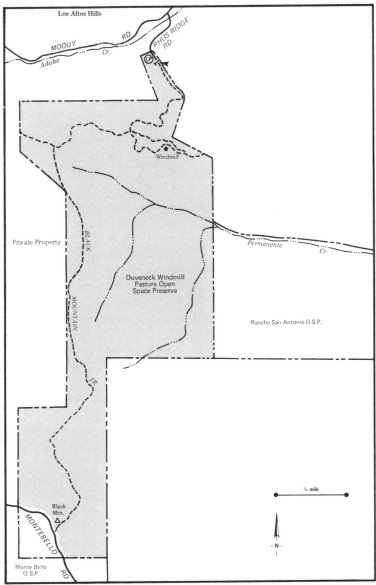

Duveneck Windmill Pasture Area

Duveneck Windmill Pasture Area

These 880 acres are part of the Rancho San Antonio Open Space
Preserve. Lying immediately west of Rancho San Antonio and
extending south to the heights of Black Mountain, the Duveneck
Windmill Pasture Area makes up more than one third of the
preserve's total acreage.

The original 430-acre Windmill Pasture was the generous gift of
Frank and Josephine Duveneck to the Midpeninsula Regional Open
Space District. The Duveneck's Hidden Villa Ranch is well-known
for its environmental education programs, its farm tours and its
youth hostel, the first in the West, which celebrated its 50th anniversary in 1987. Since the death of the Duvenecks, the Hidden Villa
programs and its ranch and wilderness lands are now owned and
operated by a private, nonprofit corporation, the Trust for Hidden
Villa.

Six miles of trails wind through the preserve's fragrant bay-tree
and oak woodlands, across sloping, grassy meadows and up the
steep shoulder of Black Mountain.

Jurisdiction   Midpeninsula Regional Open Space District.

Facilities   Trails for hikers and equestrians.

Park Rules   Open from dawn to dusk. No bicycles on Black Mountain Trail.

Maps   MROSD brochure *Duveneck Windmill Pasture Area,*
USGS topo *Mindego Hill.*

How To Get There   From Freeway 280 take the El Monte Avenue
exit west; just beyond Foothill College turn left on Moody Road,
then in 0.5 mile turn left on Rhus Ridge Road. Continue for 0.2
mile, then turn right down to a small parking place at the gated trail
entrance.

Trip 1.   A Short Hike to a Secluded Meadow

A half-hour's hike takes you to a high, hidden pasture in the
shadow of Black Mountain.

Distance   1 mile round trip.

Time   1¼ hours.

Elevation Gain   500′

TRAIL NOTES

From the preserve entrance in a forested glade, take the trail, which is an old road, up a wooded canyon. In spring, flowers bloom along the trail, and ferns—wood fern, gold back and maidenhair—line the road banks. By summer the gold back and maidenhair have dried, but the wood fern still clothes the hillsides with green.

As you round the last bend, pause on the threshold of the meadow, which the Duvenecks named the Windmill Pasture. Behind you are the cities of the Santa Clara Valley. But take a few more steps along the trail and you'll find yourself in a secluded pasture remote from that urban scene. Handsome oaks border the pasture, and Black Mountain rises beyond.

This is a place to enjoy at your leisure. Short trails through the pasture invite you to explore it and to find hilltop spots to sit in the sun or watch the changing light on Black Mountain. The windmill? Look along the lower border of the pasture for the shaft that supported the vanes, long-missing from this unused structure.

In the mid-1800s the pasture was a part of the Rancho San Antonio, an early Mexican land grant. Before that time, these woodlands and meadows, so rich in fruits, berries, seeds and game,

Frank and Josephine Duveneck stand in the windmill pasture, their gift to Midpeninsula Open Space District.

were the territory of the Ohlone Indians, who had a village beside
Adobe Creek in the valley below. A summer day might have found
them gathering seeds here or beating the grass to round up grass-
hoppers, which they considered a delicacy when lightly roasted.

Nowadays, early-rising residents with a thermos of coffee, a roll
and an orange in a backpack find this a great site for a breakfast
walk. And it is just right, too, for a leisurely picnic supper at the end
of a warm summer day.

Trip 2.   Trek to Black Mountain

From the Windmill Pasture hike up a steep trail to the highest
mountain in the Sierra Morena.
Distance   7 miles round trip.
Time   5 hours.
Elevation Gain   2 380'
Connecting Trails   Trails in Monte Bello Open Space Preserve

TRAIL NOTES

Plenty of water in your pack and an early start are requisites for
this trip. From the Rhus Ridge parking area, take the ½-mile trail to
the Windmill Pasture. After pausing there to survey the peak you
will be climbing, veer right to dip into a shady oak woodland. You
traverse a chaparral ridge and then go back into a clump of trees,
where you watch for the trail junction on your left. Take this route,
the Black Mountain Trail, through a swale that drains into one of
Permanente Creek's tributaries. Keep left at the first trail junction
and begin your steady upward climb.

Shortly, out on the open ridge that divides the drainages of Adobe
and Permanente creeks, your views on both sides are of wilderness
lands, too steep to have been farmed. Across the deep canyons to the
left lie the High Meadow trails of Rancho San Antonio, not yet
accessible from the Duveneck Windmill Pasture Area. To your right
are the private wilderness lands of Hidden Villa.

After about 1½ miles of this unrelenting ascent with very little
tree cover, you enter a wooded plateau. Here on a wide transverse
ridge is a forest of tall madrones and oaks, where trailside glades,
free of heavy underbrush, invite you to pause.

Tall towers anchored on this ridge support the powerlines spanning the upper reaches of Adobe and Permanente Creek canyons.
You cross under the powerlines and emerge from the woods on a
broad, bare service road cut through chaparral. Now, with the airway
beacons in view and a second wind in your lungs, you head for the

2800-foot top of Black Mountain. From the summit there are
marvelous views west into Stevens Creek Canyon and thousands of
acres of open-space lands on the Skyline ridge. Turn around to
behold the entire Bay Area spread out before you.

After a lunch break here you can explore the MROSD backpack
camp, downhill to the right near the farmhouse on gated Monte Bello
Road. With an advance reservation, you could stay there overnight.
For your return trip, you could arrange a shuttle to meet you at the
west end of Monte Bello Road or you could return the way you
came. Whatever your route, you have the satisfaction of having
climbed the highest mountain in the northern Santa Cruz Mountains.

Within the next five years the Midpeninsula Regional Open
Space District plans to re-align the Black Mountain Trail to alleviate
serious erosion.

Stevens Creek County Park
Picchetti Historic Ranch
Fremont Older Open Space Preserve

The park, preserve and historic ranch together make a 2500-acre
expanse set aside for public use. Stevens Creek Park, Santa Clara
County's first park, acquired over a half-century ago, was protected
and enhanced by the Midpeninsula Regional Open Space District's
acquisition of the adjoining Fremont Older Preserve and the
Picchetti Ranch during the 1980s. The park and the preserve, now
linked by trails over the high ridges between them, offer the hiker a
wide range of foothill environments—the lovely creek and its
canyon, the ridges, sheltered valleys, orchards and rolling hayfields.

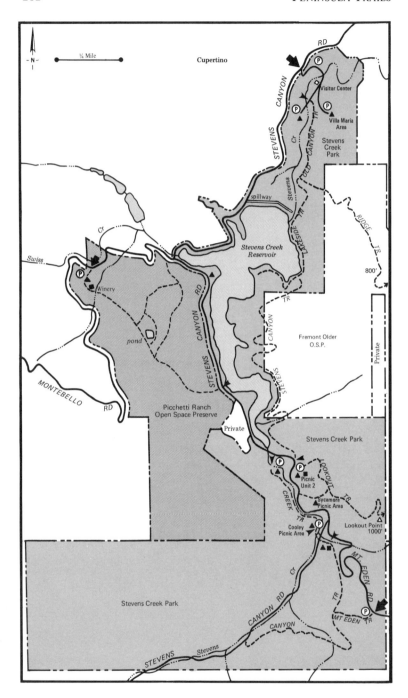

Stevens Creek County Park

The park encompasses a foothill canyon surrounding a reservoir fed by year-round streams. In an early description of this rugged area, Padre Petres Font, a cartographer who accompanied Colonel DeAnza to California in 1776, wrote, "This place of San Joseph Cupertino has good water and much firewood, but nothing suitable for settlement because it is among the hills very near the range of the cedars . . . and lacks level land." Later, the Arroyo de San Joseph de Cupertino, which included Stevens Canyon and the Villa Maria, was named Stevens Creek after Elisha Stephens (the spelling was later changed), who lived here in the 1850s. The Jesuits of the University of Santa Clara purchased the Villa Maria, a 30-acre farm and winery, in 1893. It contained a chapel, villa house, winery and barn, with grape vineyards and orchards of walnuts, apples and chestnuts. The buildings are gone, but remnants of the orchards and vineyards can still be seen.

Hiking trails originate from (1) the north entrance to the park off Stevens Canyon Road in what is known as the Villa Maria Area, below the dam and its spillway, and (2) upstream above the reservoir near the intersection of Stevens Canyon and Mt. Eden roads. In the north and south ends of the park are connections with trails in the adjoining Fremont Older Open Space Preserve.

Jurisdiction   Santa Clara County.

Facilities   Visitor center, picnic areas for families and groups, trails chiefly for hikers. Equestrians allowed on part of Old Canyon Trail and on Mt. Eden Trail.

Park Rules   Park open from 8 A.M. to ½ hour past sunset. No bicycles except on Canyon Trail connection to Fremont Older Preserve. Pets on leash in picnic area, no pets on trails.

Maps   Santa Clara County *Stevens Creek Park;* MROSD brochures *Fremont Older Open Space Preserve, Picchetti Ranch;* USGS topo *Cupertino.*

How To Get There   From Freeway 280 take Foothill Boulevard south, which becomes Stevens Canyon Road, and reach the well-designed north entrance of the park in about 2 miles. For Villa Maria Area and visitor center, turn left at park entrance sign. For other trails, continue on Stevens Canyon Road, which runs through the park and intersects Mt. Eden Road near the south end.

Trip 1.   Hike Up Old Canyon Trail
to the Reservoir and Climb the Hills Above
on Stevens Canyon Trail

From the visitor center the trail under the oaks rises on a gentle grade toward the dam and circles partway around the reservoir to the 2-mile Stevens Canyon Trail.

Distance   2.7 miles one way.

Time   1½ hours.

Elevation Gain   200′

TRAIL NOTES

Start up the Old Canyon Trail past the visitor center on an old roadbed under tall spreading oaks, climbing gently for ¼ mile toward the dam. Near the spillway you pass a trail that turns left to the Ridge Trail in adjoining Fremont Older Preserve.

Beyond the spillway cross a small meadow to the level trail that circles partway around the reservoir to its junction with the Stevens

Jogger takes the Old Canyon Trail under tall oaks.

Canyon Trail. This pleasant walk through oak groves by the water makes an easy excursion for those who may not want to make the climb above the reservoir. The Old Canyon Trail goes on around the reservoir for another 300 yards to an oak-shaded flat—a good place for a picnic.

But to continue over the hill above the reservoir turn up onto the Stevens Canyon Trail, built in 1987–88 by volunteers under the sponsorship of the Trail Center. As the trail winds in and out of ravines through oak woodlands, you glimpse the water below through the trees. After rounding an open chaparral-covered ridge, you descend into oak forest again near the upper end of the reservoir. The trail ends at Stevens Canyon Road near picnic unit #2. You can pick up the Lookout Trail from here for a loop trip of 6½ miles, returning to the visitor center by way of the Ridge Trail in Fremont Older Preserve (see Trip 1 in Fremont Older section).

Trip 2.   Lookout Trail

A climb from Stevens Creek through the woods reaches ridgetop Lookout Point for views of Stevens Creek Canyon and the Fremont Older Open Space Preserve, where you can walk on connecting trails.

Distance   0.8 mile one way.
Time   ¾ hour.
Elevation Gain   440′

TRAIL NOTES

Take Stevens Canyon Road past the reservoir and turn left into picnic unit #2. Find the trail entrance behind the restrooms. The trail crosses a small ridge that separates this picnic area from the Sycamore Picnic Area. Another trail comes up from behind the Sycamore Picnic Area and joins this one about 200 yards up a small ravine.

The trail ascends a steep hill on switchbacks under oaks and toyons, a shaded walk for warm weather. In spring the hill is lush and green when ferns and undergrowth are fresh from the rains and irises, wild currants and roses are in bloom. In fall and winter, toyons are bright with berries.

In 15 minutes you are at the first ridge, from which you can look south to the park's Mt. Eden Trail. Then, at 1000′ high Lookout Point, you can see west far up the canyon and east over the Fremont Older Preserve. At Lookout Point go through the stile leading out of the park into the preserve. Before returning, walk along the ridge to a

Lookout Point has wide view into Fremont Older Preserve.

lunch spot overlooking the meadow, where you will often have the pleasure of watching horses cantering over the trails.

For a loop trip, continue across the meadow and up to the south Ridge Trail and head north for 2½ miles back to the Old Canyon Trail and the visitor center.

Trip 3.   Creek Trail

This creekside trail is just right for a short walk before a picnic lunch.

Distance   1 mile round trip.
Time   ½ hour.
Elevation Change   Nearly level.

TRAIL NOTES

At the intersection of Stevens Canyon and Mt. Eden roads, find the trail going downstream from the Cooley Picnic Area. This trail makes for a leisurely stroll under alders and sycamores. From parts of the trail you can look down from the high banks of the creek into its pools and watch for fish in its depths. If you see perched in a tree a blue-grey bird somewhat larger than a jay, with white stripes and a rumpled crest on his outsized head, it is a kingfisher, who is also watching for fish in the creek.

Trip 4.   Mt. Eden Trail and Canyon Fire Trail to the Ridgetop

The short Mt. Eden Trail leads to the Canyon Trail over the ridge for striking views of the Santa Cruz Mountains.

Distance   3 miles round trip.
Time   2 hours.
Elevation Gain   300'

TRAIL NOTES

From the parking area off Mt. Eden Road at the south end of the park the Mt. Eden Trail climbs briefly, then levels off to a gentle grade. It is an easy stroll under great bay trees and oaks. Blue wild lilacs bloom here in summer. In ¼ mile you meet the Canyon Fire Trail, which turns uphill sharply here to climb a chaparral-covered slope.

Along your way on the right is a great craggy limestone outcrop, a good place to pause for the views up the canyon and down the reservoir. In ¼ mile from the junction you reach the high point of the trail and sweeping vistas of the Santa Cruz Mountains.

You can continue down the fire road if you welcome the exercise of the climb back. But you may want to linger near the summit, where there are several fine spots for spreading out your picnic.

Beyond the ridgetop the slopes are covered with oaks, bays and buckeyes. There are firs here and there on the way down to Stevens Canyon Road. However, the trail is washed out near its lower end, so the trip should be taken as a round trip from Mt. Eden Road.

Picchetti Ranch Area

A visit to the Picchetti Ranch is an opportunity to enjoy the flavor of a foothill winery and ranch of the late 1800s, an experience now all but vanished. The ranch was in the Picchetti family from the 1870s until the Midpeninsula Regional Open Space District acquired it in 1978. Vincenzo Picchetti came to the Santa Clara Valley from Italy in 1872, and soon after bought the ranch and planted orchards and vineyards on its hillsides. Early family quarters, the family home, the winery, the vineyards and the orchards remain.

The old brick winery, now operated by a private party, is open for wine tasting three days a week. Nearby are inviting picnic tables under spreading oaks. Call for wine-tasting hours (408-741-1310).

The ranch's 300 acres extend through orchards and up gentle hills. Two miles of trails take you to oak groves, meadows and wooded slopes. A 10-minute spring stroll through a flowery orchard brings you to a small, tree-shaded pond. Another 5 minutes along the trail and you are in a parklike meadow dotted with oaks.

Jurisdiction   Midpeninsula Regional Open Space District.

Facilities   Trails for hikers and equestrians, historic winery, wine tasting, picnic tables and restroom.

Preserve Rules   Except for winery and adjacent buildings, the preserve is open from dawn to dusk. No dogs.

Maps   MROSD brochure *Picchetti Ranch Area* and USGS topo *Cupertino.*

How To Get There   Go south on Foothill Boulevard from Freeway 280. It becomes Stevens Canyon Road, which you follow for about 1 mile beyond the entrance to Stevens Creek Park. Turn right, uphill, on Monte Bello Road and go ½ mile to the Picchetti Ranch.

Trip 1.   A Stroll to the Pond
and the Oak Grove Beyond

A short easy trail takes you uphill through the old orchard.

Distance   ½ mile round trip.

Time   ¼ hour.

Elevation Gain   120′

TRAIL NOTES

Start on the trail behind the winery heading uphill through the orchard. In 5 minutes you are at the top of a rise looking northeast over the Santa Clara Valley. The Meadow Loop branches left, but you continue ahead over the brow of the hill to a delightful spring-fed pond framed by spreading oaks and ringed by reeds. The grassy slopes by the water are an idyllic picnic destination in spring while the pond is still full.

After a 5-minute walk beyond the pond you come to a parklike oak grove, another fine picnic site, good through summer and fall. You can choose sun or the shade of spreading trees. The trail goes on from here to the Meadow Loop branching left, downhill. You could return the long way around on this trail but it is best taken in the other direction.

Trip 2.   The Meadow Loop Trail

This route circles around the hill behind the pond to views down the valley.

Distance   1-mile loop.
Time   ½ hour.
Elevation Gain   360'

TRAIL NOTES

Begin this trip on the trail up from the winery through the orchard. Turn left (east) up along the edge of the orchard and over the shoulder of the little hill behind the pond. From here the trail turns straight downhill through high chaparral. In less than ¼ mile you bear right (south) on a trail coming from Monte Bello Road, where there is equestrian access to the preserve. As you continue around the hill you reach a meadow sloping east. A stub trail goes a short way down this meadow, which looks out over Stevens Creek Reservoir and across the Santa Clara Valley. This is yet another good spot for a picnic or as the destination of a brisk walk before or after a wine tasting. Return to the trail around the hill and turn left. It soon veers uphill under a canopy of oaks and takes you back to the trail south of the pond.

In addition to these trips, you can explore the steep trail down the south part of the preserve and out to Stevens Canyon Road near the upper end of the reservoir.

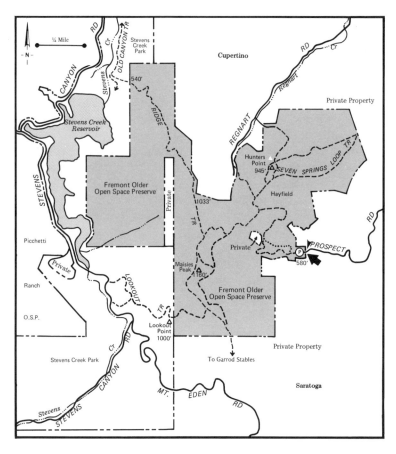

Fremont Older Open Space Preserve

The preserve is part of the old William Pfeffer Ranch, later owned by Fremont Older, a noted San Francisco newspaper editor, and his wife Cora Bagley Older. Mrs. Older designed their ranch home, known as "Woodhills," with a flat roof and many pergolas, a departure from the prevailing style of the times. The house, in a state of disrepair when the district acquired the ranch in 1975, was restored by a leaseholder and is now listed in the National Registry of Historic Places. Woodhills is open for house tours three times a year. (Call the district for information on the tour schedule.)

Meanwhile the ranchlands are open to hikers, who can take the old ranch roads that make easy trails across the rolling hayfields, orchards and ridges.

Jurisdiction Midpeninsula Regional Open Space District.
Facilities Trails for hikers, equestrians and bicyclists.
Preserve Rules Open from dawn to dusk. Dogs on leash allowed in designated areas only.
Maps MROSD brochure *Fremont Older Open Space Preserve,* Santa Clara County *Stevens Creek Park* and USGS topo *Cupertino.*
How To Get There From Freeway 280 take Freeway 85 south. At Stevens Creek Boulevard turn left, then turn right at Stelling Road and go 2 miles. Turn right again on Prospect Road and go 1.3 miles to the MROSD parking area.

Trip 1.   Ridge Trail to Stevens Creek Park

For a hike with exhilarating views take the trail that climbs the steep west ridge of the preserve and then descends to Stevens Creek Park at the Villa Maria Area.
Distance 4.6 miles round trip.
Time 3 hours.
Elevation Gain 400'
Connecting Trail Old Canyon Trail south in Stevens Creek Park.

TRAIL NOTES

Leave the parking lot on a road that goes along the creek under oak and bay trees. Beyond the first bend take the marked hiker's trail up the creek (no horses or bicycles allowed on this trail). After about a 15-minute walk the trail leaves the creek to emerge on a farm road past private inholdings, then winds uphill beside rolling hayfields to a saddle. In the spring the green of the sprouting grass in the fields is brilliant against the trunks of old fruit trees. As the oat grass dries, these round hills are golden and billowing for a brief time.

Turn left at the saddle and go uphill on the ranch road lined with old walnut trees. On the way from the hayfields to the ridgetop you pass a trail on the left marked GARROD STABLES, but continue uphill on the ranch road. In a last steep climb from this junction you reach the Ridge Trail, running north and south along the spine of the preserve.

Bear right at the ridgetop to reach the Villa Maria Area. This trail goes through tall chaparral—wild cherry, wild lilac, mountain mahogany and scrub oak. This brush gives cover to any number of wild creatures, most of which you will not see because they are nocturnal or shy. But when the path is dusty or muddy, you can see by the tracks that it is a busy thoroughfare—the pointed, wedge-shaped hoof prints of deer, the pads of coyotes, the engaging little handlike

Baling hay on "the 80" in 1917.

prints of raccoons, and bird tracks, particularly quail. You may even see these plump birds scurrying across the trail ahead of you. And remember this is rattlesnake country.

Along with the tracks of small animals there will be horseshoe prints, bicycle treads and marks of hiking boots. There are other signs of man, too, on the ridge. The preserve skirts a subdivision, so in some places the trail is close to houses built on these hills.

As the trail turns and starts around a ridge toward Stevens Creek Canyon, the views of the valley and the mountains are sweeping—golf clubs, subdivisions and quarries below, straight ahead the hangars of Moffett Field, the San Francisco Bay and the East Bay hills. To the northwest Monte Bello Ridge rises from the bend in Stevens Creek and extends to its summit at Black Mountain. Its quarry-scarred face seen from the trail belies the name given to the ridge at a time long before our needs for cement and gravel resulted in the massive excavations. However, the rest of the ridge *is* beautiful indeed, and someday even the quarry will be grown over with chaparral and trees.

About ½ mile along the ridge the trail makes a switchback, and then it descends rapidly into Stevens Creek Park. A short, winding service road leads to the Old Canyon Trail by the reservoir. Turn right on the Old Canyon Trail toward the visitor center and perhaps have a creekside lunch in the shade at the nearby Bay Tree picnic area. A car left at the Bay Tree parking lot could make this a shuttle trip and, of course, a much shorter hike.

For a longer trip you can take the Old Canyon and Stevens Canyon trails south. They go partway around Stevens Creek Reservoir, up the hillside and down, returning to Fremont Older Open Space Preserve by way of the Lookout Trail, which connects to the southern Ridge Trail. This makes a loop, adding almost 5 miles to your trip. See Trip 2, Fremont Older Preserve, and Trips 1 and 2, Stevens Creek Park, for detailed directions and trip descriptions.

Trip 2.   Loop Trip to Maisie's Peak on the South Ridge Trail

Skirt the east side of the southern ridge and return over the top of the preserve's highest point.

Distance   4½ miles round trip.
Time   2½ hours.
Elevation Gain   580'
Connecting Trail   Lookout Trail west in Stevens Creek Park.

TRAIL NOTES

Start this hike as in Trip 1, turning left at the saddle. In about ¼ mile from the saddle, take the trail that veers left toward the Garrod Stables and the southern ridges. Past tall eucalyptus and in and out of secluded canyons you contour along the east side of the ridge. In spring, pink-blooming wild currants and blue wild lilacs brighten the trail. Here and there blossoming fruit trees remind you of earlier ranching days.

At the first junction a trail veers right through a wooded canyon, crossing over to the Ridge Trail. But you continue left and go ½ mile, traversing a hillside of chaparral interspersed with patches of oaks. Then out in open, rolling meadowlands you meet the Ridge Trail near the south end of the preserve. This is horse country. You may meet riders from the Garrod Stables, which are just beyond the preserve boundary.

Here you turn north on the broad, well-used Ridge Trail, following the ridgetop up and down over high vista points. Crowned with spreading oaks, these hilltops make good picnic destinations.

Many side trails worn by horses veer off west toward the grasslands below, which can be explored at your leisure. However, to reach the park's 1160' high point, stay on the broad ridgetop to a fork in the trail marked by a sign for Maisie's Peak, named for Maisie Garrod. She and her brother, R. V. Garrod, purchased this property in 1910, grew hay, pastured horses and planted orchards here. Their heirs sold these southern ridgetop acres to the MROSD in 1980.

A rocky trail goes straight up one side of the peak and down the other, but the 360° view from the top is worth the steep climb. To the southwest is Lookout Point, on the boundary between Stevens Creek Park and Fremont Older Preserve. A trail from the point joins this Ridge Trail. (See Trip 1 for a description of a loop trip through these parklands.)

Now, return to the Ridge Trail from your summit climb and follow it north. At the second trail junction you turn right and descend to the hayfields past the old walnut trees, where deer often rest in the shade. At the saddle in the hayfields you turn right and walk back to the preserve entrance.

Trip 3.   Hunters Point

This trip across hayfields to an apricot orchard is an easy walk, especially recommended for an early supper hike.

Distance   2 miles round trip.
Time   1 hour.
Elevation Gain   365'

TRAIL NOTES

Start from the Prospect Road parking lot, as in Trip 1. At the saddle in the hayfields turn right and take the trail to Hunters Point. You will pass two trails on the left that go down off the ridge, but you head straight for the hilltop, where the trees of an old apricot orchard still have a foothold. Here on the knoll called Hunters Point you can see the whole Santa Clara Valley spread out before you. To the west is the steep ridge that crosses the preserve; beyond are the heights of the Santa Cruz Mountains.

In summer, when the days are long, the short walk to Hunters Point is ideal for a picnic supper. With a festive spread in your pack you can walk to the top of the hill and have enough time left to enjoy a leisurely supper as you watch the sunset and its glow on the East Bay hills. When the lights begin to go on in the valley, it is time to pack up to get back to the parking lot by dusk, when the park closes.

**West from Hunters Point is the ridge traversed by the
High Country Trail, with Monte Bello Ridge beyond
and the forested Skyline ridge in the distance.**

Trip 4.   Seven Springs Loop Trail

This trip descends steeply into the canyon east of Hunters Point
and returns on a sharp spine to the point before returning through
hayfields to the Prospect Road entrance.

Distance   3-mile loop.

Time   1½ hours.

Elevation Gain   365'

TRAIL NOTES

Follow the trail directions to Hunters Point in Trip 3. Just as you
come to the hilltop apricot orchard through which the trail leads up
to Hunters Point, the signed Seven Springs Loop Trail turns right,
downhill. It goes down an old ranch road with poison oak bordering
it and occasional trees shading the way.

The name "Seven Springs" refers to the numerous springs in the
lower canyon that once provided water for adjacent ranches. Moisture from the springs seeps down to the canyon floor. A clump of bay
trees stands tall on the hillside, and an old walnut orchard still
thrives at the bottom of the canyon near the preserve boundary.

The return leg of the loop veers north a little and then climbs west
up the nose of Hunters Point. About halfway back you find yourself
on a hilltop encircled by large oak trees with a toyon understory.
Beyond this tree-sheltered hilltop a small flat supports a little apricot
orchard. A short, steep climb from the orchard brings you to Hunters
Point and the downhill return to the parking area.

The Bay Trails

Introduction

San Mateo County's trails by the Bay are as varied as its convoluted 100-mile shoreline. Altogether 40 miles of trails are in place and more are under construction. Although there are a number of gaps between these trails, a Bay-Area-wide plan for bicycle and hiking trails circling the Bay envisions a continuous trail down San Mateo County's Bay shoreline.

Today landscaped paths overlook blue Bay waters that reflect massive airline buildings and tall storage tanks. Promenades edge lawns by restaurants and hotels. Paths through neighborhood Bayside parks are busy with bicyclists and strollers. Trails over a reclaimed trash mountain give walkers a perspective on the geometry of salt ponds below. Boardwalks beside sloughs take birdwatchers through wide expanses of marshes to find avocets, willets, and long-billed egrets probing for food in the mud.

The original Bay margin from the rocky promontory of Candlestick Point to Coyote Point was a series of low points of land and protected coves. South of Coyote Point to Palo Alto were broad marshes crossed by sloughs extending as much as 3 miles into the Bay.

Two hundred years ago Spanish explorers coming up the Peninsula found the marshes an impassable barrier and followed inland paths worn by Indians on the solid ground near the alignment of present-day El Camino Real. From their villages on creeks, Indians travelled in reed boats, finding abundant fish, shellfish and birds along sloughs.

During Spanish and Mexican times the boat trip to San Francisco from landings along navigable sloughs was easier than travel on the rough, muddy roads. Then Anglos built more landings and channeled sloughs to improve shipping, and by 1863 a railroad extended to San Jose. Here and there the newcomers drained the marshes for pastures and crops, and around the turn of this century dikes built around marshes impounded Bay waters for salt ponds.

As Peninsula communities grew, marshes gave way to subdivisions, industrial parks and freeways. The Bay's edges became sites of city dumps, sewage-treatment plants and an international airport. The Bay became smaller and more polluted.

Concern for the Bay and recognition of the values of marshlands gave rise to a Save-The-Bay campaign that resulted in passage of the Bay Conservation and Development legislation in 1968. This law not only limited filling of the Bay but also required public access to the Bay.

A trend toward trails by the Bay gained added momentum from the 1987 state legislation that mandated a plan for a continuous recreational corridor with a bicycle and hiking trail around San Francisco and San Pablo bays by 1989.

From Candlestick Point State Recreation Area just north of the county boundary down to the international airport several short segments of trail take bicyclists and walkers beside the Bay waters. As construction continues in Brisbane and in South San Francisco, gaps in the trail will be filled. South of the airport through Burlingame are only a few breaks in the landscaped paths. From Coyote Point Recreation Area down San Mateo's shore and around Foster City a bicyclist can ride an unbroken paved shoreline path for 12 miles. Only Belmont Slough separates these paths from the long levee path around Redwood Shores. From Redwood Shores to Menlo Park there are significant gaps in the Bay Trail. From the Bayfront trails in Menlo Park south, planned trail segments will be constructed in the next few years. These trails will complete an unbroken bicycle path to Palo Alto in Santa Clara County. From there continuous paths extend to Moffett Field.

By the early 1990s we can look forward to trails from San Francisco down the Peninsula to the South Bay at Alviso. Walking these trails we can appreciate the magnificent setting of San Francisco Bay, enclosed and delineated by the Coast Range mountains. Bicyclist, runner, walker and neighborhood stroller can enjoy the outlook across broad marshes or open water.

**The San Francisco Bay Conservation
and Development Commission
requires public access
at intervals along the Bay.**

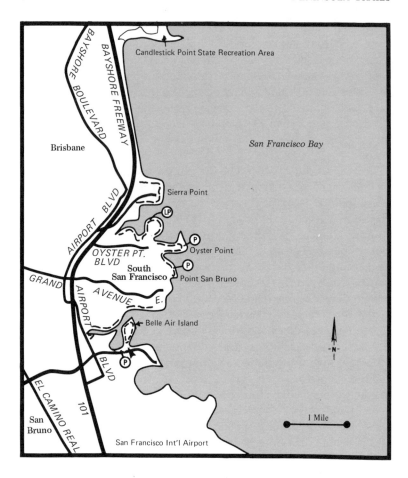

Brisbane

At the Sierra Point industrial park, sidewalks along the main roads and a paved path on the riprap seawall take the bicyclist and the walker out to a marina and a fishing pier. Although no trail exists from the Candlestick Point State Recreation Area at the San Francisco boundary south along the Bay east of the Bayshore Freeway causeway, bicyclists can ride in the bike lanes along Marina Boulevard west of the freeway to reach Sierra Point.

Trip 1.   Circling Sierra Point

A walk or a bicycle ride around the landscaped perimeter of an industrial park takes you to the edge of the Bay.

Distance   1 ½-mile loop.

Time   1 hour.

Facilities   Landscaped picnic areas and restrooms, paved paths for pedestrians and bicyclists.

Map   USGS topo *San Francisco South.*

How To Get There   From Bayshore Freeway 101 take Sierra Point Parkway and continue east to the marina. Park in any of several parking bays facing the marina at both the north and south ends.

TRAIL NOTES

Walk down to the quayside promenade from your parking area to enjoy the boating scene—sailors working on their boats, others lunching on deck or motoring out to set sail on the open Bay. Over the masts you see Mt. Diablo rising above its foothills.

From the marina take the paved path north to the fishing pier and continue west around the shoreline of Sierra Point. One gets a sense of spaciousness here beside the expanse of Bay water.

Past high-rise office buildings the path deadends below Bayshore Freeway at a small fisherman's park. To complete the circle around Sierra Point, retrace your steps to the first path on the right and continue on the paved sidewalks toward the south shoreline. You will cross palm-lined, sidewalk-bordered Sierra Point Parkway, which offers a shorter route back to the marina parking. However, if you continue to the south shore, you'll find the unpaved route along the riprap seawall easily passable on foot. This shore is more protected from strong Bay winds than the north shore.

South San Francisco

From the trail around Sierra Point in Brisbane through South San Francisco to the San Francisco International Airport, there are altogether more than 5 miles of Bayside paths. They take you on a number of short trips beside yacht harbors, through Point San Bruno Park, along Colma Creek and around Belle Air Island. Because of the present gaps between completed trails, these trails are more interesting for walkers than bicyclists. However, as new building construction fronting the Bay is approved, trails will be required and gaps will be filled.

Trip 1.   A Stroll around Oyster Point and Its Yacht Harbors

This walk takes in quayside boating activity and offers long views over the open water.

Distance   4 miles round trip.

Time   2 hours.

Jurisdiction   Oyster Point Marina, San Mateo County Harbor District; Oyster Cove Marina, part of private industrial park.

Facilities   Fishing pier, parks, two marinas, picnic areas, restrooms. Paved pedestrian and bicycle paths.

Map   USGS topo *San Francisco South.*

How To Get There   From Bayshore Freeway 101 take Oyster Point Boulevard east for 0.9 mile. Turn right on Marina Boulevard and go through the marina to the public parking area near the fishing pier. Day use fee: $3 per car.

TRAIL NOTES

From the parking area walk out onto the fishing pier, installed by the San Mateo County Harbor District and the California Department of Fish and Game. At your approach, flotillas of white-faced black coots swimming near the pier take off with noisy flapping of wings and splashing, yet they barely leave the water. Soon they settle again, resuming their search for food beneath the surface.

From the pier walk around to the south side of the point on a path at the top of the sloping bank for a spectacular vista of Bay and distant mountains. The 80-foot tree-topped knoll of Coyote Point juts out into the Bay and the 182-foot hill above Point San Bruno stands just across the cove from you. The ridges of the Santa Cruz Mountains that you see above you on the west extend from San Bruno Mountain in the near foreground to Black Mountain in the south.

Your path curves right, crosses the road to the Harbormaster's office and returns beside the marina to the pier. (Someday this path will also go south along the Bay to Point San Bruno.) On the path beside the marina you pass a fleet of boats berthed in the East Basin behind the breakwaters. Near the fishing pier you will find picnic tables tucked behind protective plantings.

The West Basin, scheduled for completion in summer 1988, will have a trail continuing west from the Harbormaster's office and then north past the swimming beach to the trails around the office and industrial parks of Oyster Point.

To extend your trip, walk back along the Marina Boulevard sidewalk or the new yacht-basin path for ½ mile. Turn right on the

Oyster Point Boulevard sidewalk and continue on it for 200 feet to a path on your right marked PUBLIC TRAIL.

Now you walk on a wide, landscaped, paved path at the edge of the Bay. Flanked by acres of parking lots, the high-rise buildings in this industrial park are deserted on weekends. From the benches along the trail you can see downtown San Francisco and, across the Bay, the wooded ridgetops behind Oakland and Berkeley. Just a few feet beyond the seawall white-winged terns wheel and dive for fish.

Continue around to the Oyster Cove Marina west of the point, where the blue of canvas sail covers repeats the blue roofs of the adjoining buildings. The trail goes around the marina past a strip of marsh and mudflat where avocets and egrets stand on long, thin legs. Two 8-foot slabs of marble placed beside the trail serve as benches from which to observe the marsh life. Shortly beyond the marsh the paved path terminates. Marina parking is permitted only on weekends and holidays. Then you can park at this end of the trail and do this trip in reverse.

On the way back to your car you see different views of harbor and Bay. You may also see sunbathers and swimmers enjoying the beach just south of the high-rise buildings. This little beach, one of only two bathing sites in San Mateo County, will be restored when the boat basin is completed.

Trip 2.   Point San Bruno Paths

The views are splendid from this short stretch of trail.
Distance   2 mile round trip.
Time   ½ hour.
Facilities   Picnic tables, parcourse.

Picnic tables at Point San Bruno overlook the Bay.

How To Get There From Oyster Point Boulevard turn right on Eccles Boulevard and then go east on Forbes Boulevard to its intersection with Pt. San Bruno Boulevard. Here is a little park Bayward from a large industrial plant complex. Ten parking spaces at this plant are reserved for midweek trail users. On weekends there are many parking places available close to the trail.

TRAIL NOTES

At Point San Bruno is a tiny park of manicured lawns, cypress trees, picnic tables and paths. In an ideal location for workers in the nearby commercial and industrial buildings and for weekend visitors, the park's gravelled trails wind among lava boulders and seabreeze-tolerant plantings close to the Bay.

From the park, where a parcourse begins, paths lead north to the other exercise stops and to Bayside picnic tables and benches. At the end of the trail, although there is no path, you can walk north on a little pebbled beach at low tide to the park at the Oyster Point Marina. Here at the water's edge the resting shorebirds—egrets, gulls and willets—will fly off before you get close enough for a picture, no matter how quietly you advance.

Trip 3.   Some Short Walks on the Trails beside Colma Creek

Views of marshes and the open Bay reward you for seeking out the several short paths along the banks of Colma Creek.

Distance Two paths, round trips of 1½ miles and 1 mile.
Time ¾ hour and ½ hour.
Facilities Paved path for pedestrians, benches.
How To Get There From Bayshore Freeway 101: (1) Take South Airport Boulevard and continue to Utah Avenue, where you turn east. Shortly after crossing Colma Creek, turn south on Harbor Way. At the curve where the street name changes to Littlefield Avenue, turn right onto the 20-foot-wide access road to parking behind the commercial buildings beside the trail. (2) Take South Airport Boulevard, turn east on Belle Air Road, and then turn left into the parking area for a large discount store.

TRAIL NOTES

For the first stroll beside the wide channel of Colma Creek and its fringes of marsh, park behind the commercial buildings at Harbor Way and step across the railroad tracks to the trail. Surfaced with blue rock and removed from the buildings, the trail runs through a broad band of fill for about ¾ mile. At high tide the creek is full to its pickleweed-and-cordgrass borders. Ducks, mudhens and seagulls near the banks dive for food in the water. At low tide, flocks of sandpipers and willets scamper at water's edge ready to pluck worms or clams from the mud.

As you walk east beyond the mouth of the creek, a few low islets of marsh dot the water, havens for the waterfowl. Across the channel lies the SamTrans maintenance facility on Belle Air Island and beyond is the San Francisco International Airport.

The trail is interrupted for a short stretch, but it can be reached again from the end of Haskins Way, which runs south from East Grand Avenue. Boulders and huge blocks of cement between the industrial buildings and the trail make convenient perches for Bayside viewing. Here the creek widens and you look out to the open waters of the Bay, across to Hayward and south to the airport. The expanse of water is a tranquil scene, attracting workers from nearby plants.

Another stroll, particularly suited to those who stay in the airport inns of South San Francisco or who shop at the discount store, is a ½-mile paved path along the landscaped south bank of Colma Creek. It begins east of the bridge over Colma Creek on South Airport Boulevard, edges the parking areas and skirts the back of the store. Then it goes through a narrow, fenced aisle adjacent to the Water Quality Control Plant. Notable are the salt-tolerant plantings of native shrubs, yellow lupine, gray salt bush, and daisylike grindelia, or yellow gum plant. When these plants mature, this will be a pleasant path for noon-hour exercise or an after-shopping stretch.

Trip 4.   A Parcourse and Hike on Belle Air Island

This well-surfaced loop path offers views of creek, Bay and airport activity as well as a fitness course.

Distance   1-mile loop.

Time   ½ hour to walk, longer if you use the parcourse.

Facilities   Paved path for pedestrians and bicyclists, picnic tables, parcourse, benches.

How To Get There   From Bayshore Freeway 101 take the North Access Road exit east past the first signal light. Turn left on the causeway to the SamTrans facility on Belle Air Island. Park on the left side of the entrance.

TRAIL NOTES

This little island, now connected to North Access Road by a causeway, is circled by a paved path and parcourse built for the employees of the SamTrans maintenance station but also open to the public. The island lies off the mouth of Colma Creek between Point San Bruno's industrial-park development and the airport. The large-scaled white buildings with their blue and red trim lend a lively air to the island.

To the left of the entrance is parking for the public. By the water's edge young trees frame picnic tables for lunching in the sun. The 1-mile landscaped path has enough parcourse equipment along the way to keep the SamTrans staff in top condition. Benches at intervals accommodate those not so exercise-minded who want to enjoy the views of water and bird life. A run around the path is enlivened by the sight of planes from the airport taking off just beyond the tanks and hangars, by the view of ducks and coots feeding in the creek channel and, on still days, by the reflections of the strong patterns of the industrial plants in the water.

The path circling Belle Aire Island includes a parcourse.

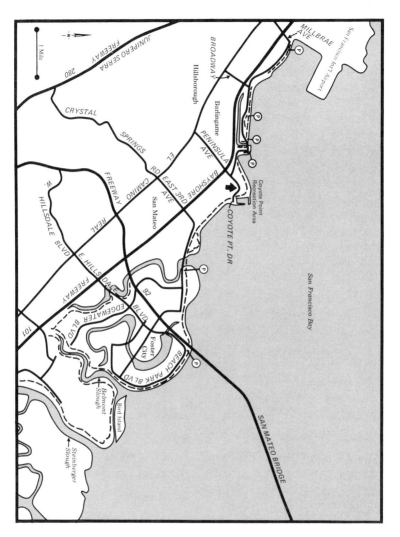

Burlingame

One of the first cities in San Mateo County to meet BCDC's public shoreline access requirements, Burlingame has waterfront walkways along much of its 3 miles of Bay frontage. These paths cross bridges over sloughs, pass an array of hotels and restaurants and reach parks with lawns, trees and playgrounds.

The paths, though not continuous, follow the Bayside from Mill-brae Avenue southward to the west end of Coyote Point Recreation Area. Where the waterside path is interrupted, pedestrians can use the sidewalks along Bayshore Highway and Airport Boulevard and bicyclists can ride in the bike lanes.

Described here are two walks along the Burlingame shoreline.

Facilities   Paved paths for bicyclists and pedestrians. Fishing pier, benches, restrooms. Some paths lighted in the evening.

Map   USGS topo *San Mateo.*

How To Get There   From Bayshore Freeway 101: (1) North Shoreline: Take the Millbrae Avenue exit and go east. Turn right on Bayshore Highway. Past Cowan Road turn left into the first parking lot north of the high-rise hotel on the Bay. (2) South Shoreline: Take the Broadway exit east, then turn right on Airport Boulevard, which curves east around Burlingame's Bayside Park. At Anza Place turn left toward the Bay, and continue to parking areas near hotels beside the Bay.

Trip 1.   North Shoreline—
Millbrae Avenue to Broadway

This walk takes you across two marshy inlets and in front of Bayfront establishments before continuing on sidewalks to the south-shoreline paths.

Distance   2 miles round trip.

Time   1 hour.

TRAIL NOTES

When you step out of your car at the north end of the hotel parking area, you look across a cove to the San Francisco Airport runways and their extensions. Start your walk by going north along the cove for a few hundred yards toward Millbrae Avenue to the handsome redwood pedestrian/bicycle bridge spanning an inlet. The marsh-bordered inlet attracts shorebirds, particularly the snowy white egret. Beyond the bridge an unpaved path continues to Mill-brae Avenue, offering more views of airport activity.

If you turn southward from the hotel parking lot, take the paved landscaped path beside the Bay that winds along past hotels and in front of car-rental establishments and motor inns. The restaurants beyond here, set back from the zigzag seawall, will install a path when the seawall is replaced.

For now, leave the Bayfront, go back out to the Bayshore Highway sidewalk and cross the new pedestrian/bicycle bridge over the mouth of Mills Creek at Burlingame's Shoreline Bird Sanctuary. From this bridge you have an outstanding vista of tidal marsh and open Bay. The paved path continues on the south side of the creek in front of restaurants, hotels and businesses as far as One Bay Plaza, almost 1 mile from your starting point. You can retrace your steps from here or take the sidewalk along Bayshore Highway to continue south.

Trip 2. Stroll Along the South Shoreline— Broadway to Coyote Point Park

Take this delightful Bayfront walk following a paved path fringed by lawns, shrubs and trees and furnished with benches facing the Bay.

Distance   4 miles round trip.

Time   2 hours.

TRAIL NOTES

At the parking area at Anza Place, BCDC signs note that the landscaped area and path curving along the Bay's edge in both directions is public shore. To the west the path goes in front of high-rise hotels and commercial buildings. Beyond these structures you must cross Airport Boulevard and use the path there for 1000 feet, then return to the Bay's edge for ¼ mile Bayward of Burlingame's Bayside Park. The path ends just beyond the park, near the Broadway exit from Freeway 101.

If you go in the other direction from the Anza Place parking area and east of the first high-rise hotel, you will find pleasant, landscaped paths along the Bay and around the Anza Lagoon linking hotels and restaurants. These paths, well-lighted in the evening, make for delightful strolls. The Bay waters reflect lights from the airport and shorefront hotels. Around the lagoon pathside lights shimmer on the water.

For a daytime walk from the Anza Place parking area you will find a fishing-access pier arcing out over the water. Even if you don't care about fishing, you can sit on the nearby benches and watch the fishermen's attempts to hook a big one. There are fish-cleaning sinks here and a restroom.

Where the Bayfront path meets the mouth of the lagoon, a striking pedestrian bridge vaults across the inlet, taking you to a shoreside restaurant on the other side. Here is 2-hour public parking at Bay View Place, from which you could start a walk.

Continuing farther east along the water, you can make your way along a strip of land in front of undeveloped property and soon come to the inlet for the Burlingame Recreation Lagoon. The lagoon, a slough resculptured by fill, is edged with cordgrass and pickleweed and inhabited by snowy white egrets stalking fish and frogs.

Moored at the mouth of this lagoon is an old Oakland ferry, the *Frank M. Coxe,* now refurbished as a restaurant. Plantings edge the Bay and a parking area provides another access to the Bay Trail. The paved path resumes here, extending to the vehicle bridge across the inlet. On the far side and south along the waterfront a broad band of fill behind the seawall serves as an unpaved path.

Along the seawall at the point where it angles south is still another access point, a paved parking area edged with plantings and picnic tables provided by San Mateo County and the Anza Corporation. Fishermen cast their lines from the seawall, and on breezy days windsurfers skim the waters of the cove between here and Coyote Point. You can make your way along a rough path by the riprap seawall for 0.3 mile, paralleling Airport Boulevard. Then turn east to follow the paved Coyote Point Park paths.

You have come 2 miles from your starting point at Anza Place, but if you want to walk or ride your bicycle farther, there are many miles of continuous, paved trails farther down the Bay.

Long-billed avocet feeds in shallow Bay waters.

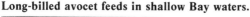

Coyote Point County Recreation Area and City of San Mateo

(Map on page 235)

Six miles of continuous paved paths edge San Mateo and Foster City's Bayfront from Coyote Point County Recreation Area to Little Coyote Point at the San Mateo/Hayward Bridge. These paved paths for runners, walkers and bicyclists connect four parks, passing a bathing beach, marshes, and a yacht harbor.

Maps San Mateo County *Coyote Point Recreation Area* and USGS topo *San Mateo.*

How To Get There Access points from north to south from Bayshore Freeway 101: (1) Coyote Point Recreation Area— (a)southbound, take Poplar Avenue exit, turn right on Humboldt, right on Peninsula Avenue and go across the freeway to the park entrance; (b) northbound, take the Dore Avenue exit, turn left on North Bayshore Boulevard to Coyote Park Drive and the park entrance. (2) Harborview Park—From North Bayshore Boulevard, south of Coyote Park Drive, turn east on Monte Diablo Avenue to the end. Limited parking on the street. Access to trail on levee. (3) Ryder Park—Take East Third Avenue exit from Bayshore Freeway for ½ mile to limited parking on the left. (4) Tidelands Park—From East Third Avenue turn south on Anchor Road. Park on north side of Third Avenue near the bridge over Marina Lagoon.

Trip 1.   An Outing on Trails through Coyote Point Recreation Area South to San Mateo Creek

This trip can be a leisurely stroll on part of the trail or a vigorous round trip through the park and along the high dike path to Ryder Park by the creek. For bicyclists it can be part of a 12-mile round trip ride to the San Mateo/Hayward Bridge.

Jurisdiction County of San Mateo and City of San Mateo.

Facilities Bathing beach with showers, restrooms, picnic areas with barbecues, playgrounds; Coyote Point Museum; yacht harbor. Access for physically limited. Two city parks with picnic areas and play equipment.

Park Rules Coyote Point Recreation Area: $3 per car. Open from sunrise to sunset. No pets allowed. City parks: Open until 9 P.M.

Distance 6 miles round trip.

Time 3 hours.

TRAIL NOTES

Coyote Point Recreation Area, the County of San Mateo's 670-acre park, has a 2-mile shorefront trail, as well as a network of interior trails. The shorefront trail is for pedestrians only, but bicyclists can use a paved path that skirts the south edge of the park and emerges at its easternmost tip near a restored marsh.

For this trip drive to Coyote Point Recreation Area's west parking area near the beach promenade. Pick up the broad, paved path and follow it eastward along the swimming beach. The beach at Coyote Point Recreation Area and the point itself are almost the only remaining fragments of the county's original shoreline. Here by the beach are a bathhouse, a special ramp for physically limited swimmers' access, picnic areas, and playing fields. After this promenade reaches the tree-topped knoll in the center of the park, it follows the bluff to two observation platforms overlooking the Bay. From the first you look northwest through the trees to the San Francisco Airport; from the second overlook you see sailboats cutting through the water, and below you are more boats at their berths in the yacht harbor.

Atop the eucalyptus-covered knoll you'll find the Coyote Point Museum, the only Bay interpretive facility in San Mateo County. Don't miss the permanent exhibits about Bay ecology, featuring dioramas of birds in the marshes and aquariums of marine life.

Continuing through the park you descend past the yacht harbor to an elegant little marsh, restored and now attracting resident shorebirds and migratory waterfowl. At the marsh you are 2 miles from the parking area. You could turn around and retrace your steps or continue down the 1-mile dike trail of Shoreline Park.

The City of San Mateo's Shoreline Park extends east from the Coyote Point marsh on a straight dike under the powerlines. On top of the dike the paved path is popular with walkers, runners, bicyclists and children in strollers. Close to neighboring homes and adjacent to Harborview and Ryder parks, Shoreline Park provides occasional benches from which to enjoy the Bay and the bird life in the band of marsh beside the dike. When you reach Ryder Park, you may want to explore the trail that continues ½ mile upstream beside San Mateo Creek.

Trip 2.   A Walk or Bicycle Ride from Ryder Park to the San Mateo/Hayward Bridge

Around a mountain of trash, beside a healthy marsh and on top of a seawall this trip takes you on San Mateo and Foster City's paths to the bridge.

Jurisdiction   San Mateo and Foster City.

Distance   6 miles round trip.

Time   3 hours on foot; 1½ hours by bicycle.

TRAIL NOTES

You can begin this trip at either Ryder or Tidelands park, or start on the far side of the San Mateo Bridge in Foster City. It is described here from Ryder Park.

On the southeast side of Ryder Park, San Mateo Creek flows into the Bay 7 miles from its source behind Crystal Springs Dam in the foothills. Spanning the creek is a handsome bridge which leads to a mile-long path around the future Seal Point Park, a mound created over the years from the city's refuse. Now the landscaped path around this landfill offers unobstructed views of the open Bay.

As the path returns to East Third Avenue another pedestrian/bicycle bridge crosses the wide inlet to Seal Lagoon, now called Marina Lagoon. It's worth a stop here to see the flocks of shorebirds wheel and dive over the mouth of the lagoon. Then continue past the broad marsh.

As you continue east on the trail beside East Third Avenue, you see across the street the green lawns and curving paths of San Mateo's Tidelands Park. Past the park you enter Foster City, where the Bay Trail stays on a levee next to East Third Avenue for about a mile. The path stays inland past an area of new construction and then near Foster City Boulevard it again follows the Bay's edge on top of a seawall for the last ¾ mile before the San Mateo Bridge. On this exposed section of the trail, waves splash against the rocks and invigorating breezes blow off the water.

After passing under the bridge you come to the San Mateo County Fishing Pier, a windswept section of the old low-level bridge, now much favored by fishermen. Also fishing are the black-winged cormorants and the slender-winged terns you may see flying overhead.

You've come 3 miles from Ryder Park beside San Mateo Creek. You can retrace your steps from here or follow many more miles of trails circling Foster City. There is ample parking south of the bridge and a few picnic tables.

Foster City

From the San Mateo/Hayward Bridge the Bay Trail continues around the perimeter of Foster City. You can walk or ride a bicycle for more than 6 miles circling the city. Marshland, where resident shorebirds congregate and migratory waterfowl rest and nest, lies between the path and the Bay.

Foster City, once a marsh and tidelands threaded by a system of sloughs, is now a city of homes and apartments, shopping centers and office complexes. In mitigation for the taking of these wetlands, BCDC required public access and marsh restoration at the Bay's edge.

Facilities   Paved paths on levees for pedestrians and bicyclists. City parks nearby with restrooms, picnic tables and play areas.

Park Rules   Open during daylight hours.

Maps   USGS topos *San Mateo* and *Redwood Point.*

How To Get There   From Bayshore Freeway 101 take Highway 92 east. Turn right on Foster City Boulevard and then left on East Hillsdale Boulevard. This street becomes Beach Park Boulevard, which you follow to a parking area on the left side of the road near the San Mateo/Hayward Bridge.

Trip 1.   Circling the City on Foot or Bicycle

Walking along beside the Bay in the company of runners, bicyclists, joggers and people pushing baby carriages, you will find a fascinating and diverse marine setting.

Distance   6+ miles one way.

Time   As long as you can spend.

TRAIL NOTES

Starting from the San Mateo/Hayward Bridge the Bay Trail is on a levee above the adjacent city street. Bayward, the tall transmission towers provide perches for birds. Especially noticeable are the large black birds sitting with outstretched wings—diving cormorants, whose feathers need occasional drying, unlike other waterfowl. An offshore lagoon is often filled with birds resting on the mudflats or probing the shallow waters with their long beaks. Avocets, distinguished by their black-and-white striped wings, sweep the water with upturned bills. The plain gray willet also has black and white stripes on its wings, seen only when it flies.

As the trail curves around the city, it leaves the water's edge, then returns to border Belmont Slough for 2 miles. This slough is a rich birding area, where great blue herons and white egrets stand tall in the marsh grasses. The tidal changes from ebb to flood attract a range of birds—those that dive in the water for their food and those that probe the mudflats.

After the path leaves Belmont Slough, it follows a levee and continues along Marina Lagoon, the former Seal Slough, until it reaches East Hillsdale Boulevard. The City of San Mateo's intermittent paths on the other side of Freeway 92 follow Marina Lagoon and will someday reach Tidelands Park on East Third Avenue.

To take this trip in reverse, which would be preferable on a windy day, start at Edgewater Park. Take East Hillsdale Boulevard from Bayshore Freeway and turn right on Edgewater Boulevard. In ½ mile park at Edgewater Park, then walk ½ mile south on Polaris Avenue to the path at the edge of the lagoon.

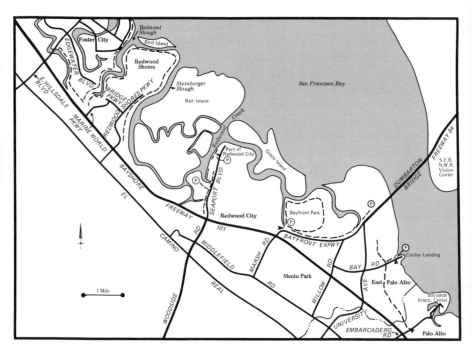

Redwood City
and Port of Redwood City

Paved paths circle the island between Steinberger and Belmont sloughs. Once marshland, much of the island is now filled and developed as Redwood Shores, but a rim of protected marsh lies outboard of the levee path.

Short paved paths by Redwood Slough take walkers to the Port of Redwood City and its marinas. From the historic embarcadero on this slough in the mid-1800s, logs from the Pulgas Redwoods were rafted or sailed by schooner to build Gold Rush San Francisco. Today the Port of Redwood City accommodates seagoing vessels and its marinas berth hundreds of yachts.

With a 1984 permit for an additional wharf at the port, BCDC required public access to the slough. Now a small park and wharfside paths invite visitors to watch port activities. A pleasant park by a new boat ramp was included in 1986 improvements at the port's marina.

Jurisdiction   Redwood City and Port of Redwood City.

Facilities   Pathways for pedestrians and bicyclists. Restrooms at the parks and Port of Redwood City Marina. Handicapped access at Marina.

Park Rules   8 A.M. to dusk. Marsh by path is protected by California Fish and Game Department. No dogs on path. Port open 8 A.M. to 5 P.M.

Map   USGS topo *Redwood Point.*

How To Get There   From Bayshore Freeway 101: (1) Redwood Shores—Take Marine World Parkway or Redwood Shores Parkway (Holly Street) exit and park at either Mariner Park at the south end of Bridge Parkway or at the north end of Shell Parkway. (2) Port of Redwood City—From the north take the Woodside Road exit, then go east under the freeway to Seaport Boulevard; from the south, take the Seaport Boulevard exit.

Trip 1.   A Bicycle Ride, Run or Stroll Along the Redwood Shores Levee

Around Redwood Shores between Belmont and Steinberger sloughs a nearly 10-mile levee path follows much of the perimeter of the island. Bayward, Bird Island, a band of protected marsh washed by the tides, provides habitat for waterfowl.

Distance   10 miles one way.

Time   5 hours.

TRAIL NOTES

Start at one of the public parks edging the pathway. Along this levee top, fringed with a band of protected marsh, you find a variety of seabirds and shorebirds, both resident and migrant. In winter months the sloughs are a resting place for ducks on their way down the Pacific Flyway. Watch the waters for the great flat-bodied skates that inhabit the sloughs. Along the path is the low-growing saltbush, which is host to the fingernail-sized pygmy blue butterfly.

The bicyclist or the energetic walker who gets to the outer rim of the path will see Bird Island across a slough. From the height of the levee you can see over the green cordgrass of Bird Island to the blue Bay beyond. The island is a protected avian habitat, a nesting ground for snowy egrets and herons.

Among many species of shorebirds, the least tern nests here, an endangered species on the California coast. This tern looks like a small, slender gull with a slightly forked tail. Also nesting here is the

The least tern dives for fish in the slough.

cosmopolitan Caspian tern, gull-sized with a red beak. These terns are fishers, so you may see them plunging headlong into the water for their prey.

The nearly 10 miles of paths circling much of this island provide bicyclists a good ride, runners a satisfying workout and walkers and birdwatchers trips of any length to suit their inclination.

Trip 2.   The Port of Redwood City

Strolls to delightful urban seascapes await you at the municipal marina and the Port of Redwood City.

TRAIL NOTES

Several short strolls around the port are described here. Each takes off from Seaport Boulevard. On your way to the Port beside Seaport Boulevard you will note a paved and landscaped path on your right, a good walk on the edge of a salt pond.

For the first stroll turn left at Chesapeake Boulevard, a new, tree-lined street leading to an industrial park. Look for the small park to your right as you reach the yacht basin. Turn into the parking space by the small, two-story building that houses the offices of the Port of Redwood City's Harbormaster. At the park are tables by the water for lunch or checkers and a long bench for sheltered sunning or boat watching. Beyond are piers and a launching ramp. Across a narrow channel are berthed large yachts in surprising variety.

From the paved court of the little park and up a short flight of steps a three-block-long boardwalk leads back out to Seaport Boulevard. This raised walk covers a slurry pipe from the salt pond to the salt company. From the walk you have more views of yachts across the channel. On a strip of marsh below you may see great blue herons stalking fish.

After lunch in the sun and a walk down the boardwalk and back, you can move on to the next marine stroll. Turning left from Seaport Boulevard onto Seaport Court, you will find parking, two restaurants, trees, an exercise course and an 800-foot strip of flower-bordered lawn beside Redwood Creek. Across Redwood Creek rises the pile of salt at the Leslie Salt Works.

The last stroll is along the wharves of the Port of Redwood City. Go two long blocks farther down Seaport Boulevard and turn left at Herkner Road. Check in with the attendant at the port gate and go on to the parking lot as directed. The port is open from 8 A.M. to 5 P.M. You will see by the ship channel the little Bay Access Park, with flower beds and benches from which to watch the action in the channel. Immediately downstream you may find a seagoing freighter or two tied up at the wharf, lending deep-sea flavor to this outing. Unless the vessel is loading or unloading, you can walk along the wharf beside it. The cargo might be redwood logs or scrap iron from a 25-foot-high pile by the wharf.

In the other direction a short path leads up the channel (left) to more wharves—for the Geodetic Survey ship and often for large yachts from other ports. It is the Bay Conservation and Development Commission requirements for public access that result in waterside parks and paths such as these all around the Bay.

Menlo Park
(Map on page 244)

The City of Menlo Park's Bayfront Park and the Bay Trail to Freeway 84 are close to populous neighborhoods and near to many offices and plants. Noontime runners and families on weekend excursions find interest in the ever-changing marsh and Bay life.

Jurisdiction   Menlo Park, Caltrans.
Facilities   Pedestrian and bicycle paths.
Rules   Bayfront Park open dawn to 5 P.M. Dogs allowed on leash.
Bayfront Expressway path open dawn to dusk.
Map   USGS topo *Palo Alto.*
How To Get There   From Bayshore Freeway 101 turn north on
Marsh Road, cross Bayfront Expressway to park in Bayfront Park.
The Bay Trail beside the Bayfront Expressway can also be reached
from Freeway 84 just north of University Avenue. Park at the utility
substation on the north side of the freeway.

Trip 1.   Bayfront Park—A Hike over the Hills or a Run by the Slough

Easy paths over gentle hills bring you to new views over marsh
and Bay.
Distance   2-mile loop.
Time   1 hour.

TRAIL NOTES

The 130-acre Bayfront Park at the end of Marsh Road is still in
the making. This park, created from the accumulation of years of
municipal refuse, brings us fresh views of the Bay from trails on its
newly landscaped heights. From experimental plantings of salt-
tolerant trees, small forests are springing up on the hills. Several
miles of paths wind over the slopes and a 2-mile trail circles the park
just above the marsh.

The park is surrounded by marshes and sloughs. Along Flood
Slough left of the entrance road, ebb tide leaves mudflats by its
banks, attracting white egrets. You cannot miss the lovely great
white egret, standing nearly 3 feet tall, and the smaller snowy egret,
which nests in reeds and cordgrass in the marsh and searches for fish
in the shallows. To the right of the road is a small tidal pool with
islands where ducks swim and broad mud flats where sanderlings
and willets find food.

Continue on the entrance road to the parking area. A gate on
your right leads to paths over the hillsides. From the vantage point of
the modest elevation of the park you can see the Santa Cruz Mountains from San Bruno Mountain down to Mt. Umunhum.

North is an expanse of marsh and Bay. Salt ponds below reflect
in their waters their end product, the tall pyramids of salt at
Redwood City. West are the curves of West Point Slough marking

the landward boundary of Greco Island, one of the largest areas of natural marsh in the south Bay.

A walk along the paths through the park is enlivened by a unique garden of "word rock poems". Read the sign at the main entrance for keys to the symbolism of the clusters of rocks you pass. Put in place by the Menlo Park Environmental and Beautification Committee in collaboration with artist Susan Dunlap, "the rocks are carefully selected to support and translate the true meaning of each word."

A walk eastward leads to a saddle, but continue over the hill beyond. If you go north through the saddle, your senses will be assailed by occasional rumblings and whiffs of gas from a methane-recovery plant operating on the site of the former sewage-treatment plant. However, this operation is temporary, a part of the process of creating a park from the dump. Meanwhile some of the profits from the operation go toward completion of the park.

In addition to paths over the hills, the trail around the park by the slough is a popular route for runners, who can enjoy a glimpse of marsh life along the way.

Trip 2.   The Bay Trail from Marsh Road to Freeway 84

Join the groups of exercise-conscious office workers for a brisk walk beside marshlands.

Distance   2 miles one way.

Time   1 hour.

Connecting Trails   Trails in Bayfront Park and bicycle lanes on Dumbarton Bridge (Freeway 84).

TRAIL NOTES

This trail runs along the marshlands next to the Bayfront Expressway. It is popular with noontime runners from nearby offices and with those who want a longer run than the 2-mile path around Bayfront Park.

It is also an important link to bicycle lanes across the Dumbarton Bridge and to trails in the San Francisco Bay National Wildlife Refuge. A freeway overpass from the SFBNWR leads to Coyote Hills Park of the East Bay Regional Parks District. A bicycle trail from there goes all the way to Niles Canyon.

In the early 1990s, after a planned-for path is constructed across a gap just south of the freeway, there will be a continuous trail down the Peninsula to Mountain View's Shoreline.

Menlo Park and East Palo Alto
(Map on page 244)

From Freeway 84 south to Palo Alto, broad marshes extend for 2 miles down the Bay. From bicycle and pedestrian paths, boardwalks, viewing platforms and benches one has panoramic views over the Bay as well as close-up sights of bird and animal life in tidal marshes and mud flats.

Until the expected trail connection is completed south from Freeway 84, the main access is from Bay Road at Cooley Landing. There is a continuous path from Bay Road to Palo Alto, paved from Runnymede Street south. During 1988 the existing footpath from Runnymede Street to Bay Road will be surfaced for bicycle use, and a system of paths and boardwalks will be constructed around the marsh north of Bay Road.

Jurisdiction   MROSD, San Mateo County, City of East Palo Alto.
Facilities   Pedestrian paths, benches, parking.
Rules   Open dawn to dusk.
Maps   USGS topos *Palo Alto, Mountain View.*
How To Get There   From Bayshore Freeway 101: (1) In East Palo Alto, turn north on University Avenue, then east on Bay Road to its end at Cooley Landing and a parking area. (2) In Palo Alto, go east on Embarcadero Road to Geng Road, then north to parking at the Baylands Athletic Center.

Trip 1.   A Walk North from Cooley Landing around a Restored Marsh

On paths and boardwalks past tidal marsh, open water and a slough you have the opportunity to examine the variety of bird life.
Distance   1½-mile loop.
Time   1 hour.

TRAIL NOTES

At Cooley Landing a small viewing plaza and bench overlook the channel of a slough. From the plaza you look across the Bay toward the narrows where Dumbarton Bridge and a railroad bridge cross to Fremont. The north side of this historic landing is approximately the original shoreline. Immediately north across the water is the high land of Coyote Hills Park of the East Bay Regional Parks District.

**The well-camouflaged but endangered clapper rail
is found in the marshes south of Cooley Landing.**

The plaza is a good point to start the trip around the salt pond on
the north side of the slough. For the western leg of the loop, go down
Bay Road 600 feet, cross the bridge over the slough and follow the
levee path straight ahead. The slough follows around the bend in the
levee. Bayward is one of the many salt ponds that ring the South Bay.
Under the direction of MROSD it is being restored to a tidal marsh.
This path is paved for bicycle riding for ¾ mile, as far north as a
bench at a bend in the levee. From this point north the pavement is
narrower, and a 6-foot boardwalk bridges some gaps in the levee.

Our path continues to circle the marsh as a pedestrian path.
However, early in the 1990s the path from the bend will be widened
to 8 feet to accommodate bicycles. A crossing over a railroad spur
will make possible the continuation of the bicycle path to join the
path along University Avenue and go on to Freeway 84 at the
Dumbarton Bridge approach.

To continue around the loop, stay on the path that circles the
outer levee to the Bay's edge. Two viewing platforms with benches
are good vantage points from which to watch ducks and other water
birds dabble or dive for food. At low tide when mud flats rim the
marsh, look for the long-billed and long-legged shorebirds that find
crabs, snails and mollusks in the shallows. When you have identified, or just enjoyed watching, the bird life, complete the loop along
the levee and down the edge of the slough to the bridge where you
started.

Trip 2. Walk or Bike to Palo Alto from Cooley Landing

Enjoy the panoramic views over this great expanse of tidal marsh.

Distance   1 mile one way.

Time   ½ hour.

TRAIL NOTES

One of our outstanding views of marsh and Bay is from the paths along the marshes of the Laumeister and Faber tracts. The expanse of cordgrass, at first glance appearing unbroken to the Bay's edge, is in fact a network of small, meandering sloughs. At low tide these ribbons of mud are alive with snails, mollusks and worms. Incoming tides bring nourishing sediments to plants of the marsh. The cordgrass, one of the most productive of all plants and an air purifier, removes much carbon dioxide and gives off much oxygen.

The marsh is home to many small and inconspicuous birds and animals. You may not see the shy and endangered harvest mouse, but keep an eye out for the chicken-sized but well-camouflaged clapper rail.

Marsh inhabitants you can spot even at a distance, of course, are the common egret, 3 feet tall, and the smaller snowy egret. Happily their numbers are increasing here. Once nearly extinct, they are now common sights, thanks to the Audubon Society, which campaigned for their survival after they were nearly hunted out of existence for their beautiful nuptial feathers.

The path down the marsh makes a slight bend at Runnymede Street, then goes straight toward San Francisquito Creek, the San Mateo County boundary. You will see the row of trees bordering the channel of the creek out to the Bay. The trail crosses the creek, then continues at the edge of Palo Alto's Golf Course to Geng Road. There is parking here, and a connection to Palo Alto's long Baylands Trail, on which you can bicycle all the way to Mountain View's Shoreline.

Appendix I
Trails for Different Seasons and Reasons
FOR THE SEASONS

SPRING FLOWERS
San Bruno Mountain Park
Crystal Springs Trail at Edgewood Road
Edgewood Park
Rancho San Antonio Preserve
    High Meadow on Wildcat Loop Trail
Los Trancos Preserve
Monte Bello Preserve
    Indian Creek Trail, Canyon Trail
Purisima Creek Redwoods Preserve
    Purisima Creek Trail
Russian Ridge Preserve
Coal Mine Ridge
Duveneck Windmill Pasture Area

SHADY TRAILS FOR HOT SUMMER DAYS
Junipero Serra Park
    Nature Trail
Mills Canyon Park
Laurelwood Park
Stulsaft Park
Huddart Park
Skyline Trail
Wunderlich Park
Stevens Creek Park
    Old Canyon Trail
    Creek Trail
Upper Stevens Creek Park
San Pedro Valley Park
    Old Trout Farm Trail
Purisima Creek Redwoods Preserve
    Purisima Creek Trail
    Redwood Trail
El Corte de Madera Preserve
Edgewood Park
    Sylvan Loop
Skyline Ridge Preserve
    Old Page Mill Road

Monte Bello Preserve
  Stevens Creek Nature Trail
Upper Stevens Creek Park
  Grizzly Flat Trail

FALL COLOR—Time for California Gold
  Wunderlich Park—lower park trails
  Skyline Trail
  Upper Alpine Road Trail
  Stevens Creek Park
  Upper Stevens Creek Park
  Coal Creek Preserve
  Huddart Park
    Crystal Springs Trail
  Windy Hill Preserve
    Windy Hill Loop Trail
  Monte Bello Preserve
    Stevens Creek Nature Trail
    Canyon Trail

WINTER WALKS—For a breath of air between show-
  ers on surfaced paths
  Sweeney Ridge GGNRA
    Sneath Lane
  San Andreas Trail—to Larkspur Drive
  Sawyer Camp Trail
  Laurelwood Park
  Alpine Road Hiking, Riding and Bicycle Path
  Dwight F. Crowder Memorial Bike Path
  Sand Hill Road Paths
    Santa Cruz Avenue to Freeway 280
  Arastradero/Foothill Expressway Hub Trails
  Rancho San Antonio Park
  The Bay Trails
  San Bruno Mountain Park
    Bog Trail and Guadalupe Trail
  San Pedro Valley Park
    Weiler Ranch Road

HOW FAR IS IT? FROM SHORT WALKS TO LONG HIKES

SHORT WALKS ON NEARLY LEVEL
  TRAILS   Less than five miles
San Bruno Mountain Park
  Saddle Loop Trail
Junipero Serra Park
  Live Oak Nature Trail
San Andreas Trail
Sawyer Camp Trail from south end
Laurelwood Park
  Main paved trail from Shasta Drive
"The Loop"—Alpine, Portola, Sand Hill Road
  trails—any segment
Arastradero Bike Path
Varian/Bol Park Path
Palo Alto/Los Altos Bike Path
Rancho San Antonio Park and Preserve
  Trail to Deer Hollow Farm
  Rogue Valley Trail
Stevens Creek Park
  Mt. Eden Hiking and Riding Trails from Mt. Eden
    Road to Canyon Trail junction
  Creek Trail
  Old Canyon Trail
The Bay Trails
San Pedro Valley Park
  Weiler Ranch Road
Crystal Springs Trail
  Freeway 92 to Edgewood Road
Burleigh Murray State Park
Purisima Creek Redwoods Preserve
  Purisima Creek Trail from west entrance
Skyline Ridge Preserve
  Loop trip around Alpine Lake

LONG HIKES   Five to ten miles
Sawyer Camp Trail
Waterdog Lake, Sheep Camp and Crystal Springs
  trails to Edgewood Road
Huddart Park
  All-Day Hike Circling the Park

Wunderlich Park
  Figure-Eight Loop Trip
Skyline Trail
Fremont Older Preserve to Stevens Creek Park and
  return on Hayfields, Ridge, and Old Canyon Trails
Saratoga Gap to Monte Bello Preserve Canyon Trail
San Bruno Mountain Park
  Summit Loop and East Ridge Hike
Sweeney Ridge GGNRA
  Mori Ridge Trail to Discovery Site
Purisima Creek Redwoods Preserve
  Loop Trip from north entrance on Whittemore Gulch
    or Harkins Ridge trail to west entrance and return
    on Purisima Creek, Soda Gulch and Harkins
    Ridge trails
El Corte de Madera Preserve
  Main Haul Road Trail
Huddart Park main entrance to Purisima Creek
  Redwoods Preserve west entrance with car shuttle
  on Dean, Crystal Springs and Purisima Creek trails
Windy Hill Preserve
  Windy Hill Loop Trail
  Spring Ridge and Hamms Gulch Loop Trip
Loop Trip through Upper Stevens Creek Park, Monte
  Bello, Long Ridge and Hickory Oak preserves on
  Charcoal Road and Canyon, Grizzly Flat, Peters
  Creek, Long Ridge and Hickory Oak trails
Loop Trip from Monte Bello Preserve through Skyline
  Ridge, Russian Ridge and Coal Creek preserves on
  Stevens Creek Nature Trail, Stevens Creek, Skyline
  and Ridge trails, Trail to Coal Creek Meadows,
  Upper Alpine Road and Monte Bello Boundary Line
  Trail
Loop Trip through Monte Bello, Skyline Ridge and
  Long Ridge preserves and Upper Stevens Creek Park
  on Stevens Creek Nature Trail and Stevens Creek
  Trail, Skyline, Grizzly Flat and Canyon trails
Loop Trip from Stevens Creek Park through Fremont
  Older Preserve on Lookout, Ridge, Old Canyon,
  Stevens Canyon trails
Rancho San Antonio Preserve
  Loop Trip on Deer Hollow, Meadow Ridge and
    Utility service road trails

EXPEDITIONS   Trails combined for hikes of more than
    ten miles
    Highway 92/Cañada Road to Wunderlich Park Skyline
        Boulevard entrance on Crystal Springs and Skyline
        trails
    Belmont to Wunderlich Park, a 2-day trip with car shuttle
        on Waterdog Lake, Sheep Camp, Crystal Springs
        trails to Huddart Park trail camp for overnight; next
        day, Crystal Springs, Skyline and Alambique trails to
        Wunderlich Park main entrance on Woodside Road.
    San Andreas, Sawyer Camp trails round trip
    Skyline Trail from Huddart Park to Wunderlich Park and
        return
    Huddart Park main entrance to Purisima Creek
        Redwoods Preserve west entrance and return—on
        Dean, Crystal Springs, Skyline and Purisima Creek
        trails or take in reverse and overnight at Huddart
        Park trail camp
    Duveneck Windmill Pasture Area through Monte Bello
        Preserve to Saratoga Gap on Black Mountain, Indian
        Creek and Canyon trails or take in reverse and over-
        night at Hidden Villa Hostel

DOWNHILL ALL THE WAY   With a car shuttle
    Waterdog Lake Trail from St. James Road to Lyall Road
    Wunderlich Park, Skyline Boulevard entrance to
        Woodside Road entrance on Alambique Trail or
        Skyline, Alambique and Bear Gulch trails
    San Bruno Mountain Park
        Either leg of Summit Loop Trail from top of mountain
    Junipero Serra Park
        From upper picnic area on Quail Loop Trail to lower
        picnic areas or continue to San Bruno City Park
    Huddart Park From Skyline Boulevard entrance on
        Chinquapin Trail to Miwok picnic area
    Windy Hill Preserve
        From Skyline Boulevard entrances on Spring Ridge,
        Hamms Gulch or Razorback Ridge trails to Alpine
        or Portola roads
    Monte Bello or Coal Creek Preserves
        From Page Mill Road or Skyline Boulevard on Upper
        Alpine Road to lower entrance gate

SPECIAL DESTINATIONS

VIEW POINTS   Hikes to high places
  San Bruno Mountain Park
  Sweeney Ridge GGNRA
  Edgewood Park
  Wunderlich Park
    Skyline Trail
    Alambique or Bear Gulch trails to "The Meadows"
  Los Trancos Preserve
  Fremont Older Preserve
    Hunters Point and Maisie's Peak
  Stevens Creek Park
    Lookout Trail to Lookout Point
    Canyon Trail
  Sheep Camp Trail
  McNee Ranch State Park to Montara Mountain
  San Pedro Valley Park
    Hazelnut Trail
  El Corte de Madera Preserve
    Main Haul Road Trail
  Windy Hill Preserve
    Loop Trip Around Knobs
  Russian Ridge Preserve
    Trip to Borel Hill
  Monte Bello Preserve
    Indian Creek Trail to Black Mountain
  Skyline Ridge Preserve
    Skyline Trail to Vista Point
  Long Ridge Preserve
    Trip to Long Ridge Saddle
  Hickory Oak Ridge Area
  Rancho San Antonio Preserve
    Upper Meadow Ridge Trail
  Duveneck Windmill Pasture Area
    Trek to Black Mountain

ALMOST WILDERNESS, CLOSE TO HOME
  Huddart Park—Trails in upper park
    Skyline Trail
    Dean Trail
    Crystal Springs Trail
  Wunderlich Park
    Alambique Trail in upper park

Monte Bello Preserve
  Canyon Trail
Duveneck Windmill Pasture Area
Rancho San Antonio Preserve
  Wildcat Loop Trail
Purisima Creek Redwoods Preserve
  Whittemore Gulch Trail
El Corte de Madera Preserve
  Main Haul Road Trail

CREEKSIDE TRAILS
Mills Canyon Park
Laurelwood Park
Huddart Park
  Richards Road and Crystal Springs trails along West
    Union Creek
Stulsaft Park
Alpine Road Hiking, Riding and Bicycle Trail
Rancho San Antonio Preserve
  Wildcat Loop Trail
Stevens Creek Park
  Creek Trail
San Pedro Valley Park
  Old Trout Farm Trail
Purisima Creek Redwoods Preserve
  Purisima Creek Trail
  Whittemore Gulch Trail
Burleigh Murray State Park
El Corte de Madera Preserve
  Creek Trail
Windy Hill Preserve
  Eagle Trail on Windy Hill Loop
Monte Bello Preserve
  Stevens Creek Nature Trail

GLIMPSES OF 19th CENTURY RANCHES
Monte Bello Preserve
  Indian Creek Trail or Monte Bello Road to Morrell
    Ranch on Black Mountain
Fremont Older Preserve
Picchetti Historic Ranch
Rancho San Antonio Preserve
  Deer Hollow Farm
Burleigh Murray State Park

MEADOWS AND HILLTOPS FOR KITE FLYING, HAWK WATCHING, PEACEFUL PICNICKING
San Bruno Mountain Park
Sweeney Ridge GGNRA
Sheep Camp Trail
Wunderlich Park
  "The Meadows"
  Upper Meadow on Skyline Trail
Los Trancos Preserve
  Page Mill Trail
Monte Bello Preserve
  Indian Creek Trail
  Knolls near Page Mill Road
Rancho San Antonio Park and Preserve
  Wildcat Loop Trail
  Loop Trip to North Meadow
Fremont Older Preserve
  Hunters Point
La Honda Creek Preserve
Russian Ridge Preserve
Pulgas Ridge Preserve
Coal Creek Preserve
Windy Hill Preserve
  Trail to the Knobs
  Spring Ridge Trail
Hickory Oak Ridge Area

NATURE TRAILS AND SELF-GUIDING TRAILS
Junipero Serra Park
  Live Oak Nature Trail
Huddart Park
  Chickadee Trail
  Redwood Trail
Rancho San Antonio Preserve
  Docent trip to Deer Hollow Farm
Los Trancos Preserve
  Self-guiding and Docent Trips—San Andreas Fault Trail
San Bruno Mountain Park
  Bog Trail
Monte Bello Preserve
  Stevens Creek Nature Trail

TRAILS ON HISTORIC ROUTES
  Sawyer Camp Trail
  Sheep Camp Trail
  Huddart Park
    Richards Road Trail
  Arastradero Bike Path
  Alpine Road Hiking, Riding and Bicycle Trail
  Upper Alpine Road
  Sweeney Ridge GGNRA
    Portola Discovery Site of S.F. Bay
  Purisima Creek Redwoods
    Purisima Creek Trail
  Skyline Ridge Preserve
    Old Page Mill Road

BIRDWATCHING BY THE BAY   By marshes and
    sloughs
  Point San Bruno Park
  Burlingame Shoreline Bird Sanctuary
  Coyote Point Recreation Area—restored marsh
  San Mateo Shoreline Parks
  Foster City Trails
  Redwood Shores
    Trail at east end opposite Bird Island
  Menlo Park Bayfront Park
  Trails from Cooley Landing

TRAILS THROUGH PENINSULA FORESTS
  Purisima Creek Redwoods Preserve
    Purisima Creek Trail
  Huddart Park
  Wunderlich Park
    Bear Gulch Trail and Alambique-Skyline Trail Loop
  El Corte de Madera Preserve
  La Honda Creek Preserve
  Skyline Trail from Huddart to Wunderlich Park
  Windy Hill Preserve
    Windy Hill Loop Trail

HIKING TRAILS OPEN FOR BICYCLISTS, EQUESTRIANS AND WHEELCHAIR USERS

FOR BICYCLISTS
  On Paved Paths
    Almost all the Bay Trails
    San Bruno Mountain Park
      Radio Road to summit
    Sweeney Ridge Golden Gate National Recreation Area
      Sneath Lane
    San Andreas Trail
    Sawyer Camp Trail
    Arastradero Hub Trails
    The Loop
    Rancho San Antonio County Park
      To Deer Hollow Farm
  On Unpaved Service and Fire Roads
    Purisima Creek Redwoods Preserve
      Purisima Creek Trail
    El Corte de Madera Preserve
    Fremont Older Preserve
      All trails but footpath from Prospect Road
    Windy Hill Preserve
      Spring Ridge Trail
    Upper Alpine Road
    San Pedro Valley Park
      Weiler Ranch Road
    Skyline Ridge Preserve
    Monte Bello Preserve
      Canyon Trail
    Los Trancos Preserve
      Page Mill Trail
    Long Ridge Preserve
    Hickory Oak Ridge Area
    Arastradero Preserve
      All Trails except the Perimeter Trail

EQUESTRIAN TRAILS (**equestrian parking)
  (Some trails closed in wet weather)
    San Bruno Mountain Park
    Sweeney Ridge
    Crystal Springs Trail
    Edgewood Park

Pulgas Ridge Preserve
Huddart Park**
Wunderlich Park**
Skyline Trail
The Loop—Alpine, Portola and Sand Hill Road trails
Windy Hill Preserve
Monte Bello Preserve**
  All trails except Stevens Creek Nature Trail
Los Trancos Preserve
  Page Mill Trail only
Upper Alpine Road
Arastradero Preserve
Rancho San Antonio**
  Except Wildcat Canyon Trail
Duveneck Windmill Pasture
Fremont Older Preserve
  Except for Foot Trail from Prospect Road
Long Ridge Preserve
Hickory Oak Ridge Area
Purisima Creek Redwoods Preserve**
  Except for Whittemore Gulch, Soda Gulch and
    Grabtown Gulch trails
El Corte de Madera Preserve
Russian Ridge Preserve

FOR WHEELCHAIR USERS   Level, surfaced paths
San Andreas Trail, north end
Laurelwood Park, Shasta Street entrance
Alpine Road Hiking, Riding and Bicycle Trail (some
    parts)
Dwight F. Crowder Bike Path (some parts)
Varian/Bol Park Path
Palo Alto/Los Altos Bike Path
Rancho San Antonio Park and Preserve (Call MROSD
    for permit parking)
San Bruno Mountain
  Bog Trail
Purisima Creek Redwoods
  Redwood Trail
Huddart Park
  Chickadee Trail
Coyote Point Recreation Area
  Bathing Beach

The Bay Trails
   most are surfaced and almost level
Monte Bello Preserve
   First part of Stevens Creek Nature Trail

SPECIAL OCCASIONS

OUTINGS WITH YOUNG CHILDREN   Try a birthday
party with no crumbs on the rug. Short walks, picnic tables,
some barbecues and restrooms.
   San Bruno Mountain Park
   Junipero Serra Park
   San Pedro Valley Park
   Laurelwood Park
   Stulsaft Park
   Huddart Park
   Rancho San Antonio County Park
   Purisima Creek Redwoods Preserve
      Redwood Trail
   Edgewood Park Day Camp Area
   Stevens Creek County Park
      Old Canyon Trail and Bay Tree Picnic Area
   The Bay Trails
      Sierra Point Marina
      Oyster Point Marina and Beach
      Point San Bruno Park
      Coyote Point Recreation Area

OVERNIGHT IN THE PARKS AND PRESERVES
Youth groups and backpack camps and hostels by
reservation
   San Bruno Mountain Park—youth groups
   Junipero Serra Park—youth groups
   Huddart Park—youth groups and backpackers
   Monte Bello Preserve—backpackers
   Hidden Villa Hostel (closed in summer)

PARKS AND PRESERVES WITH MUSEUMS AND
VISITOR CENTERS
   San Pedro Valley Park
   Coyote Point Recreation Area
   Junipero Serra Park
   Stevens Creek Park

Appendix II

Selected References

History

Bogart, Sewall, *Lauriston; an Architectural Biography of Herbert Edward Law,* Alpine House, 1976.

Brown, Alan K., *Sawpits in the Spanish Redwoods, 1787–1849,* San Mateo County Historical Association, 1966.

————, *Place Names of San Mateo County,* San Mateo County Historical Association, 1975.

Cupertino Chronicle, California History Center, De Anza College, Local History Studies, Vol. 19, 1975.

Fava, Florence M., *Los Altos Hills, A Colorful Story,* Woodside, California: Gilbert Richards Publications, 1976.

Margolin, Malcolm, *The Ohlone Way, Indian Life in the San Francisco-Monterey Bay Area,* Berkeley, Calif: Heyday Books, 1978.

Regnery, Dorothy F., *An Enduring Heritage, Historic Buildings of the San Francisco Peninsula,* Stanford, Calif: Stanford University Press, 1976.

Stanger, Frank M., *South From San Francisco, San Mateo County, California, Its History and Heritage,* San Mateo County Historical Association, 1963.

————, *Sawmills in the Redwoods, Logging on the San Francisco Peninsula, 1889–1967,* San Mateo County Historical Association, 1967.

Natural History

Crittenden, Mabel, and Dorothy Telfer, *Wildflowers of the West,* Millbrae, Calif: Celestial Arts, 1975.

Iacopi, Robert, *Earthquake Country,* Menlo Park, Calif: Lane Books, 1971.

McClintock, Elizabeth, and Walter Knight, *A Flora of the San Bruno Mountains, San Mateo County, California,* Proceedings of the California Academy of Sciences, Vol. XXXII, No. 20, November 29, 1968.

Peterson, Roger Tory, *A Field Guide to Western Birds,* Boston: Houghton Mifflin Company, 1972.

Thomas, John Hunter, *Flora of the Santa Cruz Mountains of California,* Stanford: Stanford University Press, 1961.

California Natural History Guides, Berkeley, Calif: University of California Press.

Berry, William D. and Elizabeth, *Mammals of the San Francisco Bay Region,* 1959.

Ferris, Roxana S. *Native Shrubs of the San Francisco Bay Region,* 1968.

Gilliam, Harold, *Weather of San Francisco Bay Area,* 1966.

Grillos, Steve J., *Ferns and Fern Allies of California,* 1966.

Howard, Arthur D., *Evolution of the Landscape of the San Francisco Bay Region,* 1972.

Metcalf, Woodbridge, *Native Trees of the San Francisco Bay Region,* 1959.

Sharsmith, Helen K., *Spring Wildflowers of the San Francisco Bay Region,* 1965.

Smith, Arthur C., *Introduction to the Natural History of the San Francisco Bay Region,* 1959.

Stebbins, Robert C., *Reptiles and Amphibians of the San Francisco Bay Region,* 1960.

Appendix III

Where to Call For Information on Sponsored Hikes

American Youth Hostels, Golden Gate Council	415-863-1444
Audubon Society, bird walks	
Sequoia Chapter	415-593-7368
Santa Clara Valley Chapter	415-329-1811
Committee for Green Foothills	415-494-7158
Companions of the Trail—Call Trail Center	415-968-7065
Coyote Point Museum	415-344-7755
Filoli Center	415-364-2880
Golden Gate National Recreation Area	415-556-0560
	415-556-8371
Midpeninsula Regional Open Space District	415-949-5500
Parks and Recreation Departments	
Palo Alto	415-329-2261
Palo Alto Baylands Interpretive Center	415-329-2506
San Mateo	415-377-3340
Peninsula Conservation Center	415-494-9301
San Francisco Bay National Wildlife Refuge	415-792-0222
Santa Cruz Mountains Trail Association	415-968-4509
Sempervirens Fund	415-968-4509
Senior Centers	
Little House	415-326-2025
San Carlos	415-592-9986
Senior Coordinating Council	415-327-2811
For others, see local numbers	
Sierra Club, Loma Prieta Chapter	415-494-9901
Trail Center	415-968-7065

Index

(Page numbers in **boldface type** indicate where park, preserve or trail is featured in Part II)

Hiking in the backcountry entails unavoidable risk that every hiker assumes and must be aware of and respect. The fact that a trail is described in this book is not a representation that it will be safe for you. Trails vary greatly in difficulty and in the degree of conditioning and agility one needs to enjoy them safely. On some hikes routes may have changed or conditions may have deteriorated since the descriptions were written. Also trail conditions can change even from day to day, owing to weather and other factors. A trail that is safe on a dry day or for a highly conditioned, agile, properly equipped hiker may be completely unsafe for someone else or unsafe under adverse weather conditions.

You can minimize your risks on the trail by being knowledgeable, prepared and alert. There is not space in this book for a general treatise on safety in the mountains, but there are a number of good books and public courses on the subject and you should take advantage of them to increase your knowledge. Just as important, you should always be aware of your own limitations and of conditions existing when and where you are hiking. If conditions are dangerous, or if you are not prepared to deal with them safely, choose a different hike! It's better to have wasted a drive than to be the subject of a mountain rescue.

These warnings are not intended to scare you off the trails. Millions of people have safe and enjoyable hikes every year. However, one element of the beauty, freedom and excitement of the wilderness is the presence of risks that do not confront us at home. When you hike you assume those risks. They can be met safely, but only if you exercise your own independent judgment and common sense.

Peninsula Trails
1990 Update

Page 81, Pulgas Ridge Open Space Preserve The 1-mile Polly Geraci Trail, built in 1989, up Cordilleras Creek to the ridgetop, leaves the valley just before the turn of the paved road to the gated preserve entrance. For a short distance the trail follows the creek near its west bank, and then it ascends on switchbacks through an oak forest. Ferns cover the hillside, and shade-loving flowers blossom here in spring.

As the trail rounds a ridge, leaving the creek far below, madrones and manzanita appear in a tall chaparral cover. The ridge across the canyon comes into sight, along with a scattering of houses in the subdivision on the ridgetop in neighboring San Carlos. At a bend in the trail a bench offers a welcome stopping place to take in the view.

Page 97, Purisima Creek Redwoods Open Space Preserve In May 1989 MROSD dedicated part of the Harkins Ridge Trail, the Soda Gulch Trail and the upper section of the Purisima Creek Trail as an official 5.7-mile segment of the Bay Area Ridge Trail. The narrow Soda Gulch Trail, contouring through steep-sided, fragile forests, is open to hikers only. Bicyclists and equestrians ride to the preserve's west entrance, using the Purisima Creek and Harkins Ridge trails. Bay Area Ridge Trail signs and directional arrows mark the route, which can be taken from either entrance. Trips 1 and 2 describe these trails.

Page 105, Huddart Park A new 0.8-mile trail, built by Trail Center volunteers, contours through the redwood and fir forests along the west boundary of the park. The trail extends from the park's Skyline Boulevard entrance (opposite the Purisima Creek Trail) north to the west end of the Richards Road Trail.

Page 113, Skyline Trail Between Huddart and Wunderlich Parks This trail was dedicated and signed in 1989 as an official segment of the Bay Area Ridge Trail. In 1990 San Mateo County re-aligned a 1.1-mile section just south of Kings Mountain Road. Now on a gentler grade, it swings east through evergreen forests and then, heading west, it emerges on chaparral slopes before continuing south on the old route to Wunderlich Park. The new route opens up many vistas over the Bear Gulch Watershed.

Page 127, El Corte de Madera Open Space Preserve Trails covered in the text are now named and signed, trailheads are numbered and some new trails have been opened in recent timber-cutting areas.

   Trip 3. Loop Trip into the Preserve's Canyons
The old haul road from Skyline Boulevard Trailhead (CM02) offers a spectacular trip south to the lower end of the preserve. Leading through a narrow, forested, fern-lined canyon, over an oak-and-fir-covered ridge to views west and south, the trail descends to join the Gordon Mill Trail in the canyon near Lawrence Creek. A loop trip down the Timberview Trail and a return up the Gordon Mill Trail requires a 1/2-mile car shuttle or roadside walk back to the trailhead.

   Other trails are open which explore the Sierra Morena ridgetop. A new map of the preserve is available from MROSD, 415-949-5500.

Page 136, Windy Hill Open Space Preserve From the main Skyline Boulevard entrance at the Spring Ridge picnic area to the preserve's southernmost entrance is the signed and dedicated 2.7-mile segment of the Bay Area Ridge Trail. It includes the Lost Trail section of the Windy Hill Loop Trail, described in Trip 1, and a 0.4-mile connector to Skyline Boulevard, where there is limited parking.

Page 148, Upper Alpine Road San Mateo County repaired the creek crossing and removed the landslide from this road, making it again passable for hikers, equestrians and bicyclists.

Page 151, Russian Ridge Open Space Preserve From the recently constructed parking area northwest of the Skyline Boulevard/Alpine Road intersection a new trail goes up to the trail along Russian Ridge.

   Additional trailhead and roadside parking on Alpine Road 0.8 mile southwest of Skyline Boulevard leads to trails along hillsides above Alpine Road and reaches the main trail along Russian Ridge. From the high grasslands and fine canyon-oak groves are wide vistas east down the Skyline and southwest into Alpine Creek Canyon.

Page 159, Skyline Ridge Open Space Preserve The north parking area at the northwest corner of Skyline Boulevard and Alpine Road, completed in 1990, provides access to the preserve through a tunnel under Alpine Road. A gently graded trail, suitable for the physically limited, follows the east side of Alpine Lake to a new observation platform, funded by the Peninsula Open Space Trust.

Page 163, Trip 3. The Skyline Trail Completely re-routed in 1990 from the north parking area to the Horseshoe Lake entrance, the Skyline Trail is now the hiker's route through the preserve and an eventual Bay Area Ridge Trail segment. (Bicyclists and equestrians will continue to use the old farm roads.) After passing Alpine Lake, this beautiful new trail enters a fir-and-canyon-oak woodland, then contours along southwest-facing grassy slopes. After passing a short spur trail that reaches the preserve's highest point, the trail continues around some sandstone boulders that offer trailside viewing platforms. Then, on a gradual descent along the east side of the preserve's central promontory, it goes through an oak, madrone and bay forest to reach the parking area near Horseshoe Lake. South of Horseshoe Lake the Skyline Trail continues as described.

Page 210, Trip 2. Trek to Black Mountain A new trail from the oak-madrone woodlands at the west end of the Windmill Pasture skirts around south-facing ridges to meet the new Black Mountain Trail in the shady swale of a Permanente Creek drainage. Bear left on it and follow this new, well-designed trail along the east side of a shoulder of Black Mountain. After many switchbacks you reach the south side of the wooded plateau where the powerline service road leads to the summit. From here the route is as described in the text.

Page 250, Trip 1. A Walk North from Cooley Landing At Cooley Landing the trail does not circle the marsh as previously planned, but crosses the slough on a bridge, then extends for 3/4 mile along the marsh. Concern for nesting areas in the restored marsh required this change. However, the future connection to trails along University Avenue to Highway 84 is still scheduled.